Dialogue in Palestine

SOAS Palestine Studies

This book series aims at promoting innovative research in the study of Palestine, Palestinians and the Israel–Palestine conflict as a crucial component of Middle Eastern and world politics. The first ever Western academic series entirely dedicated to this topic, *SOAS Palestine Studies* draws from a variety of disciplinary fields, including history, politics, media, visual arts, social anthropology and development studies. The series is published under the academic direction of the Centre for Palestine Studies (CPS) at the London Middle East Institute (LMEI) of SOAS, University of London.

Series Editors:
Dina Matar, PhD, Chair, Centre for Palestine Studies, and Reader in Political Communication, Centre for Global Media and Communications, SOAS
Adam Hanieh, PhD, Reader in Development Studies and Advisory Committee Member for Centre for Palestine Studies, SOAS

Board Advisor:
Hassan Hakimian, Director of the London Middle East Institute at SOAS

Current and Forthcoming Titles:
Palestine Ltd.: Neoliberalism and Nationalism in the Occupied Territory, Toufic Haddad
Palestinian Literature in Exile: Gender, Aesthetics and Resistance in the Short Story, Joseph R. Farag
Palestinian Citizens of Israel: Power, Resistance and the Struggle for Space, Sharri Plonski
Representing Palestine Media and Journalism in Australia Since World War I, Peter Manning
Folktales of Palestine: Cultural Identity, Memory and the Politics of Storytelling, Farah Aboubakr
Dialogue in Palestine: The People-to-People Diplomacy Programme and the Israeli–Palestinian Conflict, Nadia Naser-Najjab
Palestinian Youth Activism in the Internet Age: Social Media and Networks after the Arab Spring, Albana Dwonch

Dialogue in Palestine

The People-to-People Diplomacy Programme and the Israeli–Palestinian Conflict

Nadia Naser-Najjab

I.B. TAURIS
LONDON • NEW YORK • OXFORD • NEW DELHI • SYDNEY

Centre for Palestine Studies

Published in association with the Centre for Palestine Studies,
London Middle East Institute

I.B. TAURIS
Bloomsbury Publishing Plc
50 Bedford Square, London, WC1B 3DP, UK
1385 Broadway, New York, NY 10018, USA
29 Earlsfort Terrace, Dublin 2, Ireland

BLOOMSBURY, I.B. TAURIS and the I.B. Tauris logo are trademarks of
Bloomsbury Publishing Plc

First published in Great Britain 2020
Paperback edition published 2021

Copyright © Nadia Naser-Najjab 2020

Nadia Naser-Najjab has asserted her right under the Copyright, Designs and Patents Act, 1988, to be identified as Author of this work.

For legal purposes the Acknowledgements on p. xii constitute an extension of this copyright page.

Cover image © HAZEM BADER/AFP/Getty Images

All rights reserved. No part of this publication may be reproduced or transmitted in any form or by any means, electronic or mechanical, including photocopying, recording, or any information storage or retrieval system, without prior permission in writing from the publishers.

Bloomsbury Publishing Plc does not have any control over, or responsibility for, any third-party websites referred to or in this book. All internet addresses given in this book were correct at the time of going to press. The author and publisher regret any inconvenience caused if addresses have changed or sites have ceased to exist, but can accept no responsibility for any such changes.

A catalogue record for this book is available from the British Library.

A catalog record for this book is available from the Library of Congress.

ISBN   HB: 978-1-8386-0384-7
       PB: 978-0-7556-4503-9
     eISBN: 978-1-8386-0386-1
      ePDF: 978-1-8386-0385-4

Series: SOAS Palestine Studies

Typeset by Newgen KnowledgeWorks Pvt. Ltd., Chennai, India

To find out more about our authors and books visit www.bloomsbury.com and sign up for our newsletters.

To my daughters Leen and Nadine, my nephew Akram and my niece Haya, hoping they will one day read this book during a time of peace.

Contents

Foreword to the SOAS Palestine Studies Book Series	viii
Foreword	x
Acknowledgements	xii
Abbreviations	xiii
Introduction	1
1 The context of P2PP	31
2 The colonial context of P2PP	45
3 Contact between 1967 and 1987	67
4 Contact during the First *Intifada* (1987–93)	83
5 The 'Oslo years' and 'facts on the ground'	97
6 'From Both Sides': A case study of the programme	111
7 The P2PP – a critical assessment	131
8 The P2PP during and after the *Al-Aqsa Intifada*	147
Conclusion	173
Notes	187
Bibliography	199
Index	223

Foreword to the SOAS Palestine Studies Book Series

The question of Palestine – with its corollaries, the Israel–Palestine and Arab–Israeli conflicts – has been a key issue of world politics and a major source of world tension since the 1917 Balfour Declaration. Few global issues have attracted so much attention over such a long period of time.

As a result, despite its small territorial size, Palestine has become a key component of Middle East studies in the academic community as well as a field of study in its own right, in the same way that France and Germany are each the subject of individual study while being part of European Studies. This 'disproportionate' status of the Palestine topic is due to several factors.

First is the strategic location of Palestine at the Mediterranean door of the Middle East and the 'East of Suez' world. This strategic position – the source of British interest in Palestine at the beginning of the twentieth century – has been enhanced by the greater importance of the broader Middle East in global affairs as manifested by the high frequency of wars and conflicts in the region since the Second World War and even more since the end of the Cold War.

Second is the very particular fact of what has been described as a 'settler-colonial' project in Palestine that was boosted by the huge human tragedy of the Nazi genocide of European Jews in 1941–5. The result has been a complex mingling of the Holocaust, which the Zionist movement claims as legitimizing its actions, with what Palestinians call the *Nakba*, or 'catastrophe', which describes the 'ethnic cleansing' of Arab Palestinians from great swathes of Palestine in 1948 by the Zionist drive towards the creation of Israel.

Third is the sheer complexity of the Palestine question engendered by the *Nakba* and the subsequent occupation by the state of Israel of the West Bank and Gaza following the Six-Day War in 1967. As a result of these, the Palestinian people today are living under very different conditions and legal regimes: they encompass those who remained in Israel after the state's establishment in 1948; those, including refugees, under direct Israeli occupation or indirect Israeli control in the West Bank and Gaza; those displaced by the wars of 1948 and 1967 to the eastern bank of the Jordan River, some of them still living in camps and most of whom became Jordanian citizens; those living in the refugee camps of Lebanon and Syria; those of the diaspora living in other Arab countries; and those of the global diaspora.

Finally, the question of Palestine plays such a major role in Arab politics in general and represents such a major trauma in collective Arab memory that it has been the focus of prolific artistic and literary energy, a drive that goes beyond Palestinians to include creative minds and talents from all Arabic-speaking countries.

This complexity and the unparalleled diversity of contemporary Palestinian locations and situations help to explain Palestine's 'disproportionate' status and account for the abundance of publications on Palestine and its people. And yet, surprisingly, there has until now been no university-based English-language book series specifically dedicated to Palestine Studies. The SOAS Palestine Studies series, published by I.B. Tauris in collaboration with the SOAS Centre for Palestine Studies (CPS) at the London Middle East Institute (LMEI), seeks to fill this gap. This series is dedicated to the contemporary history, politics, economy, society and culture of Palestine and the historiographic quarrels associated with its past.

The subject of Palestine has aroused intense passions over several decades. On such a topic it is very difficult to exclude passion, and the pretension to be 'neutral' is often disqualified by both sides. But we will make sure that none of our books stray beyond the realms of intellectual integrity and scholarly rigour. With the Palestine Studies series we hope to make an important contribution towards a better understanding of this most complex topic.

Professor Gilbert Achcar
SOAS, University of London

Foreword

Among the many hopes associated with the Oslo Accord was one that focused on people's ability to transcend beyond past animosities and build together, from below, a better future in the torn land of Palestine. Thus, the agreement between the politicians was accompanied by a set of initiatives funded from the outside under the promising title 'People to People'. While the negotiations from above continued, on the ground, people from all walks of life, on both sides of the divide, were coached by outsiders how to cement from below the accord signed by the politicians.

The accord itself failed dismally. It was based on wrong assumptions about the nature of the conflict in Palestine, and hence the prognosis was as far-fetched as the diagnosis of the conflict. As 'the People to People' programmes were an integral part of the accord, they also were based on the same misconceptions. These included the view of the conflict as one fought between two equal parties and one which is bereft of any historical context or a moral dimension. The imbalance on the ground was not only ignored but was cynically manipulated in turning the 'peace process' into an international attempt to force the Palestinians to accept the Israeli version of a solution. The absence of a historical context meant that the 'peace process' ignored the 1948 ethnic cleansing of Palestine by Israel and reduced Palestine into the West Bank and the Gaza Strip and the Palestinians into the people living there (ignoring the Palestinian refugees and those living inside Israel). The criminal nature of Israeli policies in the past and present was also not a factor in the attempt to bring peace and reconciliation to Israel and Palestine.

This excellent book is written by someone who took part in these initiatives and lived through the First *Intifada* that brought to the fore the clear Palestinian struggle for statehood and independence that was crushed by the Oslo process. This is thus both a profound analysis of how much 'the People to People' programme represented the Oslo Accord and how much was there a potential and desire for a more genuine reconciliation of the two sides. This is a must read for anyone who wants to understand why the Oslo Accord failed and what one can learn from the attempt to build bottom-up a reconciliation process.

This is a book about good intentions gone awry as well as a tale of manipulation and coaptation disguised as a genuine endeavours for peace and reconciliation. This human fragility and insincerity will accompany any future attempt at peace and therefore needs to be properly studied and indeed is offered here in this book. This is the first ever attempt to deconstruct this most optimistic part of the botched Oslo Accord and hence an essential research that complements the already existing poignant critique of the political and economic aspects of the accord. What is very clear is that unless one understands the colonial, indeed the settler colonial, reality in the 1967 occupied territories, one would not be able to produce an appropriate mechanism, from above or from below, effective enough to bring an end to the inhumanity suffered by Palestinians there since 1967 and elsewhere from even earlier on. Nadia has not lost her faith in a dialogue or human contact, but it seems she offers us a more sober and realistic way forward than the one attempted since 1993.

Very little that happened recently in Palestine leaves us with any hope for a more meaningful and successful process of decolonization and liberation. But at least an incisive analysis, such as the one provided here, of the failures of the past attempts will maybe produce, when the time is ripe, a more successful accord that would bring justice to the torn land of Palestine.

Professor Ilan Pappé

Acknowledgements

There are many people who supported and inspired me while writing this book, including family, friends and colleagues.

I am indebted to Professor Ilan Pappé, Professor of History and Director of the European Centre for Palestine Studies, for reading the book proposal and suggesting aspects that escaped my mind. Professor William Galois, Associate Professor of Middle Eastern and Mediterranean History and Head of Research, provided invaluable support, guidance and access to important resources. I would also like to thank Professor Tim Niblock, Emeritus Professor at the University of Exeter for his constant support.

Christine Robins, the director of the Institute of Arab and Islamic Studies at the University of Exeter, was a source of constant support and encouragement, and so too were my colleagues at the institute, who are too numerous to mention here.

The anonymous reviewers provided valuable, detailed and constructive comments that encouraged me to do more research and improve the book.

My family helped to sustain me during the writing process. My husband Walid Al-Najjab, despite experiencing and enduring a dire situation, gave me the space and support I needed. My daughters, Leen and Nadine, gave me a sense of the value of my work, proudly telling their friends about my book.

My late father Arafat and mother Aisha gave me the gift of a strong belief in education, especially for women. They raised me to be open-minded, to accept the other and to renounce prejudice.

My late father-in-law Abdul Rahman Al-Najjab inspired me by publishing a book on Palestine at age 93, showing me that it is never too late to publish. My aunt Ruqia, my sister Ghada and her husband Samer Obaid were invaluable sources of strength during difficult times. My humble thanks to my sister Layla and sisters-in-law Salwa and Najwa for believing in my work.

My editor Ben Boulton was patient and available at any time. And last, but most certainly not least, my students at Birzeit University and the University of Exeter continually challenged me to think anew and to think critically.

Abbreviations

AATW	Anarchists Against the Wall
ASS	Arab Studies Society
BDS	Boycott, Divestment and Sanctions
BNC	BDS National Committee
CAWL	Committee Against the War in Lebanon
CIDA	Canadian International Development Agency
CMM	Conflict Management and Mitigation
COP	Culture of Peace
CPRS	Centre for Palestinian Research and Studies
CRB	Karen Kerev Foundation
DAPL	Dokota Access Pipeline
DFLP	Democratic Front for the Liberation of Palestine
DOP	Declaration of Principles
ECF	Economic Cooperation Foundation
EU	European Union
EU PI	European Union Peacebuilding Initiative
FBS	From Both Sides
FCO	British Foreign Office
ICAHD	Israeli Committee Against House Demolitions
ICIPP	Israeli Council for Israel-Palestine Peace
IPCRI	Israeli/Palestinian Centre for Research and Information
IPPC	Israeli–Palestinian Peace Committee
JMCC	Jerusalem Media and Communication Centre
JVP	Jewish Voice for Peace
KATU	Finnish Citizens' Security Council
NGO	Non-governmental organization
OCHA	United Nations Office for the Coordination of Humanitarian Affairs
ODSC	One Democratic State Campaign
OPT	Occupied Palestinian Territories

PA	Palestinian Authority
PCBS	Palestinian Central Bureau of Statistics
PCP	Palestinian Centre for Peace
PFLP	Popular Front for the Liberation of Palestine
PLO	Palestine Liberation Organization
PNA	Palestinian National Authority
PNC	Palestinian National Council
PNGO	Palestinian NGO Network
PPIC	Palestinian Peace Information Centre
PRIME	Palestinian Research Institute in the Middle East
P2P	People-to-People
P2PP	People-to-People Programme
SCC	Standing Cooperation Committee
SIT	Social Identity Theory
UN	United Nations
UNLU	Unified National Leadership of the Uprising
UNSC	United Nations Security Council
UPWC	The Union of Palestinian Women's
US	United States
USAID	United States Agency for International Development
WIB	Women in Black
WOFWPP	Women's Organization for Women Political Prisoners

Introduction

This book initially requires a shift of political perspective, in which attention moves from a relentlessly bleak present to a past that was, at least in its initial phases, inscribed with a sense of hope and optimism. It seems strange, and almost perverse, to reflect that, in 1993, some Palestinians had presented Israeli soldiers with roses.

When the Oslo Agreement and the Declaration of Principles (DOP) were signed in September 1993, there was a sense of 'cautious optimism'. The director of the Centre for Palestinian Research and Studies (CPRS) cited polling evidence that suggested 51 per cent of Palestinians supported peace negotiations in January 1994. This support peaked at over 65 per cent in early to mid-1995, when the appearance of progress in peace negotiations contributed to growing public optimism (Shikaki, 1999: 32). By September 1995, these results had effectively inverted, with 60 per cent of respondents claiming there would be no lasting peace between Palestinians and Israelis.

Later polling revealed that just over four-fifths (81 per cent) of Palestinian respondents did not trust the intentions of the Israeli government (ibid.: 45). Despite this, Palestinian and Israeli public opinion continued to broadly support the peace process (Ma'oz, 1999). Palestinian polls in October 1999 showed that 58 per cent of respondents supported the peace process and 70.7 per cent remained optimistic that peace could be achieved (JMCC, 1999). Shikaki, in rendering this uneven and sometimes contradictory state of affairs, spoke of a Palestinian public opinion that 'cautiously' blended optimism and pessimism (1999: 46).

Oslo II, which was signed in 1995, divided the West Bank and Gaza Strip (excluding Jerusalem) into three areas. Area A, which accounted for 4 per cent of the West Bank, covered six cities: Bethlehem, Jenin, Khalil (Hebron),

Nablus, Ramallah and Tulkarm. Area B included 450 Palestinian villages and accounted for 27 per cent of the West Bank – the Palestinian Authority was responsible for civil administration in this area, while the Israelis were responsible for security. Area C included mainly Israeli settlements and land under public ownership, unpopulated areas (or *masha*) and Israel's strategic security zones (Shehadeh, 1997: 71). It accounted for 69 per cent of the West Bank.

The political terrain radically shifted when the *Al-Aqsa Intifada*[1] broke out in September 2000, following on from the collapse of direct negotiations between Palestinian and Israeli representatives a few months earlier. Contrary to the established 'wisdom' of the mainstream media, Yasser Arafat did not walk away from a political solution to the conflict. Rather, he chose to reject a deeply flawed proposal that exposed the objective limitations of the Israeli government's 'commitment' to peace. Bishara cites four 'red lines' (1967 borders, settlements, Jerusalem and Palestinian sovereignty) that were pre-emptively handed down by Israeli negotiators during the Camp David talks (2001: 56). Israeli positions repeatedly failed to approximate, even loosely, to the international consensus (embodied within the relevant UN resolutions) or minimum Palestinian requirements.[2]

International observers, in frequently celebrating the 'concessions' made by Israeli negotiators, which were admittedly significant when compared to what preceding Israeli governments had been willing to countenance, failed to recognize that Arafat's own political survival would have been jeopardized had he accepted what was on offer. Questions of justice, most notably those relating to the social, economic and historical impact of the occupation (see Bishara, 2001: 90), were not on the agenda. Israeli negotiators actually advanced positions that were more conservative and cautious than Israeli public opinion.

The Oslo process collapsed and disintegrated when a violent popular uprising broke out. The bleak farce of the peace process rapidly transformed into an ongoing tragedy. For international observers, Palestine became a series of vivid and immediate snapshots. As in other conflict environments, images of human suffering and despair militated against meaningful analysis. This was particularly apparent in Israel, where news coverage of Palestinian suicide bombings coincided within a marked hardening of Israeli public opinion, even among those who had previously been committed to a peaceful settlement of the conflict. Israelis increasingly expressed the view that there was 'nobody to talk to'.

This development was particularly negative because, in many respects, the unravelling of the peace process had been essentially foretold. It can even be argued that the enterprise was doomed from the outset, having originated in what were little more than illusions and deceits. In retrospect it is surprising to reflect that, even after the *Al-Aqsa Intifada* broke out, the peace process did not collapse entirely but instead found renewed impetus within a series of abortive and ill-conceived initiatives, which included the Arab Peace Initiative (2002), the Roadmap for Peace (2002), the Annapolis Conference (2007) and the most recent peace talks (2013–14).

In this difficult and immensely draining environment, international actors appear less interested in engaging Palestinian concerns than in reiterating their own beliefs and reading of the conflict. A recent controversy is instructive in this respect. In February 2015, a group of British artists published a letter calling for a cultural boycott of Israel (Guardian, 2015a). In response, a second group of British artists, including the British children's author J. K. Rowling, indicated their intention to establish a network that would promote a culture of coexistence. This network would, in their words, 'buil[d] bridges, nurtur[e] freedom and [promote] positive movement for change' (Guardian, 2015b).

It is significant that the signatories saw no need to refer to the past history of similar initiatives. To the same extent, their contribution lacked an assessment of the obstacles that could conceivably impede such an aspiration. From a Palestinian perspective, it was similarly noticeable that there was no acknowledgement of the deeply rooted Palestinian opposition to normalization. The signatories essentially offered what was little more than a series of normative assertions.

This book offers an important corrective by engaging with the P2PP programme, which was in process during the mid- to late 1990s. During this period, various international donors poured money into a people-to-people diplomacy programme (P2PP) that sought to foster public engagement and remove deeply embedded barriers. Its designers believed that broad-based public engagement would, through a series of joint projects and initiatives, produce positive attitudinal change. In my role as a coordinator for a Palestinian

NGO, I was well placed to perceive its ongoing development. Perhaps more importantly, I was also able to directly observe its weaknesses, which were so numerous that they provided the basis for my PhD research project, which I began in 2000.

In my reading, there is a close resemblance between the network initiative and the P2PP. To this extent, the P2PP does not ask if contact is a realistic aspiration or situate it within the wider context of an ongoing conflict. Rather, it instead takes the answer for granted and instead asks how contact can be more concretely embodied and evidenced. To put it differently, it approaches contact as a practical imperative.

The contributors also implicitly take the view that the establishment of contact would be an achievement in itself. But, as I will demonstrate, this overlooks the fact that there was already a pre-existent, albeit largely latent, tradition of contact. I subsequently came to see that the P2PP lacked a clear 'theory of change' – that is, an explanation of precisely how contact would contribute to lasting and significant change. In no small part, this was attributable to the very limited number of participants.

It is also noticeable that both the network's and the P2PP's advocates approach peace as an unconditional imperative. But this overlooks the extent to which 'peace' has become intertwined with strategic interests within the region's past history. The 1978 Camp David agreement between Egypt and Israel confirms this point. Under these circumstances, there is a clear danger that 'pacification' may become indistinguishable from 'peacebuilding', with 'peace' coming to function as little more than a conduit for the achievement of wider strategic objectives. Both the P2PP and the wider peace project of which it was a part were clearly exposed to this criticism.

This book therefore has much in common with contributions to the critical peacebuilding literature that conceptualizes and theorizes the enactment of peacebuilding and state-building in conflict and post-conflict settings. This branch of the literature, in emphasizing that such interventions are frequently taken in the absence of a sustained engagement with underlying assumptions, further reiterates that the P2PP was particularly vulnerable to co-option because it remained conceptually and theoretically underdeveloped.

After the *Al-Aqsa Intifada*, the soil in which the P2PP was supposed to take root has become increasingly infertile. The decline of the Israeli Left has closed up opportunities for political engagement, and on the Palestinian side there is little desire for direct engagement – on the contrary, the rise of the BDS (Boycott, Divestment and Sanctions) movement is in many respects a rejection of the peace process and its dubious achievements.

Despite these internal changes and adjustments, international observers continue to retain an abiding belief (perhaps 'faith' would be a more appropriate word) in the virtues of contact. In apparent defiance of a past history of drawn-out failure, these observers advance an essentially ideological position by insisting on the transformative potential of contact. Rendered in this idealized form, contact operates independently of historical or political context.

At the current point in time, it would be no exaggeration to say that contact has become one of the central points of contention within the Palestinian–Israeli conflict. For both local and international actors, contact has become an open question to be approached with varying degrees of endorsement, reservation and trepidation. For Israel's international sympathizers (perhaps 'supporters' is too strong a word), contact is an open question to be explored; for Palestinians, in contrast, it is part of a discredited experiment that ultimately further extended conditions of occupation.

In many respects, the BDS is a stage removed from this ongoing debate. It represents a concrete embodiment of the Palestinian debate upon contact and unconditionally rejects the proposition of normalization. In the course of its existence it has been, along with the consensus that it embodies, subject to various degrees of misrepresentation and even distortion. In many respects, this book functions as a clarification that is offered in response.

Much of the current discussion of the BDS has now shifted to the question of contact – the circumstances when contact is appropriate, the limitations that should be placed upon contact and when disengagement is necessary. A previous generation of activists and concerned international citizens once asked these same questions in relation to Apartheid South Africa.

One of the most frequently encountered criticisms of BDS is that it is divisive. These critics frequently express the view that the Palestinian–Israeli conflict will only be overcome when Palestinians and Israelis learn to work together, when barriers are broken down and common languages are spoken. BDS refuses to engage with this vision of peace and is instead diametrically opposed to it: in place of reconciliation and compromise, it instead casts blame, demands justice and openly insists upon the centrality of Palestinian rights.

All too often, criticisms of BDS can be traced back to an idealized or ideological understanding of contact that fails to acknowledge that Palestinian opposition to contact or normalization is not rooted within an inherent dislike of the 'other'; rather, as I seek to demonstrate, it is instead grounded within a principled political stance and a sound analysis of the limitations of contact. Past Palestinian contact experiences have been – as I will demonstrate in more depth – far from happy or productive. Opposition to 'normalization' should be engaged and understood in this context, as Issa Rabadi, of the Israeli/Palestinian Centre for Research and Information (IPCRI), demonstrates when he encapsulates the experiences of a substantial number of Palestinian participants, including the current author's.

He observes,

> I feel I have to explain myself and state that I do not work on normalisation. I tell people that I want to serve my cause and raise the awareness of the Palestinian identity through a peace education programme. People are usually sarcastic about the work with Israelis.[3]

In engaging with a number of the themes and issues raised by BDS, my analysis is pitched at a different level to many analyses of the programme, which instead focus on the question of attitudinal change and the resolving of negative perceptions or stereotypes. Although I do not deny that this is an aspect of the conflict, I am more predisposed to ask why international actors have accorded such questions a near-unparalleled significance. As a consequence of this prioritization, contact has taken on the appearance of an open horizon of possibility, to be exhorted and produced through a series of interventions.

I am more inclined to read this as an evasion of actually existing facts. International actors are fully aware of the fact that they have a limited ability to alter material realities. Instead of confronting an occupation and ongoing project of colonization, they have instead chosen to focus on attitudinal change. In addition to being easier to achieve, this approach also has a clear political expediency, as it sidesteps the various complexities of occupation. But an inconvenient fact lurks in the background, forever haunting this pretence: perceptions will alter when material realities change, not vice versa. In apparent defiance of a past history of protracted failure, prominent external donors (such as the United States and the EU) continue to fund P2P initiatives.

In highlighting the limitations of this self-serving arrangement by incorporating theoretical analyses of settler colonialism, I propose to critique the application of P2PP from an alternative perspective. In excavating the sedimented assumption that contact has the potential to reconfigure political realities, I propose to establish an alternative basis for theoretical and practical engagement with the Palestinian–Israeli conflict. I do not aspire to an optimal contact or to the establishment of conditions that enable contact to be more effectively enacted; rather, I instead propose to situate contact in broader context, with the intention of questioning, and ultimately undermining, its underlying assumptions.

By extended implication, I also propose to challenge the pervasive convention of objectivity, along with its pernicious influence on social science research. Edward Said previously anticipated a similar project when he sceptically regarded 'a knowledge always denying its complicities in the historical circumstances of its production (and reproduction), always proclaiming its openness, its fairness, its objectivity' (1979: 17).

In my own work, I have treated claims to objectivity with similar scepticism. For instance, my critical book review that engaged with Katz's *Connecting with the Enemy* (Katz, 2016) observed that the author's understatement and qualification of injustice was frequently couched in the form of an ongoing commitment to objectivity. I made my scepticism with this conceit quite clear: '[Katz's] commitment to impartiality and even-handedness all too frequently collapses into equivocation, occlusion and even denial' (Naser-Najjab, 2017: 312). While I was fully aware of the flaws within Katz's account, I was also aware of the likelihood that they would escape researchers accustomed to viewing 'research through imperial eyes' (Smith, 2012: 58).

Far from being a precondition for good research, objectivity more often takes the form of an unconditional demand that is imposed upon the subaltern. Fanon previously recognized this when he observed that 'objectivity is always directed against' the native (1963: 77). Objectivity, it might be said, is the product of various relations of force. Abu-Saad observes,

> The dominant group tended to know only its own understanding of reality and social relations because it had ignored, rejected, and silenced the differing perspectives of those over whom it had power. (2008: 1906) [H]ow skewed the discourse can become when neutrality is determined from the perspective of the dominant standpoint alone, in absence of an analysis of the power relations it is used to describe or disguise. (2008: 1914)

Donor attempts to enforce equanimity under the guise of objectivity elicited strong protests from Palestinian participants, who were fully aware that their acceptance of 'equal' conditions of participation in effect helped to sustain an inequitable status quo. The Israeli suggestion of a committee that would process entry to Jerusalem was a case in point. While it was ostensibly justified as a logistical measure, Palestinians were well aware that their acceptance would lend a de facto legitimacy to the occupation of East Jerusalem and would also reinforce an arrangement where Palestinians were to be granted 'concessions' by enlightened Israelis.

Palestinians resented the premise that they should be even-handed or balanced as they felt that this mitigated their claim of historical injustice. This recalls Smith's observations on the place of the native within history. She observes,

> The negation of indigenous views of history was a critical part of asserting colonial ideology, partly because such views were regarded as clearly 'primitive' and 'incorrect' [but] mostly because they challenged and resisted the mission of colonization. (Smith, 2012: 29)

The convention of objectivity also fails to problematize the fact that most research on the P2PP has been conducted by Israelis and Western academics (Chaitin, 2011; Gawerc, 2012; Hanssen-Bauer, 2000; Hermann, 2009; Hirschfield, 2000; Katz, 2016; Ma'oz, 1999). Despite the fact that the research of these academics is strongly influenced by established power relations, no consternation is elicited as long as they adhere to the sanctified customs and rituals of objectivity.

The corollary of neutrality obliges observers to be 'balanced' in their assessments (Zartman, 2007) with the consequence that an entirely artificial balance becomes superimposed on analysis. Jon Hanssen-Bauer (2005), Fafo's[4] managing director, who was fully acquainted with the P2PP's many failures and inadequacies, inadvertently makes this point when he insists that, with the benefit of hindsight, he would apply the same design again but with minor modifications. In apparent disregard of near-universal Palestinian opposition to the programme, he in turn proposes the scaling-up of participation as an additional improvement that could be introduced.

Given the extent to which the P2PP's holy trinity of 'objectivity', 'balance' and neutrality' remained loaded against them, it is scarcely surprising that so many Palestinian participants came to view it as an instrument that serves the interests of Israel (Mu'allem, 1999). The imposition of conditions by Israelis and donors (for similar analysis see Taiaiake, 2005), along with the use of the P2PP to improve Israel's public image, also reinforced this conclusion. It was not simply that P2PP did not enjoy substantial public support on the Palestinian side; rather, it was actively opposed by elements within Palestinian society. Insofar as Palestinians engaged, they were primarily predisposed to communicate aspects of their everyday existence to Israeli counterparts. As this book will demonstrate, this intention was not compatible with the P2PP's terms of engagement and reference.

In addition to being rooted in the specific failings of the P2PP, Palestinian opposition to contact is also strongly influenced by historical experience. In the current discussion of contact, observers sometimes seek to naturalize divide, invariably for their own purposes and ends. It always surprises me when I have to remind observers that the current state of affairs is not foretold but is instead the concrete product of a political project. It is, in many instances, necessary to firmly rebut and challenge the belief that contact needed to be created and engineered through an externally designed and implemented programme.

The artificiality of existing arrangements is the first issue that must be addressed. It is imperative to recall that Palestinians who remained in historical Palestine and became citizens of Israel in 1948 have always been subject to discriminatory Israeli policies that have sought to separate them from other Palestinians. After Israel was established in 1948, its Palestinian inhabitants remained under military rule until 1966. During both the First and Second *Intifadas*, Palestinians in Israel engaged in solidarity activities (Pappé, 2011; Rouhana, 1990). It is seldom acknowledged that the Oslo Agreement actually underlined this basis of cooperation by excluding this group. In reflecting on their status, Pappé observes,

> Zionism was the exceptional factor, not being a Palestinian in Palestine, or what used to be Palestine. This strong affirmation of the connection to the country and not to the state was the end product of a long internal Palestinian analysis of the predicament, crisis and nature of the community, which was followed by a prognosis and a kind of action plan for how to deal with the crisis of being a national indigenous. (2011: 195)

Even after the occupation of the West Bank and the Gaza Strip, Israelis and Palestinians still regularly came into contact. This contact was frequently voluntary – Palestinians travelled between the West Bank, Gaza Strip and present-day Israel without major restriction or impediment. This contact took a number of different forms. Palestinians visited Israel to shop, Palestinian schools and universities visited Israel, Palestinians worked in Israel and a range of solidarity activities brought Palestinians and Israelis together. West Bank and Gazan Palestinians would regularly travel to present-day Israel; Israelis would also travel to the West Bank and Gaza Strip, although to a lesser extent. These casual interactions were of course complemented by a more unwelcome form of contact – detainment in Israel prisons, encounters with Israeli bureaucracy and Israeli checkpoints.

In the 1970s and 1980s, contact between Israelis and Palestinians extended to a range of solidarity activities. These solidarity actions peaked during the First *Intifada* (1987–93). I personally worked alongside Israelis in a whole range of joint activities – these took the form of various forms of civil disobedience: demonstrations, sit-ins and vigils. Both Israelis and Palestinians stood alongside each other and were subject to the same vicious treatment by the Israeli army.

In retrospect, it is possible to see the limitations of these forms of contact. In often subtle and understated ways, the wider conditions of occupation intruded upon our interactions, influencing their dimensions and, to a substantial extent, anticipating their future trajectory.

Progressive Israelis came to these joint activities with a clear sense of what they were against but not so much what they were for. The slogans that we deployed ('End the Occupation' and 'Two States for Two People') could only thinly paper over the points of potential and actual divergence.

It seems perverse that the inauguration of a peace process should accentuate divides; but this is precisely what occurred. The Oslo Accords did change relations between Israelis and Palestinians but not in the way that was intended or popularly perceived. It would be instructive to reflect upon the reasons why the P2PP neglected to engage with this tradition of contact and instead chose to construct a largely artificial programme that was largely detached from the environment where it was implemented.

The professionalization of Palestinian civil society was an important outcome and accompaniment of this development. This was significant precisely because Palestinian participation was, in the first instance, so often preceded by the desire to enlighten Israelis about the occupation. But the P2PP made it impossible to engage on this basis and instead anticipated that participants would come together through shared cultural, professional or social affinities. The P2PP was, to this extent, detached from both local context and the motivations of Palestinian participants. When I spoke to Palestinians, I frequently found myself having to defend, explain or justify my continued participation.

I ultimately came to view the P2PP in the same way that I viewed the more general peace process. I was not predisposed to criticize either on the basis that they failed to achieve their stated aims or objectives; rather, I instead sought to criticize them on the basis that they failed to challenge, and therefore ultimately helped to perpetuate, the occupation. 'Peace', I came to conclude, has become an instrument through which a settler colonial project has found renewed purpose and impetus.

In documenting the tools and techniques through which colonial power is exerted, I am obliged to also highlight and engage points of resistance or subversion. In the final chapter of this book, I will therefore seek to demonstrate how Palestinians and Israelis are working together to challenge the colonization of Palestine. Although the number of Israeli activists is considerably smaller than during the First *Intifada*, this commitment is significant because it clearly demonstrates solidarity with the Palestinian struggle and highlights the internal limits of the colonial project. I argue that this ongoing commitment, when contrasted with P2PP, provides a more sustainable basis for the advancement of Palestinian–Israeli cooperation, not least because these activists generally recognize that the colonization of Palestine began in 1948 and not 1967.[5]

At this point, it would perhaps be useful to clarify the exact dimensions of the 'tradition' of contact that I have previously referenced. During the pre-Oslo period, Palestinians and Israelis had, as already noted, interacted across various levels. Although there were limited restrictions and impediments (for instance, Palestinians were not allowed to stay overnight in Jerusalem), Palestinians and Israelis were relatively free to move between the 1948 and 1967 areas.

But these restrictions were not as institutionalized or permanent as they came to be during the post-Oslo period. During this period, contact was both compulsory and voluntary. In the first sense, the occupation brought Palestinians and Israelis into direct contact. This included many aspects of day-to-day life and also extended to exceptional circumstances (such as the provision of birth and death certificates). Palestinians also sought paid employment in Israel. Although this contact was clearly hierarchical and sometimes exploitative in character, it nonetheless established the basis for sustained interaction.

At the political level, the Palestinian leadership remained strongly opposed to the principle of contact. Far from directly engaging with Israel, this leadership was reluctant to even acknowledge its existence. But even here the seeds of change had been planted – by as early as 1968, a few activists and leaders had begun to advocate contact.[6] Secret meetings had also been initiated at this early stage. Dialogue began to gain support from the Palestinian public in the late 1970s, when Peace Now formed and began to openly protest against Israeli settlement activity.

Meetings between Palestinians and Israelis gained momentum during the Israeli invasion of Lebanon in 1982 and the First *Intifada*, which broke out in 1987. A number of Israeli groups were established, and they began to openly challenge the occupation. Many groups were essentially pressure groups that sought to operate from within Israeli society. They included Yesh Guvl (There is a Limit), an organization made up of Israeli reservists who refused to serve in Lebanon. Parents against Silence was another significant organization made up of Israeli mothers who called on the government to stop the war and save the lives of their sons.

Palestinian–Israeli interactions peaked during the First *Intifada*. I directly participated in this mobilization, which operated on both a joint (Palestinian–Israeli) and individual (e.g. within Israeli or Palestinian society) basis. These activities took the form of demonstrations, sit-ins and talks to Israeli audience. Both Palestinians and Israelis organized solidarity and protest activities under the slogans of 'end the occupation' and 'two states for two people'. But we never discussed the political implications of these two slogans in any depth. Our discussions tended to be focused on logistical arrangements or on awareness-raising initiatives. Relations between Palestinian and Israeli activists were broadly positive, in no small part to the fact that the Israeli army did not distinguish between the two sets of protestors. Nonetheless, complications did arise at separate points, most notably during the First Gulf War.

These interactions gradually diminished in the post-Oslo period. When Israel closed Jerusalem, a permit system was established, and this restricted the movement of Palestinians in the West Bank and Gaza Strip. This meant that the 'Oslo generation', on both the Israeli and Palestinian side, grew up with minimal or very limited interaction. The main exception in this regard was the programmes that were established by the Oslo Agreement, which brought together a few hundred Palestinians and Israelis. It is something of a historical paradox, and even perversity, that the Oslo Accords instituted a physical and psychological separation.

The disjuncture between discourse and practice, which became an institutionalized feature of the peace process, was therefore, I would argue, foregrounded from the outset. Yitzhak Rabin's decision to close Jerusalem, which came into force in April 1993, served to illustrate that discourse and practice were, in many instances, contradictory or even antagonistic. Israeli settlement activity and the construction of an extensive system of bypass roads were significant in this respect. In addition to separating Palestinians and Israelis, these measures also separated Palestinians from their livelihoods, communities and land. This was the infertile soil in which the P2PP was supposed to take root. Donors repeatedly failed to incorporate context[7] into their interventions, and this further embedded the perception that the peace process was divorced from the needs, aspirations and rights of Palestinians. Given this bitter inheritance, it is scarcely surprising that the concept of 'peace' is now such discredited currency among Palestinians.

There was a clear divergence between the logic of contact and the actual practice that, at times, bordered upon the surreal. To take one example, a number of Palestinian participants who were denied access to Israel were granted special permits to travel to Europe (from Israel!) in order to participate in P2PP activities. The formal equality that each P2PP participant theoretically enjoyed was therefore undermined by wider inequalities.

This was also true when Palestinians and Israelis with shared professional backgrounds came together: here too, wider inequalities intruded and asserted themselves. As one example, Palestinians sometimes requested that Israelis indicate specific expressions of sympathy or solidarity in writing. Despite the challenges, international donors continued to insist that bringing Palestinians and Israelis together under the heading of professional cooperation would establish the basis for productive cooperation. Palestinian NGOs had limited scope to challenge this misconception, as it was a precondition for continued funding.

Inequality was not however merely a feature or attribute of P2PP implementation. Rather, it was frequently present from the outset, a point that is further reiterated by the fact that participation was, in the first instance, often underpinned by very different motivations, such as the desire to enter Jerusalem or Israel or travel abroad.

But inequality was only one among a number of factors, and it is important to acknowledge that criticism of the P2PP was being voiced by as early as 1995. Over time, it increasingly came to be viewed as a negative imposition that effectively legitimized the occupation. It should also be recognized that this concern predated the start of the P2PP, and this helped to explain why it was not initially underpinned by a strong Palestinian consensus. Over time, this and a range of other concerns coalesced into a clear agenda that was presented to donors. This fact notwithstanding, a range of P2P initiatives continued after the *Al-Aqsa Intifada*.

As an activist who had previously been engaged in solidarity-based work, I was well placed to observe that the absence of a common or overarching goal was a clear weakness. Incidentally, this weakness had also been apparent in joint initiatives during the First *Intifada*. Its absence from the P2PP was nonetheless particularly surprising because all theories of contact concur that the 'common goal' variable is the most crucial determinant of success in any given contact situation (Allport, 1954; Amir, 1969; Pettigrew, 1971). In retrospect, 'goal orientation' can be said to have been an important factor in helping to promote, sustain and legitimize participant engagement.

While participant criticisms were in many respects entirely legitimate, they do not provide the angle from which I seek to critically engage with the P2PP. I also view theories of social psychology as providing an insufficient basis for such an engagement, in no small part because they lack an analysis of power.

Ultimately, I orientate towards theories of settler colonialism, which map onto the precise exigencies of the Palestinian–Israeli conflict. This emphasis is characterized by a very clear distinction between colonialism and settler colonialism (see Veracini, 2010; Wolfe, 2006). Whereas the former seeks to exploit the host society, the latter instead seeks to replace it (in Veracini's (2010: 97) words, in settler colonialism the 'settlers come to stay' (see also, Wolfe, 2006: 388).

Because the P2PP failed to directly address the occupation it often reproduced it, albeit in more insidious form. In my reading, the ostensible neutrality of P2PP served to circulate and reproduce colonial attitudes, mentalities and predispositions. Its transformative potential, which was invested in by, inter alia, actors as significant as the Canada Fund, the European Union and USAID, is therefore rejected from the outset. While being presented in the benign vernacular of peacebuilding, P2PP ultimately came to function as a means through which relations of control and domination were perpetuated. It 'achieved' this by, to take just two examples, delegitimizing Palestinian narratives of struggle and constructing Palestinians as inferior subordinates. Knowledge played an essential role in the construction of this architecture, as Edward Said had anticipated in advance. He observes,

> There is, after all, a profound difference between the will to understand for purposes of co-existence and humanistic enlargement of horizons, and the will to dominate for the purposes of control and external dominion. (Said, 2003: xiv)

The overlap between power and knowledge is the central theme that Said expounded in *Orientalism*. Meetings under the P2PP served to legitimize particular forms of knowledge and delegitimize others. The structuring of the P2PP along external lines made it quite clear that Palestinians were to engage upon terms that were not their own, and the actual implementation of the programme made it quite clear that they were to engage as subordinates.

The pronounced failure to fully appreciate and incorporate this insight significantly impacted Palestinian disengagement. To this extent, many of the workshop activities were afflicted by a pronounced sense of artificiality and by a related sense that the activities had little relation to everyday experience and preoccupations.

Inadvertently, the P2PP underlined that differences between groups should be brought to the fore and not marginalized. It is unrealistic and indeed unreasonable to ask groups in conflict to ignore reality and focus on unrelated topics. But ideological renderings of contact continue to resist this insight, along with the fact that the two-state solution is increasingly an impossibility. While international protagonists remain beholden to the static and increasingly obsolete two-state framework, local actors have increasingly begun to explore alternative political possibilities.

The overwhelming impression is of an 'international community' that is captive to obsolete policy commitments. The most recent Palestinian–Israeli peace negotiations, which began in July 2013, resulted in deadlock after the Israeli government responded to the Fatah-Hamas[8] reconciliation agreement by suspending negotiations. But this could not conceal the fact, which was even acknowledged by US officials, that the Israeli government is actually the main impediment to a lasting solution. During an April 2013 meeting, the US secretary of state informed senior officials that Israel risked becoming an apartheid state if it failed to commit to a two-state solution (Rogin, 2014). Anonymous US officials also privately express the view that the construction of Israeli settlements is the main obstacle to peace talks (Barnea, 2014). In this respect, the United States is far behind local actors – after all, Peace Now was formed in the late 1970s in response to Israeli settlement activity in the Occupied Palestinian Territories (OPT).

In March 2014, John Kerry, the former US secretary of state, therefore claimed that the level of mistrust between the respective parties had reached the highest level that he had ever seen. Perversely, he then proceeded to claim that 'narrative' was the main obstacle that impeded a peaceful resolution of the conflict (Ravid, 2014).

Here Kerry reproduces the trope that holds the conflict is a misunderstanding, and that improved mutual interaction will help to establish the basis for more productive interaction and relations. This suggests that the root of the problem is more psychological than political. Having trained in social psychology, I know that conflict resolution frameworks are poorly suited to the Palestinian–Israeli conflict.

While it is admittedly difficult to conceive of circumstances in which an incumbent US secretary of state could admit that settler colonialism lay at the heart of the continuing conflict, it is clear that this would be a considerably more helpful intervention that would, at the very least, acknowledge the development of the conflict since 1948. In contrast, Kerry and his predecessors have scarcely begun to acknowledge the extent to which 'peace' has been grafted onto settler colonial dynamics.

This deteriorating political situation reminds us that the peace process has been, from its outset, defined by an essential dichotomy. Ostensibly, it has been justified as a process of reconciliation, in which former adversaries unite and move towards a better future. Here the powerful symbolism of conflict resolution is rendered in its full intensity. But at the same time the peace process has also been sustained by the desire of each party to separate and pursue their own national projects *in isolation*. It is an infrequently observed irony that Palestinians and Israelis actually came into contact more frequently *prior* to the onset of the peace process. To the same extent, the existence of a peace movement grounded within universal principles and values is also often overlooked (Hermann, 2009: 224–32).

Far from providing the basis for a sustainable resolution of the conflict, the two-state solution has instead become tied up with the perpetuation of various forms of injustice. It has given rise to the misconception that the conflict began in 1967. It has also shifted the focus away from questions of historical justice and towards the proposition of a limited territorial compromise. The fact that Zionism is a colonialist project (Hanafi, 2013; Lloyd, 2012; Piterberg, 2008; Sayegh, 2012) that achieved, and retrospectively justified, the expulsion of 80 per cent of historical Palestine's population is, as a consequence, conveniently set aside and disregarded.

The two-state solution has become implicated in the perpetuation of the conflict. It is not merely that there is a gap between the image and reality of the peace process; it is more that the very idea of 'peace', as embodied within the two-state solution, has become deeply intertwined with the extension of relations of dominance and control. This is shown by the fact that the refugee issue is regarded as a 'final status' issue rather than as something which is integral to the very conflict itself; it is embodied within the fact that the formal peace process makes Palestinian rights an object of political negotiation; it is embodied within the fact that Palestinians are, in a variation of 'divide and rule', split into different cantons and small sections of territory.

At the same time as the two-state solution is deteriorating, the two sides are increasingly drawn together in hostile union. Meron Benvenisti[9] openly states his view that 'Israel and the Palestinians are sinking together into the mud of the 'one state' (Benvenisti, 2003). This originates a strange dichotomy: as the two peoples conjoin physically, their collective psychologies become increasingly divided. If they persevere in their attempt to 'work around' the occupation, both the United States and the EU will persist in being part of the problem rather than the solution.

My own research has gradually moved towards the conclusion that the two-state solution is an inadequate response to the conflict. But, until recently, this sentiment was very much inconsistent with the consensus that had been established since the mid-1970s, when the two-state solution became synonymous with 'compromise', 'mutual recognition', 'negotiation' and, perhaps most crucially of all, 'peace'. The two-state framework, concepts and theories of conflict resolution and the P2PP are in many respects a series of concentric circles, which overlap and intersect at different points. The analysis of the P2PP (see Chaitin, 2011; Gawerc, 2012; Kaufmann and Salem, 2006) engages with these wider reference points.

In conclusion, it can be asserted that the Palestinian–Israeli peace process has been sustained by numerous illusions, including good faith, partnership and reconciliation. Contact has been an essential accompaniment to each illusion. It was clearly embodied in the famous handshake between Yitzhak Rabin and Yasser Arafat on the White House Lawn. For international observers, this symbolized the point at which the respective leaders set aside their mutual enmity and agreed work towards a brighter future. More than two decades have now passed, and contemporary Palestine presents a very different picture. The two national communities live in isolation from each other, and their separation is vividly embodied by the brutal architecture of the so-called separation wall, which Israel began constructing in 2002, and closures. But the divisions are as much mental as physical and extend across individual, social and political levels.

Researching under occupation

As both a Palestinian and coordinator of P2PP projects, my research is clearly situated within a specific context. It should be established from the outset that this book does not seek to emulate the 'objectivity' that is so frequently invoked in conventional social science research. In drawing upon questionnaires and interviews, I have nonetheless sought to retain a degree of detachedness in relation to my subject matter.

This research is intended as a contribution to the literature on P2PP. It is first important to recognize that this literature has been influenced to a disproportionate extent by Israeli researchers and grass-roots activists. This research has tended to assess and evaluate the P2PP from within a conflict resolution lens (Endresen, 2001; Hirschfeld and Roling, 2000; Maoz, 2004; Rosetti, 2005/6). Most Palestinian participants, in contrast, have been more predisposed to discuss colonial structures and imbalances of power. This further reiterates the importance of research that seeks to retrieve 'peace' from the interests and priorities of elite actors (Richmond, 2007). Other research highlights the limitations of conflict resolution frameworks that promote apolitical dialogue and overlook historical context (Thiessen, 2016).

The imbalance within the literature is important because, rather than engaging in a sustained questioning of underpinning assumptions and concepts, analysts of the P2PP have instead been predisposed to engage at the level of practice and to ask how existing interventions should be refined and adapted. The literature on P2PP often lacks an analysis of power. Theorists of the post-Oslo contact, whose work often developed within the field of social psychology, are often predisposed to conceive of contact as a self-contained consensual interaction. This contact is invariably theorized with reference to general models that are divorced from specific contexts. Even in instances where contact does not accord to prior expectations there is, by virtue of this feature, an expectation that it can be realigned.

This is an important oversight because I would suggest that the core issues are not logistical but are instead conceptual and theoretical. To take one example, the lack of a conceptualization or theorization of inequality (and here I would maintain that this oversight was in large part attributable to the predominance of Israeli perspectives within the literature) significantly detracted from implementation.

Most observers tend to operate within a problem-solving framework that is focused on implementation. Even when it acknowledges the wider political context, along with its assortment of impediments and obstacles, it ultimately orientates back towards the question of how the programme should have been applied. The concerns and priorities of Palestinian participants, including the closure and permit system (Darweish and Rigby, 2015: chapter 5; Maoz, 2000, 2004), appeared as 'externalities' that were problematically engaged and incorporated.

A closer engagement with this literature reveals that there is a clear lack of Palestinian perspectives. I view my own engagement with the subject matter as a clear advantage that would enable me to bring out novel perspectives and insights. But it was possible to anticipate situations where the converse might apply – it was, for instance, conceivable that interviewees might, because of our shared nationality, instinctively orientate towards the middle ground. It was similarly possible to conceive of circumstances where their Israeli counterparts would be reluctant to express negative views about the Palestinian approach to P2PP.

In May 2000, I left Ramallah and travelled to Exeter to begin my PhD studies. It had been six years since the Oslo Agreement had been signed, and this had inaugurated a qualitative shift in the relationship between Palestinians and Israelis. But this shift had been far from positive or conducive to the promotion of peace.

In summer 2001, about one year after the *Al-Aqsa Intifada* started, I began to collect data in Palestine and Israel. In responding to the tense political situation, the Israeli authorities imposed various impediments upon Palestinian movement. Israeli tanks besieged Palestinian cities and villages, and Palestinians experienced considerable risk when moving from one area to another. It was often necessary for me to navigate side roads when conducting interviews. Shooting incidents also made it very difficult to travel from one area to another. One interview had to be postponed when it was interrupted by tank shelling. It was sometimes necessary to conduct interviews by telephone, and the Jerusalem Media and Communication Centre (JMCC)[10] sometimes helped me to distribute questionnaires in areas outside of Ramallah.

Lee Perlman was the Israeli coordinator of the 'From Both Sides' joint project, and he worked as my opposite number during the project. On 9 August 2001, Perlman arranged for me to meet participants at Melitz's[11] offices in Tel Aviv. During the meeting there was a suicide bombing in Jerusalem, and there was a noticeable air of tension in the city. I was conducting my interviews at the Melitz office and four Israeli staff members were listening to the Hebrew news programme. But they simply carried on and did not say anything. Nor did the Israeli staff in Melitz change their plans as a result. Lee had arranged for us to have lunch with two Israelis from Melitz. The event did not influence our interaction, and we talked about my research and our joint projects; however, I began to feel rather uncomfortable in the restaurant when I started to receive phone calls from worried relatives and friends who urged me to go back.

I became increasingly anxious and decided to leave Tel Aviv immediately, only to discover that a high security alert had been declared. In the end it took me three hours to travel from Tel Aviv to Ramallah, a journey that normally takes forty-five minutes. With the help of an Israeli facilitator, I was able to distribute questionnaires by mail to the Israeli participants who had been unable to make it to Tel Aviv.[12]

In the later stages of my research the situation deteriorated further, and I was unable to travel back to Palestine to collect more data. During this period, Israeli restrictions upon Palestinian movement became even tighter. In working around these obstacles, I began to conduct interviews by telephone. I conducted my fieldwork in September 2003 at a time when even the minor roads had been closed. It was impossible for Palestinians to travel between Palestinian areas without a permit. I therefore decided to conduct face-to-face interviews in Ramallah City. When interviewees were unable to access Ramallah, I instead conducted interviews by telephone.

I had extensive experience of peacemaking, whether as a coordinator, facilitator or participant. It was nonetheless often challenging to engage with the challenges and questions of dialogue under these circumstances, especially as no solution or reconciliation was in sight. I was on personal terms with most of the people whom I interviewed (in some instances I did not need to arrange meetings), and most interviewees were identified through a 'snowball' method. Interviewees were also a vital source of information, who kept me up to date on new developments in the P2PP field (e.g. conferences, publications and/or seminars). Although the number of interviewees was limited by the intensification of the conflict, I do not believe that the quality of my data was negatively affected. In those instances where potential problems arose, I was able to take corrective steps.

While the book draws extensively on the material that was collected for my PhD research, it offers an important innovation by drawing on theories of settler colonialism, which have profoundly influenced the recent study of the Palestinian–Israeli conflict, to bring out ingrained power relations and dynamics. These theories help to sustain a critique of conflict resolution and social psychology theories (Zartman, 2007) and also extend the terms of discussion beyond limited donor agendas.

This book is primarily based on interviews, with both Palestinians and Israelis, that were conducted over the course of 2001 in the West Bank and Israel. These interviews were conducted under hugely challenging circumstances and were undertaken at a time when the security situation remained uncertain and precarious. In arranging interviews, I had to take account of the fact that violence could potentially erupt (during the course of one interview with a Palestinian facilitator, our interview was interrupted by tank shelling). At times, I had to rely on colleagues at the JMCC to distribute questionnaires on my behalf and sometimes I undertook telephone interviews.

The creation of Israeli 'facts on the ground' has made it near-impossible to entertain, let alone establish, a two-state solution (Hilal, 2007; Karmi, 2011; Peled, 2006; Sussman, 2004; Tilley, 2005, 2006; Yiftachel, 2005). This development has profoundly altered Palestinian–Israeli relations at both the macro and micro levels. Both Ahmad Qurei, the former Palestinian prime minister, and the former UN secretary general have observed that the one-state solution is increasingly becoming an inevitability (Associated Press, 2004; Sherwood, Willsher and Sparrow, 2012). Ilan Pappé, a figure who operates far outside of this policy horizon, further affirms that 'there is no chance of getting out of the deadlock in Palestine without tearing apart the façade of a fake peace process and the two-state solution' (Chomsky, Pappé and Barat, 2015: 177–8).

The P2PP provided an extra layer to this 'fake' process by instituting an arrangement in which Israeli participants were not required to engage uncomfortable topics or questions. This is why Palestinian citizens of Israel and Palestinian refugees were excluded from the terms of discussion (Hermann, 2009). This also brought to light tensions within the peace movement that had coalesced during the First *Intifada*. When the Oslo Agreement was signed, Israeli peace activists frequently voiced the opinion that peace had been achieved (ibid.). It is therefore not difficult to appreciate why tensions arose whenever the inconvenient subject of Palestinian refugees arose – on one occasion, an Israeli coordinator even claimed that it would be impossible for us to continue to work together if the issue of Palestinian refugees continued to arise.

The deployment of the settler colonial lens will provide an alternative framework of analysis and will also bring to light future opportunities for cooperation, thereby moving the terms of discussion beyond the limitations imposed by P2P. Settler colonial analyses also enable an inversion of power dynamics that became established in the aftermath of the Oslo Agreement. During the First *Intifada*, Palestinian needs were foremost. This changed in the post-Oslo era, as Israeli coordinators expanded their influence, thereby further compounding the various comparative advantages that Israeli NGOs possessed.

In the First *Intifada*, solidarity activities were highly politicized. P2P activities in the post-1993 era were however highly depoliticized, and participants were actively encouraged to engage on an apolitical basis (Hanafi, 2007). Palestinian acquiescence to this agenda should be understood in the wider context of Arab dependency on the United States and the growing orientation towards normalization and alignment with US-sponsored neo-liberalism (Hanieh, 2016).

In the First *Intifada*, Palestinians cooperated with Israeli solidarity groups in an effort to influence public opinion and pressurize the Israeli government. This agenda was indigenous to Palestinian constituencies. In contrast, P2P was to all intents and purposes an external imposition. Palestinian resistance to this imposed agenda grew as 'facts on the ground' were established and this ultimately culminated in the 2005 establishment of the BDS movement that called for the boycotting of P2P meetings.

This book builds up these developments to demonstrate how this alternative framework will advance the Palestinian–Israeli aspiration towards a better future defined by common goals and an arrangement where all 'enjoy full rights, equality and partnership' (Chomsky, Pappé and Barat, 2015: 178). In responding to the Israeli colonization of Palestine, actors have increasingly emphasized the one-state solution. In 2012, the *Israeli Committee Against House Demolitions (ICAHD)* issued a statement in support. Jeff Halper, ICAHD's director, explains,

> We must see ourselves as political actors[;] following the lead of our Palestinian partners we must formulate and pursue solutions that will provide justice, peace and the full range of human rights – civil, political, social, economic and cultural – guaranteed by international law. (Halper, 2012)

In April 2018, academics, activists, intellectuals and students launched the One Democratic State Campaign (ODSC) initiative. I was personally involved and helped to arrange a workshop that was held at the University of Exeter between 16 and 18 February. Members held events across Palestine and put together a ten-point draft platform that was published on social media. It has been officially launched in Spring 2018 (MEMO, 2018).

This is a significant initiative because Palestinians, including citizens of Israel and refugees, have taken the lead. The platform calls for a just solution grounded on equal rights with Jews and Palestinians living together in a democratic state. ODSC has also committed to influence Israeli public opinion on the one-state solution and the Palestinian Right of Return.

In contrast to the artificial encounters between Palestinians and Israelis within the context of P2P, this and similar initiatives have the potential to create lasting cooperation. Israeli activists responded to the Great Return March in Gaza, which began on 30 March 2018, having been organized by Gazan civil society to protest the Israeli blockade and demand the Right of Return. On the following day, the Coalition of Women for Peace organized a joint protest. These initiatives are significant because they reject the assumption that partition is a peaceful act. On the contrary, the partition of Palestine was an act of destruction, conducted under the veneer of a UN 'peace plan' that attracted no international reaction or condemnation (Chomsky, Pappé, and Barat, 2015).

The Orwellian peace

The word 'Orwellian' suggests a situation in which words are inverted and become fundamentally opposed to their actual meaning. Far from conveying or embodying reality, words are instead a form of violence inflicted on reality.

In the absence of a sustained analysis of either preponderant political realities or deeply entrenched power relations, the initial expectations invested in P2PP were always destined to be both misplaced and essentially illusionary. To a similar extent, the conflict resolution framework that external actors imposed on these interactions inflicted a false and wholly artificial sense of equanimity. Questions of historical justice and injustice, of dispossession and exile were problematically reconciled with, and even excluded from, a framework that was more predisposed to emphasize reconciliation.

In my role as a coordinator, I also frequently encountered the objection that Israeli participants appeared to think that peace was already in place, a misconception that appeared to derive from the premise that peace had already been achieved. This mistaken impression derived from the fact that, because Israeli and Palestinian participants were sitting and talking together, the only question that remained to be resolved was how they would build a common future. It slowly dawned upon the Palestinian participants that their participation within peace initiatives effectively legitimized the occupation – this created a resentment and suspicion that continues, to this day, to inform Palestinian resistance to normalization.

In failing to acknowledge, much less engage, these political realities, the P2PP took on a strangely detached and almost surreal appearance. The formal equality that the framework of engagement bestowed upon its participants could not have been more diametrically opposed to a political reality inscribed by occupation, dispossession and institutionalized violence. Edward Said had previously acknowledged this discrepancy in *Peace and Its Discontents: Essays on Palestine in the Middle East Peace Process*. He observes,

> The thought that by working out an arrangement whereby the occupation might continue while at the same time a few Palestinian and Israelis could nevertheless cooperate on a friendly basis, struck me as false and misleading. (1993a: 36)

The conceptual and practical shortcomings of the initiative were numerous: this point is reiterated by the fact that they provided more than sufficient material for my subsequent PhD thesis. As has already been noted, the framework failed to engage the occupation, failed to engage with uncomfortable historical realities and failed to acknowledge deeply embedded asymmetries of power and privilege. At a conceptual level, the initiative was also undermined by a series of simplistic assumptions that had an intuitive appeal (e.g. that contact and dialogue will reduce hostility) but which evaporated when they were transferred beyond a textbook.

There was also a range of logistical challenges – the Israeli authorities had imposed closures on the OPT just prior to the Oslo Accords, which made it much more difficult for Palestinians to attain the necessary permission to attend events held in Israel or Jerusalem (it was actually easier for Palestinian participants to travel abroad than it was to visit Jerusalem). In a particularly savage irony, the arbitrary impediments that the Israeli authorities imposed on Palestinian participants became a topic of discussion engaged during joint meetings. Donors continued to fund the P2PP, even after the actions of the Israeli authorities made it impossible to operate in any meaningful sense (a point which is further reiterated by the fact that internal restrictions upon movement made it necessary for us to arrange some joint events outside of the country).

External donors appeared to view established realities as an inconvenience that would be magically transformed once Israeli and Palestinian participants came into contact. But this overlooked the fact that both sets of participants engaged on a very different basis. Throughout the period of my participation in many of the post-Oslo joint projects, I could see that the Israeli side was initiating projects while the Palestinian side remained passive and reactive. Moreover, Palestinians involved in such projects were always critical and dissatisfied with joint meetings. Palestinian participants left these encounters with a strong sense of anger and disappointment.

My experiences have not shaken my commitment to the values that informed my initial commitment to reconciliation. I still believe that Palestinians and Israelis should work together to establish a shared future. But I cannot surrender myself to the naïve and simplistic assumption that these moral commitments will assume a force of their own, that they can overcome the material apparatus that sustains a system of occupation. If Israelis and Palestinians are to find a common cause and future, it must be in opposition to the occupation, not in an illusionary, transient and abortive 'peace'.

This book argues that the P2PP should be reconceptualized and understood in relation to a settler colonial project that sought to suppress Palestinian resistance by establishing the basis for a series of apolitical interactions that were phrased in the vernacular of peace and reconciliation.

To all intents and purposes, P2PP legitimized the occupation and helped to sustain it. This book works 'backwards' to question underpinning assumptions. It seeks to provide critical insight, with a view to shining a light onto contemporary debates about contact and its potential contribution to the resolution of the Palestinian–Israel conflict. It is not therefore intended as a work of history that provides insight into a particular feature of the past. Rather, it is forward-looking and predisposed to engage contemporary challenges.

It is driven by the belief that the research of the native, which is pre-empted by a rejection of any claim to neutrality, should work to achieve decolonization and disrupt a status quo rooted within 'competition, accumulation, and exploitation' (Grande, 2004: 30). As part of this project, it is essential to challenge dominant knowledge and its sustaining power relations (Abu-Saad, 2008: 1907; Smith, 2012). As al-Hardan recognizes, the researcher, and his or her position, has performed a crucial role in sanctioning the production of truths that sanction research participants' 'ongoing colonized and stateless realities'. By implication, he or she also has a central role in contributing to the truths that Palestinian communities produce as they contest these forms of power (al-Hardan 2014: 66).

As a Palestinian, I enjoy a number of advantages that leave me better placed to offer solutions to the dilemmas that confront indigenous communities (Smith, 2012: 151). My rootedness within the everyday experience of Palestinians is key in this respect (Abu-Saad, 2008: 1915), and my continued exposure to unequal power relationship (al-Hardan, 2014: 67) further enables me to explore points of resistance (Smith, 2012).

As a Palestinian, I am clearly distinct from what Tamari (1995) has termed 'a tourist' (or international researcher) and this leaves me better placed to answer the questions that Smith raises: 'Whose research is it? Who owns it? Whose interests does it serve? Who will write it up? How will results be disseminated?' (2012: 10)

As a Palestinian, I am also well placed to offer perspectives that challenge colonial relations and structures. My work has a clear parallel in the contribution of Elias Nasrallah (2016), a Palestinian citizen of Israel, whose autobiography explores the colonization of Palestine and its people. My research is grounded within resistance (Smith, 2012) and the possibility of a justice that will be achieved through decolonization, a goal that is rarely acknowledged, let alone pursued, in Western, mainstream research. It is about the power to imagine alternatives to the reality of colonialization that fragments and isolates natives (Smith, 2012: 125–6).

My research draws extensively on my own experience of a contact-based initiative. Much of the material that is referenced here was initially engaged in my PhD thesis, which was submitted to the University of Exeter. It also incorporates more recent innovations within my own work, which has increasingly drawn on concepts and theories of settler colonialism. In this respect, this book can be said to be a 'bridging point' that joins the two phases.

The first chapter situates the key features of P2PP in the wider context. The chapter also provides a critical analysis of the social psychology theories that donors adopted as a basis for the P2PP. The second chapter sets out theories of settler colonialism and seeks to demonstrate how they enable the programme to be reconceptualized as a settler colonial tactic or manoeuvre. This contribution seeks to provide insight into specific features or dimensions of the programme, such as power relations and established terms of participation. Chapter 3 puts the programme in historical perspective. The following chapter then considers the events of the First *Intifada* – this is a particularly important development because it clearly questions the assumption that contact needed to be created. Chapter 5 focuses on contact in the post-Oslo period and demonstrates how power imbalances and asymmetries between Palestinian and Israeli NGOs directly impacted the implementation of the P2PP. It will emphasize the donor role in defining contact and will also seek to demonstrate how the programme adapted to wider political changes. Chapter 6 refracts these general themes through a specific case study before Chapter 7 then provides a critical assessment of the programme. Chapter 8 focuses on changes and alterations in the aftermath of the *Al-Aqsa Intifada*. It also outlines alternative forms of cooperation that have emerged in opposition to colonial conditions. In the concluding phases, the outlines of future resistance are traced in closer detail.

While this book is focused on a specific P2P initiative, it ultimately speaks to a wider literature that includes area (Middle East), conflict and peace studies, international relations and social psychology. It will be of interest to activists, donors and policymakers who are engaged with the Palestinian–Israeli conflict; in cutting across each of these levels, it will ultimately contribute to productive debate and will enrich the policy discussion.

The book will also be of interest to those with a general interest in the Palestinian–Israeli conflict, which continues to be a subject of public debate in Britain, Europe and the United States. While the issue of Palestine continues to mobilize anti-war and peace activists around the world, a substantial part of the news coverage is incomplete and superficial. This book will make an important contribution by providing the basis for more in-depth analysis and discussion.

1

The context of P2PP

The Oslo II Agreement envisaged that dialogue would 'foster public debate and involvement and remove barriers to interactions'.[1] The P2PP sought to establish the basis upon which Palestinians and Israelis could engage within a neutral and non-threatening environment and participate in projects that worked towards common ends and purposes.

The P2PP emerged as a subcomponent of a wider peace project that sought to achieve a lasting resolution of the Palestinian–Israeli conflict. Although it initially made allowance for the direct participation of formal political actors, it became established, over time, as a micro-level initiative that sought to engage grass-roots actors on both sides of the conflict. It was grounded within an apolitical vision of contact and the belief that personal and professional affinities would encourage Palestinian and Israeli participants to set their differences aside and engage on a cooperative basis.

The P2PP was essentially the grass-roots component of the peace process (although initially it had incorporated an official dimension – see below) that would bring pressure from below.

Madeline Albright, the then US secretary of state, would later commit $8 million to P2PP projects,[2] in the form of the Wye River Memorandum, in support of this vision.[3] During an October 1998 press conference, she observed,

> The reason I think there is a desire to be more pro-active on the people-to-people activities is that if you get business people together or teachers together or children, that it helps to change the atmosphere. So you really have something coming from two directions: the mood of the leadership and then the mood of the people.[4]

Here Albright invokes participation, which can be said to be one of the defining attributes of P2PP. In the first subsection of this chapter, I engage with its features and seek to explain how the P2PP emerged as a largely externally sponsored project that ultimately developed into a grass-roots project. I then proceed to engage with theories of social psychology, which can be conceived as the conceptual or theoretical underpinning of the P2PP. The chapter's third subsection discusses the implementation of the P2PP and therefore identifies and sets out key stages. Equally importantly, it also engages externalization as a continuity that extends from the P2PP's inception to its later stages.

The key attributes of the P2PP

The P2PP focused upon attitudinal change – that is, upon challenging and changing negative perceptions and attitudes about the 'other'. It was grounded within theories of social psychology and therefore sought to establish optimal conditions for contact, in the expectation that this would fundamentally alter the ways in which the two sides perceived each other. After being launched and funded by the Norwegian Ministry of Foreign Affairs, it attempted to establish the principle of cooperation, further the exchange of information and contribute to the development of concrete projects.

The P2PP clearly states its intention to

> promote initiatives in areas which are likely to have an impact on people's everyday lives and welfare, including practical activities which will promote communication and understanding by demonstrating the advantages of working together for mutual benefit and tangible results. (Partnership for peace, 2014: 1)

The European Commission further clarifies,

> The specific objective of [P2PP related activity] is to strengthen civil society actions aimed at promoting peace and confidence building in order to broaden the base of support [for] a negotiated solution of the conflict. The programme intends to support practical actions [thereby] building mutual trust, building capacity for conflict resolution, launching joint development

initiatives [and] empowering marginalized groups. (Partnership for Peace, 2012: 4)

The origins of the P2PP can be traced back to 1994, when Uri Savir, the then director general of the Israeli Ministry of Foreign Affairs and one of the Israeli negotiators in the Oslo talks, suggested the idea to Jon Hanssen-Bauer, who was then Fafo's managing director. Savir suggested that it would be beneficial to create an environment in which Israelis and Palestinians could come together and conduct peaceful dialogue (Hanssen-Bauer, 2000).

The P2PP was established by Annex XI of Oslo II (entitled 'Protocol Concerning Israeli-Palestinian Cooperation Programme'), which came into force in 1995.[5] The Norwegian government funded the first initiatives, and other funding agencies subsequently provided further funding assistance. The term 'P2P' was originally used to reference Norwegian-funded initiatives and was then expanded to refer to all donor-funded activities in this field.

The P2PP was initially funded by the Norwegian Ministry of Foreign Affairs, although the European Union, USAID and the Canada Fund later provided financial support. These donors set out clear funding criteria in order to ensure that joint (Israeli–Palestinian) projects functioned in accordance with the general principles set out in Article VIII (Annex VI) of Oslo II. In establishing the programme, the Norwegian Ministry of Foreign Affairs asked the Oslo-based Fafo Institute for Applied Social Science Centre for International Studies[6] to assume various managerial functions. In addition, the Norwegian government also assisted in the formation of a 'Standing Cooperation Committee' (SCC).[7] This committee would be made up of representatives from both sides,[8] and it would be responsible for coordinating all cooperative activities and projects. Lena Endresen[9] explains that the two-tiered organizational structure

> combine[d] governmental control and popular civic activities. One tier consisted of the governmental steering committee, made up of representatives from the Palestinian, Israeli and Norwegian authorities. On the other was the non-governmental body, which consisted of planning groups from the two parties, and a Norwegian Programme Secretariat. (2001: 9)

Day-to-day administration was implemented through Israeli and Palestinian Planning Groups,[10] while Fafo assisted with coordination. The Ramallah-based

Palestinian Centre for Peace (PCP), a Norwegian-funded non-governmental organization (NGO), which was established in 1997, provided administrative support and functioned as the Palestinian planning group. (The CRB Foundation[11] functioned as the Israeli planning group, funded the Israeli contribution to joint projects and worked closely with the Israeli Foreign Ministry.)[12]

The planning groups, PCP and CRB, along with the SCC jointly formed the hub steering committee – they contributed by screening proposals and recommending which ones should receive funding. This screening enabled both sides to control applicant access to donor funding. This had important implications for both the geographical scope and range of activities that were associated with donor funding (Endresen, 2001: 13). The guidelines that the Norwegian government set out were not always followed by other donors, and this had a substantial impact upon the structure of P2PP projects. It was relatively straightforward – subject to the usual conditions – for a joint Israeli–Palestinian application to be accepted; however, it was near-impossible for a Palestinian NGO to obtain funding without an Israeli partner.

The Planning Groups were responsible for upholding the principle of equal partnership, most notably with regard to fund distribution and implementation. They were also responsible for monitoring the political content of the project and ensuring that they did not conflict with predefined interests.

Jon Hanssen-Bauer, Fafo's former managing director, clarifies,

> The two parties run and have full control over the Programme. They have the final say and have to agree on which projects to recommend for funding. The authorities on both sides are involved in the selection of projects, and take ownership of the Programme but not the responsibility for each project. (Hanssen-Bauer, 2000: 38)

Although the P2PP was implemented by Palestinian and Israeli NGOs, it was ultimately subject to official scrutiny, in the form of the SCC. This level of official engagement distinguished the Oslo II P2PP from other people-to-people initiatives that were sponsored by other countries (Endresen, 2001; Endresen and Gillen, 2000).

A number of Israeli and Palestinian NGOs were formed and registered in response to the programme. The two main conditions were that each proposal should not exceed $20,000, and that it should be implemented jointly and at the local level. The funding limit of $20,000 was deliberately imposed in the expectation it would promote the involvement of smaller NGOs (Hanssen-Bauer, 2000: 38). Applicants were invited to apply under one of the five categories: (1) Youth; (2) Adult dialogue and seminars; (3) Culture; (4) Environment; and (5) School twinning and education.

The P2PP was advertised in local newspapers, and advertisements were presented in four languages – Arabic, English, Hebrew and Russian (in Israeli Russian newspapers).[13] The People-to-People Guidelines for Applicants set out clear assessment criteria; projects were expected to: (i) enhance dialogue and improve Israeli–Palestinian relations; (ii) be jointly implemented by Israeli and Palestinian organizations; (iii) foster wider exposure of the two publics to the peace process, both through education and by encouraging public discussion and involvement in the peace process; (iv) increase people-to-people exchange and potentially bridge the gap between large audiences on both sides; and (v) operate in the region.[14]

The underpinning elements of the P2PP: Social psychology theories

The P2PP framework was foregrounded within the guiding tenets of social psychology and sought to extend the belief that attitudinal change could make a real and lasting change to local political and social conditions. In being voiced in the vernacular of conflict resolution, it sought to enable participants to 'speak across the divide' and 'build bridges'. This confirmed that the Palestinian–Israeli conflict was, from the perspective of the P2PP's designers, conceptualized in the same way as any other conflict.

The influence of social psychology was also clearly attested to by the prominence of the contact hypothesis, which is premised on the belief that contact between members of different conflict groups will, in providing knowledge and challenging stereotypes, reduce prejudice, produce positive attitudes and establish a basis for peace. The hypothesis asserts that the four conditions for a sustainable peace are common goals, equality of status, institutional support and intimate relations (Allport, 1954). The P2PP's sponsors and participants engaged the programme with the expectation that contact would help to eliminate negative stereotypes and produce cooperative behaviour between Palestinian and Israeli participants.

The P2P-related article of the Oslo Agreement II envisaged a happy circumstance in which a consensus upon dialogue would foster public debate and remove barriers to interaction.[15] If this was to be achieved, then it was a necessary precondition for these activities to be immunized from the wider context. It was therefore no coincidence that contact-based activities were envisaged and developed in closed settings.

The P2PP sought to achieve attitudinal change. Theories of social psychology have examined inter-group contact, with the intention of reducing prejudice and reinforcing positive attitudes. Contact theory is grounded in the assumption that improved knowledge will help to eliminate stereotypes. While different theories vary with regard to their approaches and the optimal conditions for effective contact, they all ultimately converge on the proposition that interaction can help to change negative attitudes (Allport, 1954; Pettigrew, 1971; Tajfel, 1974; Tajfel and Turner, 1979). Social psychology theories were adopted by international donors before being incorporated into practical initiatives. They offer the insight that the 'common goal' variable is the most crucial factor in any contact situation.

These contributions are perhaps drawn into question by Palestinian–Israeli contact experiences from the First and Second *Intifadas* that demonstrate that productive contact can be sustained even in the absence of preconditions first identified by Allport (1954) and later refined by others (e.g. Amir, 1969; Cook, 1962; Pettigrew, 1971). Palestinians and Israelis who met during the Second *Intifada*, for instance, sought to challenge barriers and obstacles put in place by the political situation. Israelis who supported the Palestinian effort to subvert the checkpoint system met with their counterparts at the borders to show their solidarity. This occurred despite a clear lack of support from the Israeli public and a manifest lack of institutional support.

The formal equality that the P2PP was premised on was also likely to prove to be difficult to realize in practice. Brewer and Miller observe,

> In many racially and ethnically mixed settings [it] is not so easily achieved, since participants come into the situation with pre-existing status differentials

based on group membership. Even if there are no formal status differentials within the cooperative setting, ethnic identity may serve as a generalized cue for expectations of differences in ability and competence. (1996: 117)

Both authors suggest that ability differences could be resolved by compensatory measures that close the gap between lower- and higher-status groups. An enhanced access to information could, for example, improve the ability of the disadvantaged group.

Some theorists suggest that differences between groups should be recognized (Hewstone and Brown, 1986; Pettigrew, 1986) and proceed to suggest the acknowledgement of existing differences along with the adoption of a multicultural approach (see Hewstone and Brown, 1986). Brown (1988) suggests that intimate relations which encourage groups to discover shared similarities are not effective. This was not in itself sufficient as the key condition of success appeared to be the duration and length of contact between members who met as representatives of their groups.

In a study of Northern Ireland, Trew (1986) finds that short and casual contact between Catholic and Protestant would enable individuals to discover similarities without being diverted by differences (p. 10). She also emphasizes that political divisions between Catholics and Protestants are not illusory (p. 103). Differences between members of different groups in this case therefore have to be brought out in contact situations as this reality cannot be ignored (Miller, Urban, and Vanman, 1998; Trew, 1986). Institutional support is another factor that contact theorists link to positive attitudinal change (Allport, 1954; Amir, 1969; Pettigrew, 1971). Foster and Finchilescu (1986) present research results obtained from South Africa that demonstrate that positive contact experiences tend to be specific to a given situation.

Theorists also link the wider social context and laws by suggesting that the efficacy of the latter is limited when the former is hostile. Morris and Jones (1993) therefore observe that desegregation laws did not bring an end to racial tensions in the United States. Other research reiterates that a supportive social climate is an essential precondition for positive contact. Fitzduff (1999) observes that Northern Irish legislation introduced without support from the civil community was not been effective. In building on this observation, she suggests that NGOs have an essential role to play in helping to build a positive consensus through civic education, dialogue and democracy. But the contribution of Foster and Finchilescu (1986) questions whether such innovations can succeed when wider social tendencies are opposed.

A new paradigm within social psychology has sought to address problems with the contact hypothesis. Social identity theory (SIT) does not reject this inheritance but instead seeks to build upon it. SIT argues that the perception that individuals have, of themselves and others, is the key condition of successful contact. Contributions from Tajfel (1974) and Tajfel and Turner (1979) advocate the inter-group approach as a foundation for understanding the effect of contact, while suggesting that there is a positive link between the images that people have of their group and themselves. Social categorization theory and the minimal group experiment developed by Tajfel et al. (1971)[16] provide its conceptual and theoretical grounding. This provides a foundation for an understanding of how individuals assign themselves to groups, develop in-group identity and discriminate against the out-group.

Three basic models were developed to anticipate in-group bias: decategorization, inter-group contact and recategorization. These models were based on the manipulation of interaction and therefore sought to identify if positive interaction between members of different groups depended on the salience of either social or self ('decategorization') or instead attained a common in-group identity ('recategorization'). The debate basically revolved around whether contact was more successful when members of different groups met as individuals (Brewer and Miller, 1984, 1996) or as representative of their groups (Hewstone and Brown, 1986).

Self-categorization theory engages with cognitive processes and group behaviour to explain why an individual conforms to groups in order to overcome uncertainties deriving from attitude, behaviour and beliefs (Hogg and Mullin, 1999). In many joint projects, administrators and coordinators design programmes that are professional and focused. Their intention is to emphasize individual, as opposed to national or social, identity.

Dag Lonning observes that, in a real inter-group setting, personal experiences can explain the various motivations of the participants of the dialogue group. He notes that some participants have internalized symbolic interethnic meanings, and that this creates a clear challenge for those who seek to create positive contact and dialogue encounters: in some cases, it is only personal interethnic experiences that will sufficiently counter these deeply internalized systems (1995: 139). While these differences were not evidenced in the workshop described by Cohen et al. (1977), this may have been attributable to the ongoing prohibition on contact on both sides. Subsequent to the signing of the Accords, participants evidenced a greater willingness to challenge attitudes towards the out-group.

The influence of the macro level on dialogue groups and their behaviour is similar in both Palestine and Northern Ireland. Trew (1986) demonstrates that interpersonal relations between Catholics and Protestants in Northern Ireland were correlated with the political situation to the extent where the latter could not be ignored. While group loyalty could be accentuated in some instances and it was possible to conceive of instances where perceptions of the 'other' group could be reinterpreted, it was in many respects a prior consideration that impinged upon the respective participants. For this reason, it was difficult to envisage circumstances in which contact could reconfigure the fabric of society (Trew, 1986: 105–7).

It was also unclear how interpersonal contact would generalize to the group, and this led Trew to conclude that there was no link between the two. Recent theories of contact suggest that generalization, which is a key preoccupation for coordinators and advocates of Palestinian–Israeli joint projects, ultimately relates back to the question of whether contact is individual or collective. A South African study had previously made an important contribution by suggesting that the arguments that each side applies to the presence of the 'other' reflect their own views and beliefs. In seeking to make sense of contact, individuals mobilize arguments that justify certain kinds of collective/personal action and disqualify others (Dixon and Reicher, 1997: 364).

It quickly became clear that a foundation of goodwill and knowledge was not sufficient to sustain the P2PP, and it also became apparent that its appropriateness to the given context had not been interrogated to a sufficient extent (Dixon and Durrheim, 2003; Dixon and Reicher, 1997). It was therefore significant that most Israelis criticized Palestinians for raising the refugee issue and argued that the past was the past and the future should be the core focus and objective. Israeli participants also tended to prefer cultural and social engagement because this preserved their privileged position (Tajfel and

Turner, 1985). Palestinians instead orientated towards political engagement, as their intention was to bring about lasting change.

The case study research confirms that the absence of the common goal variable was, in the Palestinian–Israeli instance, the main impediment to the contact objectives. Most Palestinians engaged with P2P activities viewed them instrumentally – that is, as a means through which to challenge the Israeli occupation. The P2P programme brought to light a clear divergence of Palestinian and Israeli goals (see Chapters 3 and 4). SIT clearly identifies how the goals of the privileged group may differ radically from its underprivileged counterpart and stresses that this divergence is most likely to be evidenced in different attitudes to social change. Despite identifying this feature, SIT has not managed to propose a realistic solution (Tajfel and Turner, 1985; Turner, 1999).

The conceptual and theoretical foundations of the programme derived from the field of social psychology. Under ideal circumstances (equality of status, intimate relations, common goals and institutional support), the two sides would come together and inter-group contact would directly challenge negative attitudes towards the 'other' (Allport, 1954; Pettigrew, 1971; Tajfel, 1974; Tajfel and Turner, 1979).

The P2PP in practice: A brief history

From the outset, the P2PP was regarded with suspicion by Palestinians – this was shown by the fact that even Palestinian officials who were committed to the peacebuilding agenda were reluctant to officially endorse P2P activities. For example, the Palestinian Ministry of Education did not provide an official declaration in support of contact through joint projects and did nothing to facilitate such projects. Zakaria Al-Qaq[17] refers to the difficulties that IPCRI encountered when it attempted to implement peace education projects in schools. He reflects,

> We were unable to work with a single Palestinian public school. The Palestinian Ministry of Education refused to give us the green light. The Ministry justified this position as being due to bureaucracy, and claimed that such projects would require approval from the Council of Ministers,

due to public pressure on the official Palestinian system. Therefore, we only were able to work with private Palestinian schools. (interview with Al-Qaq, 15 December 2003, Jerusalem)

Official involvement became problematic, however, when Palestinian officials began to disassociate from the programme. Yolla Haddadin, PCP representative at the ministerial level, observed that there was a clear perception among Palestinian political elites that grass-roots activities should be detached from official peace initiatives.[18] Jon Hanssen-Bauer, Fafo's managing director, observes,

> We still had the support from the political leaders at the top on both sides, but their priorities changed. They did not want to get really involved and publicly to launch the Programme. Our solution became to 'de-couple' the activities from the events on the political level and to 'go grass-root'. We launched the NGO Programme in 1996. (2000: 37)

The 'official' dimension of the programme, which had strongly influenced the programme's development, now became an obstacle and impediment. Despite this, P2PP activities continued to take place outside of the programme. It was therefore at least partly due to necessity that the P2PP became conceived as a grass-roots initiative. The P2PP had initially made allowance for both official and grass-roots components, in the understanding that they would be mutually reinforcing; nonetheless, it was all too easy to conceive of instances where they could potentially diverge. Benjamin Netanyahu's 1996 election as Israel's prime minister was significant in this respect.[19] Naseef Mu'allem (of the Palestinian Centre for Peace and Democracy) observes,

> The Israeli peace movement doubled its activities after the fall of the Labour government, and this increase affected and activated People-to-People projects. The peace camp in Israel during Netanyahu's time used joint projects for their own benefit to strengthen their position and prepare for new elections. (2000: 11)

Endresen[20] demonstrates how the NGO level subsequently emerged as the most active programme component, and this substantially diverged from the original expectation that state institutions would play an active role in the programme and contribute to interactions between NGOs (2001: 10–11).

Fafo initiated the NGO programme in 1996. By mid-2000 the P2PP had, according to the Fafo database,[21] funded 136 projects (Endresen, 2001: 14). It established the basis for short-term projects, long-term projects, workshops, seminars and cooperative and professional encounters. However, implementation was far from straightforward and a number of obstacles were encountered.[22]

In recognizing the ongoing deterioration of the political situation, the administrators decided, in January 2004, to halt all activities. Two developments were key in this respect. First, a Likud government with no interest in P2PP was elected; second, CRB, the Israeli NGO, withdrew from the programme in response to the election of the same government. Even in the aftermath of this decision, Mahmoud Abbas (Abu Mazen), who had previously been lukewarm about the P2PP, sought to re-engage, with a view to restarting the P2PP in some form. However, while each of the respective stakeholders (notably, the Israeli and Norwegian governments) were engaged, these discussions never led anywhere.[23]

In responding to these developments, predicaments in the peace process and emerging facts on the ground, international donors incorporated the P2PP into the peacebuilding/statebuilding process in the aftermath of the *Al-Aqsa Intifada* (Bouillon, 2004; Bouris, 2010; Haddad, 2016; Khalidi and Samour, 2011). Statebuilding has been a largely elite-driven project that has been sustained by external knowledge, political commitment and financial support and might be assumed, in key and important respects, to be diametrically opposed to the logic of a grass-roots initiative.

Both statebuilding and the P2PP did nonetheless share an apolitical tenor. The latter evidenced this when it applied the assumption that contact could occur on a personal or professional basis. In meeting under the rubric of the P2PP, Palestinians and Israelis would encounter each other as individuals rather than as members of separate national groups. Neo-liberal statebuilding, for its part, is premised upon the belief that enhanced output efficiency can sufficiently substitute for a meaningful political existence. Khalidi and Samour observe,

> The statehood program encourages the idea that citizens may have to acquiesce in occupation but will not be denied the benefits of smoother

running traffic, a liberal education curriculum, investor-friendly institutions [and] efficient public service delivery. (2011, 15)

Despite a deeply problematic past history, external donors and political actors continue to fund and support P2P-based initiatives. In this respect, contact-based initiatives can be broadly said to resemble modernization and development, two other projects that found a renewed justification and impetus in failure. Indeed, despite a continually reiterated donor commitment to 'evaluation', the overriding impression is of an ideological commitment that must be sustained and perpetuated. This, I will argue, is the story of the P2PP.

Conclusion

This chapter has clarified some of the P2PP's key features and has also set out its conceptual and theoretical antecedents. The P2PP was apolitical in tone and was predisposed to work around, rather than directly acknowledge, structural political realities. In large part, this was attributable to its grounding in the contact hypothesis and other core tenets of social psychology. In this and a number of other key respects, the programme was heavily externalized and had little or no relation to the specific context where it was applied. To this extent, it represented a break with, rather than a continuation of, a tradition of contact that could be traced back to the First Intifada.

From its inception, the P2PP lacked support among Palestinians, many of whom were sceptical about its ability to attain its stated objectives and, perhaps equally importantly, its unstated objectives. The expectation that the formal political level would interweave with the grass-roots programme proved to be entirely misplaced – the converse was actually true, as the two levels actually conflicted with each other and grass-roots engagement was conceived in opposition to the impediments and obstacles created by the formal political process. It seemed somehow appropriate when the programme was ultimately subsumed into the equally flawed statebuilding project.

While it has noted this general condition of failure, this chapter has consciously and deliberately refrained from pointing out the programme's defects or weaknesses, as these will be engaged in more depth in later chapters. It has nonetheless established the basis for critique by highlighting the P2PP's ingrained orientation towards general solutions, its reliance on external resources and its highly theoretical character. Each element implicitly anticipates the critical analysis that will follow.

The key concern of this chapter has been to engage with the defining attributes and underpinning elements of the P2PP. By necessity, this has implied a neglect of wider context, not least because the programme itself had manifested a conspicuous disinterest in context, along with its various manifestations and implications. The following chapter will now offer an important corrective in this respect by engaging, outlining and developing theories of settler colonialism and critical interpretations of development.

2

The colonial context of P2PP

The preceding chapter essentially described the P2PP by setting out its defining attributes. In this chapter, I instead propose to consider the P2PP in wider context. This will be achieved by incorporating theories of settler colonialism and critical contributions to the development, both of which I interpret as being uniquely well-suited and adapted to the Palestinian–Israeli conflict.

In addition to providing further insight into the general attributes of the Palestinian–Israeli conflict, theories of settler colonialism also bring out important parallels with other settler colonial projects. The P2PP closely resembles Canadian 'native' reconciliation initiatives in many respects (Coulthard, 2014), while the contributions of Frantz Fanon, Albert Memmi and Lorenzo Veracini clearly resonate with many of the contemporary features of the Occupied Palestinian Territory (OPT) and Palestinian–Israeli relations.

As I demonstrate in this chapter, theories of settler colonialism have an essential contribution to make by linking the Palestinian struggle to native and indigenous movements that have mobilized in other contexts. They reject reducing the issue of 'Palestine' to the parameters of a two-state solution that is fixated on lands occupied after 1967 and necessitate a closer interrogation of Zionist ideology and the ability of the two-state solution to deliver on the many promises that have been advanced in its name. Given these limited goals, they require a closer engagement with 'decolonization and liberation as the imperative goal[s]' (Salamanca et al., 2012: 4), proceeding on the basis of the understanding that the settler-colonial project is a 'structure not an event' (Wolfe, 2006: 388).

The incorporation of theories of settler colonialism and critical readings of development enables the discussion to engage the range of measures that the Israeli authorities deploy to suppress Palestinian resistance. Closure, collective punishment, displacement, incursion and incarceration are applied both singularly and in combination, complementing a disjointed and inchoate peacebuilding project and a somewhat more coherent and advanced state-building project (Halper, 2015; Turner, 2015; UNHRC, 2015).

An established critical literature, grounded within contributions from Oliver Richmond (2007), Haddad (2016), Shehadeh (2015) and Hanieh (2016), establishes that it is a profound error to view peacebuilding and state-building as being emancipatory or transformative in character. In this chapter, I accordingly propose that both practices appear as technologies through which colonialism finds a renewed impetus, perpetuation and rationale. This rendering of peacebuilding and state-building as 'subtle' forms of coercion and control that work through and within the agency of local actors clearly recalls the work of Antonio Gramsci, which examined how ruling-class power was exerted within society. Gramsci relates

> the entire complex of practical and theoretical activities with which the ruling class not only justifies and maintains its dominance, but [also] manages to win the active consent of those over whom it rules. (Hoare and Nowell-Smith, 1971: 244)

I therefore echo Turner's claim that peacebuilding is a pacifying tool that 'requires serious and extensive strategies in the realm of governance, development and security' (2015: 75). Furthermore, I invoke Tartir (2017) in asserting that Israel's security has *guided* the peace process – by implication, it has not just been a preponderant consideration. As such, it has produced closures, the creation of 'facts on the ground', the fragmentation of land and restrictions on movement (Ophir, Givoni and Hanafl, 2009) and a system of surveillance (Shalhoub-Kevorkian, 2015). Each element, in individual and cumulative effect, has functioned to impede independent Palestinian economic development (Haddad, 2016; Hever, 2017).

Here I should confirm that I am not interested in the idealized concepts of peacebuilding that are frequently used to justify interventions, which were repeatedly invoked within the P2PP, to take one example. Rather, my critique is instead focused on 'neo-liberal peacebuilding' (Haddad, 2016), which I understand to be a combination of discourse and practice that orientates towards the reproduction of power and domination (Foucault, 1980).

Foucault once observed that 'discourse is the thing for which and by which there is struggle, discourse is the power [that] is to be seized' (Foucault, 1984: 110). It was as discourse that neo-liberal peacebuilding fundamentally transformed the vernacular in which Palestinian resistance was presented, signalling an abrupt shift away from inalienable rights and instead repositioning these same rights as points of contestation and dispute (Badarin, 2016, chapter 7). This discursive structure was accompanied by an enhanced and sophisticated practice that worked towards the fragmentation of Palestinian land. As Turner and Shweiki (2014) observe, fragmentation and division have been key components of the Palestinian experience since the *Nakba*. Both features were in turn reproduced within the programme, as exemplified by the requirement for Palestinian participants to obtain a permit before traveling to Jerusalem or Israel. Palestinian citizens of Israel were also excluded at the outset, before being considered as suitable participants when participation from the OPT began to decrease.

The P2PP should be engaged and understood in this wider context of neo-liberal peacebuilding and state-building and should be understood to be subject to forms of discipline and normalization that operate through the conditions and terms imposed by donors and Israel (Khalidi and Sobhi, 2011: 15). It would be no exaggeration to remark that the state-building project has not only failed (Hanieh, 2016; Hilal, 2010) but has also become complicit in colonization and dispossession. International intervention has become interwoven into a colonial project of displacement (Hanieh, 2008; Pappé, 2017).

Neo-liberal state-building has therefore succeeded in achieving a compromise with the occupation. Just as neo-liberalism institutes a sharp divide between the 'economic' and the 'political', neo-liberal state-building clearly distinguishes the Palestinian Authority's (PA's) policy interventions as an autonomous sphere that operates in accordance with its own internal logic. To the same extent, Palestinian society is conceived and theorized as an independent sphere of engagement, into which the Israeli occupation does not intrude. Insofar as it is acknowledged, the occupation is treated as an administrative inconvenience, in much the same way as a flawed legislative or regulatory environment. As Badarin notes, 'The overall institution-building and capacity-building arrangements coexisted with the operative colonial structure instead of bringing it to a close' (2016: 159). There is, as Hanieh notes, a steadfast reluctance to acknowledge that the occupation is the antithesis, and very denial, of Palestinian development (2013: 118).

In this discussion, I intend to demonstrate the contemporary resonance of settler colonialism along with its potential, and actual, application to the Palestinian–Israeli conflict. I draw upon an emerging literature to bring out themes that include elite co-option, indirect rule and the strategic deployment of reconciliation. I argue that the Palestinian–Israeli conflict should be refracted through the lens of other historical struggle and should be interpreted as a continuation of the struggle for freedom, equality and basic human dignity.

In this chapter, I engage with general theories of settler colonialism with a view to establishing core theoretical tenets and also explaining how these theories can be applied to the contemporary situation in the OPT. The discussion then proceeds to examine three key attributes of the contemporary situation that closely align to a settler colonial analysis. The first is a leadership that has been co-opted into wider strategies and priorities. While it ostensibly acts of its own accordance, the true significance of the PA's interventions and actions is only fully intelligible when regarded in wider perspective. The second is forms of government that operate through forms of consent. Here I adapt the Foucauldian notion of subjectivity to demonstrate how 'subtle' forms of control help to orientate the conduct of the Palestinian population. 'Normalising Occupation and Colonialism' then explains how international actors have – for a variety of reasons – found it more convenient to 'work around' than to confront conditions of occupation in order to demonstrate the strategic use of reconciliation as a means of control and coercion. A conclusion then summarizes key points, establishing a basis for following chapters.

Theorizing settler colonialism

Theoretical frameworks that engage with the phenomenon of settler colonialism are not just focused on forceful imposition; rather, they instead originate within the important observation that the indigenous population is displaced or eliminated by a variety of techniques, which include force (Veracini, 2010: 33; Wolfe, 2006). Coulthard's observations that relate to the 'productive' dimensions of colonial power are particularly instructive as they reiterate that colonialism is not just sustained through relations of force (see Coulthard, 2014; Fanon, 2008; Veracini, 2011: 5).

In order to gain critical purchase on the specific operations of the P2PP, I suggest that the insights of Foucault and Gramsci are of particular importance as they provide insight into 'soft' or 'consensual' forms of indirect power that operate through indirect means. Robert Cox observes,

> International institutions embody rules which facilitate the expansion of the dominant economic and social forces but which at the same time permit adjustments to be made by subordinated interests with a minimum of pain. (1996a: 138)

Mechanisms such as peacebuilding, development and even state-building can therefore be theorized as extensions of 'soft control' that help to perpetuate the existing hegemony and thereby serve established interests within the international system (Khalidi and Samour, 2011: 15). In place of the ruling class that Gramsci referred to, we can instead refer to preponderant international actors – both political and economic – that work towards the preservation of the status quo (Gramsci, Hoare, and Nowell-Smith, 1971: 244).

Gramsci's concept of hegemony does not deny agency. Instead, power is exerted when individuals 'consent' to power. Incentives and rewards help to sustain this arrangement. But coercion remains a factor – this is the key implication of Gramsci's allusion to forms of power that are 'half man, half beast' (Cox, 1996a). This finds an echo in Coulthard's account of the integration of Canada's indigenous communities during the 1960s and 1970s, which adapts Fanon and Gramsci to explain how the politics of coercion and consent results in 'internalisation, with the colonised coming to see the social relations of colonisation as "true" or "natural"'. Coulthard explains,

> In the Canadian context, colonial relations of power are no longer reproduced primarily through overtly coercive means, but rather through the asymmetrical exchange of mediated forms of state recognition and accommodation. (Coulthard, 2014: 15)

Gramsci also demonstrated how this power is exerted through and within civil society. The NGO sector, which international actors have come to realize has a considerable potential as a means through which to subtly remould political and social realities, appears as the international counterpart to this domestic civil society.

An initial distinction should first be established between colonialism and settler colonialism on the grounds that, whereas the former seeks to exploit or extract surplus value from the indigenous population, the latter instead works towards their elimination (Mamdani, 2015: 610; Veracini, 2010: 33, 101; 2011: 1; Wolfe, 1999: 1; 2006: 388–9). Patrick Wolfe argues in line with the preceding analysis by arguing that, while settler colonialism possesses a 'logic of elimination', it is 'not invariably genocidal' (2006: 387). This chapter builds on this insight to suggest that Zionism can be categorized as settler colonialist for the reason that it ultimately seeks to eliminate the Palestinians (Derek, 2004: 79; Hilal, 1976; Sayegh, 2012). When conceived in this framework, elimination can take different forms (see Veracini, 2010) and can conceivably extend to forms of education that deny the culture and history of the colonized (Naser-Najjab and Pappé, 2016). Here pacific and aggressive tendencies coexist, being embodied in applied technologies such as 'partnership'. Veracini explains,

> The language of partnership is also politically correct and persuasive. Utilising both as weapons for change remains tempting, but these strategies have proven ultimately ineffective against settler colonial structures of domination. (Veracini, 2011: 5)

Pappé (2013) observes that when Israel occupied the West Bank and Gaza Strip in 1967, it viewed both as part of 'Eretz Israel' (Segev, 2007). In support of this claim, he suggests that Israeli plans for occupation had already been drafted four years previously (Pappé, 2013). In 1968, Yigal Allon, the then deputy prime minister, put forward a set of proposals to the Israeli cabinet. These proposals, which became popularly known as the Allon Plan, suggested that Israel should annex the Jordan valley and the southern part of the West Bank (Raz, 2012: 244–7). The plan's emphasis on displacing Palestinians continues to resonate today, as the case of Khan Al-Ahmar[1] clearly illustrates (B'Tselem, 2018).

Even as it ritualistically intoned the mantra of 'land for peace' for the benefit of credulous international observers, the Israeli government began to colonize the OPT. Settlement activity then accelerated after Likud was elected in 1977, although it still remained relatively limited when the First *Intifada* broke out ten years later. Some settlement activity was explicitly supported by the Israeli government; in other instances – such as when Gush Emunim played a leading role – this activity could be traced back to a mixture of political, religious and security motivations (Weizman, 2007).The colonization of Palestine had begun decades earlier, being evidenced in the targeting of culture, language and narrative and the displacement of the indigenous population and the Judaization of the land. Colonization activities in the Galilee and Negev were particularly instructive in this regard (see Nasasra et al., 2015; Rouhana and Sabbagh-Khoury, 2015).

Other observers ascribe a similar logic of elimination to Israel's settlement activities in the West Bank (Pappé, 2013; Shafir, 1984). Badarin explains how the expansion of Israeli settlements in the West Bank facilitated control of Palestinian land and space, expanded Israeli surveillance (see Halper, 2015; Weizman, 2007) and extended a logic that is 'essentially eliminatory' (Badarin, 2015: 4).

In being applied to these developments, settler colonial theory has made numerous valuable contributions. The work of Nur Masalha (1992) and Piterberg (2008) highlights the place of transfer within Zionist thought, while David Lloyd positions the Israeli occupation in wider perspective (he describes it as an 'exemplary settler colonial project' (2012: 59)). Yiftachel, meanwhile, explores the ethnic foundations of the Israeli state ('Zionism remains a deeply ethnocratic movement [that is] premised [on its] "historic right" over the entire "promised homeland" and the associated "othering" of the Palestinians' (2005)).[2]

Colonialism is both embodied and reproduced through discourse and visual symbols. To a certain extent, colonialism appears as a psychological phenomenon, in which the colonized internalizes a sense of his/her inadequacy (Fanon, 1963; Memmi, 1974). Coulthard speaks of a 'psycho-affective' element that influences the colonized's negative perception of him or herself and therefore maintains colonial structure.

The contribution of Taiaiake Alfred (2005) also underlines how an acceptance of the colonizer's terms helps to dictate the behaviour of the colonized. Simpson further clarifies,

> Part of being Indigenous in the 21st century is that regardless of where or how we have grown up, we've all been bathed in a vat of cognitive imperialism, perpetuating the idea that Indigenous Peoples were not, and are not, thinking people. (2011: 32)

In engaging in frameworks that are defined and orientated by the terms of the colonizer, the colonized becomes hostage to a version of 'peace' that has no meaning or significance for them. In my own work on the one-state solution, I sought to demonstrate, through interviews with Palestinian political leaders, how they came to participate in a process whose outlines were framed by settler colonialism. Palestinian leaders have internalized this framing to the extent where they now reject any attempt to move beyond the parameters of the two-state solution (Naser-Najjab, 2014; also see Fanon, 2008; Taiaiake, 2005). This internalization is of course both reflected and reproduced in relations of dependency.

This reluctance to engage with the reality is in large part attributable to a pivoting of Israeli diplomacy, which reordered and realigned the basis on which external actors engaged with the conflict. Fanon, as if anticipating this development, spoke of 'a diplomacy which leaps ahead, in strange contrast to the motionless, petrified world of colonization' (1963: 78). He fully anticipated instances in which 'the enemy, in fact, changes his tactics. At opportune moments he combines his policy of brutal repression with spectacular gestures of friendship [and] manoeuvres calculated to sow division' (1963: 136).

Contemporary observers, in failing to register the truth of Fanon's contribution, all too frequently make the error of assuming that settler colonialism is a historical phenomenon, which can be engaged and studied in much the same way as any other historical event. Current-day visitors to the Palestinian West Bank will however note a clear contemporary echo. Herein lies the significance of Scott Lauria Morgensen's assertion that 'settler colonialism directly informs past and present processes of European colonisation, global capitalism, liberal modernity and international governance' (2011: 53).

The colonial structure should be theorized in relation to both the colonized and the colonizing society. In the latter instance, it is most clearly indicated in a culture of militarism whose reach extends to, and is in some cases synonymous with, civic institutions. It is no coincidence that opponents of colonialism within the colonizing society will therefore emphasize the long-term *internal* impacts of colonialism. Similarly, classical texts of colonialism, such as Franz Fanon's *The Wretched of the Earth*, focused upon both societies.

The established distribution of power, both within the international system and in the relations between colonizer and colonized, helps to explain why it is reconciliation, as opposed to justice, which tends to be prioritized. Coulthard recognizes the extent to which this desire originates in bad faith. He states,

> What is treated in the Canadian discourse of reconciliation as an unhealthy and debilitating incapacity to forgive and move on is actually a sign of our *critical consciousness*, of our sense of justice and injustice. (2014: 126, emphasis in the original)

Crucially, this preoccupation with reconciliation is implicated in what Veracini refers to as a 'specific interpretative deficiency' and a 'systematic disregard of the colonially determined characteristics of the Palestinian struggle'. Veracini (also see Kimmerling, 1983; Lockman, 1976; Shafir, 1989) is consistent in this regard – in appraising the collapse of the 2000 Camp David talks, he suggests that they ultimately highlighted Israel's inability to countenance, much less accept, full decolonization (2006: 8) – this is despite the fact that its ability to pursue settler colonial ends has arguably decreased in the aftermath of 1967 (Veracini, 2013: 28). This is why he insists that decolonization remains an option for the Palestinians of the West Bank and Gaza Strip. He also notes that options remain open to the Palestinian inhabitants of contemporary Israel (ibid.: 38).

Veracini's previous indictments of 'interpretative deficiencies' and 'systematic disregards' have a clear resonance in this context. The conflict resolution paradigm traces conflict back to flawed interpretations or communication processes. But in the case of the Palestinian–Israeli conflict both factors have a limited resonance: the fragmentation of Palestinian land and territory, the creation of sub-divisions of Palestinians and the creation and exploitation of internal political divides were clearly intended and in large part products of a colonial strategy that was quite clearly intended (Benvenisti, 2010; also see Roy, 2004).

But Veracini's abrupt treatment of the conflict resolution paradigm does not sufficiently address the question of what should be done with the 'coloniser who refuses', a figure who frequently appears in the work of Albert Memmi. During my activism, I repeatedly encountered such individuals, in the form of well-meaning Israelis who struggled to fully divest themselves of colonial assumptions. For Memmi, this essential confusion can be traced back to an inability/refusal to accept national liberation in its entirety (1974: 78).

The work of Avigail Abarbanel, which engages with the tortured experiences of Israeli activists, provides particular insight into the 'coloniser who refuses' (Abarbanel, 2012). In my reading, these activists are clearly distinguished from large sections of the Israeli Left by the fact that they have successfully questioned their own inheritance. In their accounts, I found no trace of the colonizer who 'offer[s] obscure or Machiavellian rationalizations where the simple mechanics of colonization are self-explanatory' (Memmi, 1974: 88). Similarly, I found no trace of those who were motivated more by their own 'contradiction and uneasiness' than by a sense of historical injustice (1974: 88).

In other words, liberal 'guilt' and the desire to be rid of it cannot provide a sustainable basis for peace. Simpson extends this criticism to liberalism more generally and specifically the belief that because the historical 'wrong' has been corrected, no further transformation is required (2011: 22). There is a clear insinuation here that concessions will be tolerated insofar as they do not impinge on the convenience or privilege of settler Canadians (Simpson, 2011: 24). This understanding also underpins Taiaiake Alfred's criticism of self-government initiatives that leave basic power structures intact. In referencing the Canadian example, he observes that 'the state has nothing to fear from Native leaders. [E]ven if they succeed in achieving the goal of self-government, the basic power structure remains intact' (Taiaiake, 1999: 71).

This suggests that the colonizing society frequently fails to grasp the historical or contemporary injustice of dispossession and occupation (Simpson, 2011: 21). Coulthard notes that the importance of land for the native frequently fails to be acknowledged in its full significance (2014: 59). Meanwhile, Dunbar-Ortiz relates 'encounters' and 'dialogue' that produce little more than 'apologies for one-sided robbery and murder' (2015: 5).

When well-intentioned and well-meaning Israelis sought to engage with Palestinians, they frequently found that it was not possible for them to step outside of their prior identity as an Israeli. In one workshop, an Israeli participant expressed her deep offence when a Palestinian told her that she could only see an Israeli soldier when she looked at her. The contrast with the contact experience of the First *Intifada*, when Israeli solidarity groups were warmly greeted and considered as coequals in the struggle against occupation, provides a clear and instructive contrast.

This highlights the limitations of conflict resolution theories and frameworks and suggests the need for an alternative framework of engagement. Pappé observes,

> It is time to adopt a new dictionary that views Israel as a settler colonialist state and the Palestinians as leading an anti-colonialist struggle. Decolonization is more relevant than a 'peace process' for the torn land of Palestine and Israel. (2013: 350)

In highlighting the limitation of the peace process, he adds,

> [It] was born as concept at a certain given moment, in June 1967, and was part of the settler colonialist state's attempt to reconcile the Israeli wish to remain demographically a Jewish state while at the same time expand geographically without losing the pretence of being a democratic state in the post-1967 reality. (2013: 341)

Pappé's work demonstrates the fact that Israel's 'concessions' in the name of peace have always been far from straightforward. Quite the contrary – its invocations of coexistence and mutual friendship have always been contingent and sometimes contradictory.

A co-opted leadership

The P2PP functions in the wider context of the peacebuilding framework put in place by Oslo, which was an interim agreement meant to address the conflict at each stage. From its inception, the peace process was therefore intended to respond to developments on the ground. The Palestinian Authority (PA) was established upon the principle of self-rule and was widely understood to be establishing the foundation of a future Palestinian state. But from the outset, the PA was a weak political actor with limited capacity to alter material realities, and this in turn led to the accusation that it was engaged in 'false decolonialization' (Tabar and Salamanca 2015: 12) that sought to co-opt

Palestinian struggle and resistance while creating a privileged class beholden to a neo-liberal agenda that was fundamentally opposed to the needs of the Palestinian people (Nakhleh, 2012).

The liberal peacebuilding project became synonymous with agendas that were advanced by the Israelis and donors through unequal power relations (Haddad, 2016; Shehadeh, 2015, chapter 4). The PA's endorsement of the neo-liberal donor agenda had a negative impact upon Palestinian political unity, by reinforcing divisions between the West Bank and Gaza Strip (Khalidi and Samour, 2014). The neo-liberal agenda 'hollowed out' indigenous state-building efforts and the Palestinian interest in the building of a sovereign, democratic state (Sayigh, 2009), while introducing a clear tension between the economic and political components of Palestinian state-building (Roy, 2002). The Palestinian commitment to counterterrorism astonished even Uri Savir, the chief Israeli negotiator, who noted that the Palestinian leadership evidenced a considerable willingness to influence Palestinian public opinion, leaving the Israelis to focus upon security issues (Savir 1998, 102).

Nonetheless, the PA sought to build an independent security capacity. Palestinian security forces had been established in 1994 by the Cairo Agreement. The PA then increased the size of these forces, although significantly this did not arouse any objection from Israel (Al-Shu'aibi 2012; Tartir 2015). This is one illustration of how security cooperation has been subject to ad hoc amendments and adjustments (Swisher, 2011: 53–62). Perhaps more importantly, security cooperation created the expectation that the Palestinian leadership would actively assist the colonialist agenda – the Cairo Agreement, for example, required the PA to prevent hostile acts against settlements located in Area C.

The PA's dependency on international funding enabled Israel to dictate conditions in all subsequent negotiations, which were then embodied in specific agreements (Hilal and Khan, 2004). State-building became a tool in the hands of the Israeli government, which worked closely with international donors to focus on Israeli security and interests (Dana, 2015). The Paris Economic Protocol, to take one example, permitted Israel to collect custom duties and tax revenues on behalf of the PA (Zagha and Zumlot, 2004).

The advancement of the 'peace' project enhanced Israel's control over the OPT and furthered its ability to pursue colonial ends and objectives.

Financial aid assisted categorization, fragmentation and control (Hilal, 2015; Turner, 2012). Sarah Roy explains the socio-economic dimension of the Oslo agreements, along with its negative impact upon Palestinian lives (Roy, 2012). Peace/state-building under these conditions is deeply problematic and ultimately contrary to the interests of the Palestinian people (Pogodda and Richmond, 2015). Richmond renders the Palestinian case as

> an extreme example of the statebuilding paradigm (along with Iraq). Here the state is a vehicle for regional order, to which local questions of justice and rights are secondary. This is the outcome of donor collusion with the Israeli state over a peace that is a thinly veiled occupation. (2013: 7)

Turner draws the inescapable conclusion that negotiations and peace agreements have put in place a 'colonial peace' that favours Israel (2012: 11). This 'peace' downgrades Palestinians political priorities (such as Jerusalem and refugees) and enables Israel to exert control over a fragmented population and continue its expansionist project (Veracini, 2013). This development had been anticipated in advance when the Palestine Liberation Organization (PLO) entered into negotiations through secret channels, thus weakening the influence of wider Palestinian political constituencies and resulting in crucial issues being deferred (Cavanaugh, 1999). Uri Savir, the lead Israeli negotiator, expressed surprise at the number of concessions that PLO leaders were willing to make. In registering their 'surprisingly flexible positions', he noted that they were 'far more practical' and escaped the 'legalistic tangles created by the non-PLO delegation in Washington' (Savir, 1998: 4).

The forms of control that Israel exerts through political economy clearly parallel those that are applied within the context of P2P activities. This was demonstrated when Palestinian participation was driven, sometimes in the first instance, by the exigencies of occupation – the desire to gain access to Jerusalem or Israel was one example in this respect. This also applied to NGOs, which were required to comply with donor agendas in order to access funding. When P2P is situated in the wider context of these disadvantages and impediments, it becomes easier to understand the Palestinian reluctance to engage with P2P. Donors evidenced a limited ability to engage with these objections in their full significance and sometimes suggested capacity-building as a suitable response to the various impediments imposed by occupation.

State-building reproduces the series of distortions and inequalities that derive from the wider occupation. Shir Hever (2010) reiterates this point by noting that most international aid benefits Israel by reinforcing colonial structures and increasing PA dependence (Hever 2010). The P2P programme also provided disproportionate financial benefits for Israeli NGOs and also improved Israel's international image.

Indirect rule is an established tactic and component of colonial rule. In registering the costs associated with the extension of colonial power, colonial actors came to realize the potential cost and efficiency savings that could arise from the co-option of local actors, who would then claim to rule while actually furthering and serving colonial interests. In the 'post-colonial' era, indirect rule is invoked in arrangements where largely powerless 'local' leaders serve the interests of multinational corporations and leading states within the international system.

The emergence of a 'client class' is one of the defining features and preconditions of neocolonialism, and it is clearly evidenced in the Palestinian context. Hanieh explains how the Palestinian mode of development has only benefitted a small elite, contributing to class contradictions, while deepening divisions and fragmentation in Palestinian society (2016: 42). Hanieh demonstrates how development projects coexist with the structural features of Israeli colonialism (2016: 35). For him, the PA assists this arrangement because its inability/unwillingness to challenge Israeli control over land, natural resources and population perpetuates this arrangement (also Hilal, 2010). Hilal also relates various forms of inequality (Hilal, 2010: 1) to wider colonial structures.

The PA perfectly illustrates a number of features of indirect rule, having been established after the Israelis fully registered the costs of occupation during the First *Intifada*. Israel ultimately sought an arrangement in which it could retain the benefits of occupation (economic, political, security-related) while outsourcing or subcontracting the costs. The establishment of the PA enabled it to achieve this and also served to perpetuate myths of 'autonomy' and 'cooperation', thereby helping to placate – at least initially – important international constituencies.

From the outset, the PA's structural weaknesses were clearly evidenced. It could be argued that this was intentional. In the contemporary period, the PA's pronounced dependence on external funding (see Khalidi, 2006, chapter 5) is actually an asset as it enables external actors to 'discipline' the PA (see Cox, 1996a: 138; Haddad, 2016). There is perhaps a parallel with Tania Li's account of development interventions in Indonesia, which clearly set out the ideological content of the enterprise along with its internal and external limitations.

She attributes developmental failure to an inability/unwillingness to address structural inequalities and also maintains that there is a clear analogy between those who currently claim to uphold the interests of indigenous population and 'their' colonial predecessors. She attributes this parallel to the fact that neither group envisages reversing the 'dispossessory effects of capitalism' (Li, 2000: 399).

Li's research engagement with Indonesia, an ethnographic account based on two decades of research, explains how intervention in the highland, which was justified in the name of improvement, disrupted people's lives and left them without the means to improve their own productivity. Citing Gramsci, Li observes that 'power is lived and inequality is normalized at the nexus of force, consent and the production of desires for particular ways of living' (2014: 17).

But Li aligns herself with development orthodoxy when she argues that development intervention projects didn't work because they were imposed on highlanders and failed to acknowledge the interests and needs of individuals. In failing to meet these requirements, the projects also failed to help highlanders obtain 'their' share of development resources (2014: 163). In an equally significant contribution, she rejects the teleological assumption that development is a creative (if painful) destruction (2017: 1249). In her treatment, 'development' appears as little more than a self-perpetuating myth that diverts attention from inequality and political realities.

Even if the PA were minded to challenge the core tenets of the development enterprise, its structural weaknesses would militate against this course of action. While the Accords were ostensibly based on the principle of formal equality, it is infrequently recognized that they actually helped to perpetuate various forms of inequality, which extended from the PA to the P2PP. Embedded or structural weaknesses also left the PA clearly exposed to colonial tactics of 'divide and rule'. A 2002 reform plan promoted by the United States, which focused on institutional reform, market economic and counterterrorism actions (Bush, 2002), quite clearly favoured one faction over another (Ahern, 2012: 173). The protracted power struggle between Abbas and Arafat, during which the 'international community' made no secret of its preference for the former, provided a further example.

This critique can also be extended to 'internal' Palestinian politics and specifically to the political parties that have become dependent on donor funding (Hammami, 1995). This weakness of political representation has been further exacerbated by the marginalization of the PLO (Ghanem, 2010; Hilal, 2010). Haddad observes that the integration of political parties into post-Oslo donor aid, in spite of their opposition to Oslo, has further reinforced their vertical dependence on (overwhelmingly Western) donor funding while further weakening their political and financial accountability to their grass-roots bases (2016: 199). Dependency ultimately predisposes the colonized to search for solutions within the colonial structure.

In operating within a conflict resolution framework, the PA has instead adopted an approach that owes more to reciprocal compromise. In this respect it can be clearly contrasted with the Boycott, Divestment and Sanctions (BDS),[3] which evidences a much clearer comprehension of ongoing political realities. In many respects, the emergence of BDS could be conceptualized as a local response to ongoing fragmentation, along with a number of its most important corollaries (human rights abuses, settlement expansion) (Lloyd, 2012: 66). A number of observers have therefore sought to present the BDS movement as a 'counter-hegemonic' struggle that directly challenges the neo-liberal order (see Buchanan 2000; Lloyd and Wolfe, 2016).

Governing through subjectivities and civil society

In the preceding subsection, indirect rule was largely discussed with reference to the forms of indirect control that are exerted over the PA. But indirect rule can also be exerted over groups or even whole populations. This control is not exerted directly on the subject but is instead reframed, reconfigured and circulated through their subjectivity, meaning that control becomes indistinguishable from its object. This presents a heightened efficiency and economy, requiring less expenditure and incurring fewer costs.

The work of Sara Roy, which is focused upon the political economy of the 'peace process', provides insight into indirect means of coercion and control. She explains how the 'de-development' of the Gaza Strip and the expansion of West Bank settlements are components of a general strategy that seeks to impede Palestinian national aspirations (Roy, 1995: 117).

The NGO sector is a conduit through which international resources are circulated and directed (Hammami, 1995; Hanafi and Tabar, 2005; Tamari, 1995).

Funding acts as an additional disciplinary source, helping to regulate and integrate the agency of local actors. Over time, this discipline becomes internalized and is reproduced in the acceptance of established codes and conducts (e.g. the writing of funding proposals). External knowledge also assists the legitimization and therefore the perpetuation of particular practices. In a number of key respects, P2PP can be said to function as a power/knowledge nexus (Foucault, 1991, 2002: 103–21).

In order to fully unravel this compound, it is first essential to recognize that Foucault insisted that power should not be, as in the legal-juridical tradition, understood in terms of repression or denial; quite the converse, it should instead be engaged with a clear understanding of its creative potential. He observes,

> We must cease once and for all to describe the effects of power in negative terms: it 'excludes', it 'represses', it 'censors', it 'abstracts', it 'masks', it 'conceals'. In fact power produces; it produces reality; it produces domains of objects and rituals of truth. The individual and the knowledge that may be gained of him belong to this production. (1991: 194)

Coulthard's development of Marx's concept of primitive accumulation is particularly instructive in this respect. In emphasizing the productive character of colonial power, he stresses that it does not necessarily need to be 'understood as strictly coercive, repressive, or explicitly violent in nature'. This productive dimension appears as the counterpart to the 'coercive authority of the settler state' (2014: 152). Lorenzo Veracini explains how population transfer draws on various strategies, only some of which involve physical displacement (2010: 33). His allusion to activities that fall 'within the cultural horizon of colonialism' (2006) also acknowledges this broader horizon of interventions.

Contributions from Memmi (1974) and Fanon (1963), in bringing out the complexity of interactions between the colonizer and the colonized, similarly refuse the proposition that it can be reduced to relations of force.

Foucault notes that 'power is exercised only over free subjects, [only] insofar as they are free'. The P2PP approximates to this outline because it did not – at least ostensibly – tell participants how to think or act. Rather, it attempted to subtly guide participants towards appropriate forms of conduct that they would then enact. Its influence was indirect rather than direct. Governmental technologies that operate through discourse (1991) are perfectly embodied in the contemporary operations of civil society and the NGO sector. Foucault observes,

> Governing people is not a way to force people to do what the governor wants; it is always a versatile equilibrium, with complementarity and conflicts between techniques which assure coercion and processes through which the self is constructed or modified by himself. (Foucault, 1993: 204; also see Shalhoub-Kevorkian, 2015: 6)

Normalizing occupation and colonialism

In their engagements with the Palestinian–Israeli conflict, international observers have historically evidenced an unwillingness to engage the occupation in its full significance – that is, as an underlying cause of the conflict. It has, to varying degrees, been treated as a legal violation, a political inconvenience and an impediment to normalized relations. To put it differently there is, and this feature became particularly pronounced in the 'Oslo' era, a reluctance to acknowledge that the occupation is a prior, as opposed to subsequent, consideration. This is a point that Fanon previously made in relation to colonialism. He observes,

> When you examine at close quarters the colonial context, it is evident that what parcels out the world is to begin with the fact of belonging to or not belonging to a given race, a given species. In the colonies the economic substructure is also a super-structure. The cause is the consequence; you are rich because you are white, you are white because you are rich. (1963: 40)

This was shown by a clear continuity with what had come before. This echoes Hanieh's account of development models that 'attempt to incorporate Israeli colonialism into the very practice of development itself' (2016: 35; also see Alfred, 2005: 180), and it also overlaps with Selby's analysis of water resources in the OPT. In referring to the issue of water usage, he observes that 'much of what had previously been patron-client relations under occupation were suddenly discursively repackaged and represented as instances of Israeli-Palestinian "cooperation"' (2003: 123).

He adds,

> Formalisation of Israeli-Palestinian cooperation had enabled Israel to divest itself of some of the most onerous burdens of occupation, without losing control of either water resources or supplies to Israeli settlements, and without having to forego its discriminatory pricing policy. (2003: 131)

This was part of a more general pattern, in which the 'peace process' relieved Israel of a number of burdens associated with the occupation, thus enabling it to sustain, and arguably even strengthen, its power and influence. This is clearly illustrated by the perverse situation in which EU projects in Area C, which include temporary buildings (Silver, 2016) that effectively relieve Israel of its duty to provide services to an impoverished population, are subject to Israeli demolition orders that are conducted under the pretext of security – millions of dollars of international funding have been wasted as a direct result (OCHA, 2018). In responding to Israel's flagrant and systematic violation of the most fundamental human rights in these areas of the West Bank, the European Parliament passed a bill, on April 18, 2018, that established that future EU aid will be conditional on Palestinian adherence to 'European' values of freedom, peace and tolerance (Ben-Ozer, 2018). This is the same logic that international donors delineated for funding P2PP.

Conclusion

One of the central contributions of settler colonialism theories is to confirm that the conflict began in 1948. This is not a purely academic detail as it entails a whole new reading of the conflict and a horizon of reference that stretches across the various forms of injustice and dispossession that have been inflicted by the conflict. Nor is it a historical amendment, as for Palestinians the *Nakba* has a clear contemporary resonance. The reiteration of the colonial dimensions of the conflict also demands a framework of reference that expands beyond the parameters – or perhaps limitations – of the two-state solution to explore alternative political possibilities. It also enables and sustains a critique of a peace process that has so clearly distorted Palestinian history and narratives, most notably of resistance (Hilal, 2015: 2).

It is a fundamental error to assert that the Oslo Accords brought about a fundamental change in Palestinian–Israeli relations. Theories of settler colonialism help to bring out and accentuate the continuities. In reality, the Accords brought about a redeployment of the Israeli army and a realignment of the occupation. The persistence of a settler colonial mentality and reality were in fact the main elements that undermined the prospect of a just and lasting peace. However, for various reasons (political convenience, self-interest, vested interests), the international community continues to overlook this essential fact.

During the Oslo years, peacebuilding was the main focus for the international community as it sought to engineer a peace agreement. In the post-Oslo era, it was supplanted by state-building. This marked a shift in the applied tools and technologies but did not signal a shift in the underlying desire, which was to control and possess. It was not merely that both frameworks failed to engage with the settler colonial characteristics of the conflict; rather, in key and important respects, they helped to perpetuate colonial relations.

Theories of settler colonialism also shift the terms of political reference beyond the OPT to engage with the situation of Palestinians in Israel. The compartmentalization of Palestinians in Israel, Palestinians in the OPT and Palestinian refugees, which can be said to be a defining feature of the peace process, is therefore clearly and unconditionally refused. In later chapters, I will discuss how this analysis has filtered into the practical politics of the BDS movement.

Crucially, theories of settler colonialism also enable a closer engagement with context, which was all too frequently overlooked by the P2PP on the grounds that it was more predisposed to work towards general solutions that applied *irrespective of context*. The universalism of peace and the generalizing impulse of the social sciences were both possibly influences in this respect.

The specificity of the individual context, along with the precise tools and techniques through which colonial power was rendered, therefore escaped closer attention.

In contrast, it is quite clear that the Palestinian leadership does not share this analysis of the conflict; as a consequence, it has become rootless, drifting towards solutions – such as the failed state-building project – that are not rooted within a theoretical or historical analysis. In lieu of an actual analysis, the PA attempts to turn pragmatism into a political principle. Far from challenging the colonial apparatus, the PA has actually become an essential component of it, essentially functioning as a conduit through which external and Israeli resources are circulated and reproduced.

The gap between the formal 'autonomy' of the PA and the actual reality was anticipated in key and important respects by theories of neocolonialism, which sought to explain how states that achieved formal independence in the aftermath of the Second World War still remained entrapped within relations that limited their independence. The anti-colonial struggle, as Fanon clearly foresaw, remained incomplete when nationalist leaders took the place of their former colonial masters and continued to serve their interests. Fanon's analysis, in highlighting the divergence of *de jure* and *de facto* sovereignty and the exertion of indirect political control through economic means, anticipated Core-Periphery and Dependency theory in crucial respects. As Taiaiake and Corntassel observe,

> We do not need to wait for the colonizer to provide us with money or to validate our vision of a free future; we only need to start to use *our* Indigenous languages to frame our thoughts, the ethical framework of *our* philosophies to make decisions and to use *our* laws and institutions to govern ourselves. (2005: 614)

Settler colonial theory therefore provides insight into a number of the conflict's different aspects and attributes and also provides a means through which conflict resolution theory can be critically disassembled. In being applied as a framework of analysis, it implies, and indeed necessitates, a very different approach to the conflict that clearly breaks with the illusions and deceits that have hitherto sustained the peace process. In later chapters, I will proceed to demonstrate how it can be applied and will also consider its wider application, in the form of the BDS movement.

3

Contact between 1967 and 1987

In mainstream media discourse, the famous (or perhaps infamous) meeting between Yitzhak Rabin and Yasser Arafat is presented as the point when the opposing sides resolved to overcome deeply rooted enmities and work towards a common future. This was a fundamental misconception – the meeting was actually the *culmination* of a range of interactions which substantially proceeded it. Contact, to put it differently, predated this meeting. It is a perverse irony that opportunities for contact actually diminished during the 'Oslo years' (1993–2000).

This chapter brings out the history of contact by identifying three chronological stages (1967–72, 1973–81 and 1982–86). In progressing through each phase, it distinguishes structured and unstructured contact and separates obligatory and voluntary contact. It takes care to differentiate endogenous and exogenous influences and also endeavours to convey the uneven character of contact. It observes that contact has historically taken a range of different forms, while varying substantially in terms of its overall significance.

1967–72

In the aftermath of the 1967 War, Israel occupied the West Bank, Gaza Strip, the Golan Heights and the Sinai Peninsula. In displacing Jordan from the West Bank and Egypt from the Gaza Strip, Israel exerted control over what would henceforth be known as the Occupied Palestinian Territories (OPT). Israel's occupation ironically established the basis for reunification of families that had been separated by the *Nakba* almost twenty years previously. The war displaced 350,000 refugees, with around half this figure being displaced for the second time in less than twenty years, having originally experienced the Nakba (Pappé, 2017a, chapter 6).

In Jerusalem, Israel almost immediately destroyed the Moroccan Quarter (*Mughrabi*), resulting in the forced relocation of around 650 Palestinians, thus initiating a series of policies that sought to 'Judaize' the Holy City (Pappé, 2006: 194). In responding to these developments, the UN Security Council adopted UNSC242, which called to Israel to withdraw from territories occupied during the war, recognize the right of all states to live in peace (Dajani, 2007: 31) and commit to a negotiated peace.

Israel accepted the Resolution in 1968 (with the PLO following twenty years later) but this was largely for purposes of appearance. In 1968, Yigal Allon, Israel's then deputy prime minister, proposed a plan that would link the Jordan Valley to Jerusalem. It was then unofficially adopted as Israeli government and provided the backdrop for Israel's colonization of the West Bank (Pappé, 2017a: 35). Israel's commitment to the colonial project would remain in place under the current day. Khalidi observes,

> After all, the Revisionist Zionist 'Greater Land of Israel' line incarnated by the movement's founder, Zeev Jabotinsky and his successors Menachem Begin and Yitzhak Shamir has almost completely dominated Israeli politics for more than thirty-five years. [The United States] has acquiesced in and effectively supported this radical and uncompromising position. (2013: 28)

In recognizing this political reality, the PLO mobilized regional and international support behind its aspiration to liberate historical Palestine (Sayigh, 1997: 147) and to establish a democratic state that would uphold the rights of all its citizens, including Jews.

But the United States refused to recognize the PLO as the legitimate representative of the Palestinian people on this basis and insisted that it recognize UNSC 242, which would entail recognizing Israel's right to exist (Dajani, 2007: 3). Israel, for its part, sought to marginalize the PLO by enticing residents of the OPT with illusionary promises of autonomy or the so-called Jordanian option (Khalidi, 2013; Raz, 2012).

Even as it remained ostensibly committed to the principle of 'land for peace', Israel's colonial project of settlement construction continued apace. The PLO's ability to resist these developments was limited by internal divisions within the Arab world, to which it in part contributed (Sayigh, 1997: 148).

In September 1970, a civil war, which would later be known as 'Black September' broke out in Jordan, resulting in the Palestinian leadership and its membership being forced to relocate to Lebanon. The PLO's position was later furthered weakened by Anwar Sadat's overtures to Israel, which were relayed through a US intermediary, in which he indicated his willingness to work towards a peace agreement (Sayigh, 1997: 150).

This established a recurring theme in which the United States, in acting as an intermediary on behalf of its Israeli client state (see Khalidi, 2013), pressurized Arab states, and ultimately the PLO, to acquiesce to a partial solution to the Arab–Israeli conflict (Muslih, 1990). The PLO's tentative engagement with these and other peace initiatives eventually resulted in Israeli activists engaging with the organization, and several meetings were held with Yasir Arafat in foreign locations.

At the same time, the PLO sought to extend support to Palestinian residents of the OPT. PLO political parties sought to build grass-roots organizations, with a view to helping Palestinians to confront the challenges of military rule and the general lack of services (Hiltermann, 1991; King, 2007). These interventions, as the discussion will subsequently demonstrate, crucially impacted Palestinian resistance activities and opened up opportunities for contact with Israeli solidarity activities. Non-official Israeli contact channels also began to emerge and began to explore the possibility of engaging with the PLO.

Tentative movements towards contact therefore began in the aftermath of the Six-Day War, which had delivered a hugely traumatic blow to the Arab world. It also shifted Palestinian attention away from the Arab states, whose political and military weaknesses had been brutally exposed. In its aftermath, Palestinians realized that they would have to assume responsibility for their own historical destiny.

At this point in time, contact was not on the agenda. When the PLO was founded in 1964 it had, in aligning itself with the stance of the Arab League, insisted on unflinching opposition to Israel.[1] As Ziad Abu-Zayyad emphasizes, those who proposed contact with Israelis risked ostracization and even physical harm. Israelis were to be viewed as the enemy.[2] It was unacceptable to meet with the enemy and to seek knowledge of them or their society (Abbas, 1994: 25). Abbas recalled how ignorance of Israel was openly aspired to and even celebrated.[3] At this point in time, Palestinian rejectionism was all-encompassing.

While the PLO ostensibly remained committed to this rejectionist stance it began, over the course of subsequent years, to gravitate towards a more moderate political strategy. A number of the Arab states also sought to establish secret channels of communication with Israel (Shlaim, 2000) (then, as now, this cooperation was however limited to security cooperation). By virtue of the fact that these initiatives were clearly unacceptable to Arab public opinion, they were conducted in secret.

The Israeli authorities, however, approached contact with a greater degree of openness and enthusiasm. In the immediate aftermath of the 1967 war, Israeli officials had met with political 'notables' (e.g. established families) in Bethlehem, Hebron, Gaza City, Jerusalem, Nablus, Ramallah and Tulkarem (Abdul Hadi, 1987: 6–8; Raz, 2012). The first meeting took place in 1967 and was led by Levi Eshkol, the Israeli prime minister. He met with Walid Shaka'a and Hikmat Masri, the heads of two well-known families in Nablus. Moshe Dayan held a subsequent meeting on 16 April 1968. While these meetings were initially exploratory, they were undertaken with a clear intention – to identify which sections of Palestinian society would be willing to establish peaceful relations with Israel.

It was possible, in these initial encounters, to identify the outlines of a future Israeli diplomacy that would incorporate 'peace' into its manoeuvres and strategies, conceiving of it as a means through which its interests could be advanced. At this stage, this 'diplomacy' was relatively rudimentary and unsophisticated; it was only later that it coalesced into a 'foreign policy of deception' (Raz, 2012: 4).

Raz (2012) provides a clear account which clarifies how the occupation developed in its initial phases. Even casual and employment-related contact took place within the shadow of the occupation. Moshe Dayan, the then minister of defence, had argued in favour of an 'enlightened occupation' that would permit Palestinians to travel between the OPT and Israel (Levy, 2014; also see Raz, 2012: 95). Any concessions that Israel made in this regard were far from disinterested – in the words of Fanon, the colonizer 'never gives anything away for nothing' (1963: 142). As one case in point, while Palestinians were allowed temporary residence in Jerusalem (a permit was not required but they were not allowed to stay overnight), the colonization of Jerusalem began almost immediately.

This voluntary contact was accompanied by compulsory contact. In the aftermath of the war, the Israeli army began to consolidate its influence over the Palestinian territories by issuing a series of military orders. Compulsory contact originated within the fact that the Israeli authorities controlled everything from birth to death certificates. As the occupation tightened its grip upon the Palestinian land and population, it became increasingly difficult for Palestinians to find employment. The 'de-development' of the OPT was not accidental or coincidental and instead derived from a deliberate and intentional policy on the part of the Israeli authorities. As a consequence, Palestinians were forced to seek employment in Israel. Palestinians also came into contact with Israelis upon a voluntary basis, as they were (with the exception of political activists) permitted to travel into Israel.

On the Israeli side, the main impetus towards contact came from the Israeli Communist Party, which sought to advance their ideological goals by engaging with the Palestinian Communist movement (Lockman, 1976). Michel Warschawski, a prominent member of Matzpen (the (Arab-Jewish) Revolutionary Communist League), observes, 'We were few in number when, in 1968, we went scurrying all over the West Bank in search of Palestinians who shared our opinions or who were at least willing to talk to us' (1992: 86).

Israeli communists also initiated solidarity activities[4] and participated in protests against the arrest of Palestinians.[5] More moderate elements within the Israeli labour movement also worked across the divide. Israeli trade union activists advocated on behalf of Palestinian labourers who worked in Israel. Many Palestinian defendants also subsequently maintained contact with Felicia Langer, an Israeli lawyer who represented them in court.[6] Aruri, in questioning whether these interactions can be legitimately defined as contact, makes two important observations. First, he notes that the two sets of communists did not encounter each other as Palestinians or as Israelis; rather, they came together as adherents to a shared ideology. Second, both sets of participants engaged upon a purely individual basis and did not therefore seek to advance the interests of their respective national communities.[7]

This did not, however, apply to a number of journalists, writers and students, who began to mobilize in opposition to the occupation. In contrast with Israeli communists, their protests were more rights-orientated (civil and national) and motivated by a concern that the occupation would undermine Jewish democracy (Hall-Cathala, 1990: 30). Taysir Aruri acknowledged that the contribution of a number of leftist Israeli academics helped to spark Palestinian debates on dialogue and contact and elicited a limited number of Palestinian responses.[8]

A small number of Palestinian participants also defied the Palestinian consensus and sought to engage with Israeli audiences. A variety of groups (advocacy, business and solidarity) were established, and a number of lectures, seminars and debate sessions took place. But these activities were of limited significance – at this stage, peace activism 'failed to mobilize any significant amount of public support' (Hall-Cathala, 1990: 32).

Ziad Abu Zayyad, a pioneering figure in the establishment of contact, informed me that encounters between Palestinians and Israelis during this period had not been constructive, and that the respective participants had ultimately been unable to establish the basis for a workable solution. Indeed, during most of the initial contacts that were established in the late 1960s and early 1970s, the participants were predominantly concerned with apportioning blame.[9]

While these initial contacts were of limited scope and significance, they are nonetheless often entirely overlooked by external observers, who instead present the PLO's 1974 implicit acceptance of the two-state solution as the point when Palestinians began to progress beyond a rejectionist stance (Muslih, 1990). This is a common mistake, which derives from the tendency to fetishize and elevate the actions of formal representatives, invariably at the expense of individual and civil society initiatives.

In the period between 1967 and 1973, contact between Palestinians and Israelis took three forms: first, individual Palestinians gave lectures to Israeli audiences and participated in a number of solidarity activities (these activities did not enjoy any level of public support and were isolated initiatives); second, Palestinian labourers sought work in Israel; and finally, Israeli officials and Palestinian notables established initial contact – but this contact was essentially exploratory and was not characterized by any real sense of purpose or direction.

1973-81

The October/Yom Kippur War had severely undermined Israel's deeply rooted faith in its own military abilities. It induced a sense of uncertainty and even trepidation – with considerable justification, Kaminer (1996) speaks of 'an historical upheaval, the first of its kind'. In responding to this sense of flux, a wide number of social movements mobilized, with a view to influencing wider public opinion (Bar-on, 1996; Hall-Cathala, 1990; Kaminer, 1996). While the war did not significantly alter Israeli attitudes towards Palestinians, it did assist the emergence of new Israeli political parties, a number of whom would substantially impact upon Palestinian–Israeli relations (Hall-Cathala, 1990).

Palestinians had, in the aftermath of the *Nakba*, called for the liberation of historical Palestine – it was upon this basis that they rejected the Partition Plan, which was put forward in 1948. Two decades later, limited Palestinian support for a binational state had been displaced by growing support for a two-state solution, a development that was given added impetus by the PLO's 1974 declaration (Muslih, 1990).

In addition to the October/Yom Kippur war, a number of developments at the international level also lent renewed impetus to attempts to establish a Palestinian–Israeli peace. In November 1975, the UN General Assembly recognized the Palestinian right to self-determination, reiterated the Palestinian Right of Return and awarded the PLO observer status. In the same year, the Assembly also collectively agreed that Zionism was a form of racism.

During this period, a range of peace groups began to mobilize, largely in response to the growing presence of Israeli right-wing groups in the OPT. During this period, the two poles of the political spectrum directly interacted. The emergence and development of Oz ve Shalom, whose peace activism originated in religious sources, was only intelligible in relation to Gush Emunim (Block of Faith), a religious movement that sought to advance settlement construction in the West Bank and Gaza Strip.

Towards the end of this period, the peace movement gathered added momentum when Anwar Sadat, the Egyptian president, made a historic visit to Israel in November 1977. Peace Now was also established in March 1978. Whereas previously contact had been confined to exploratory and small-scale initiatives, it now took the form of an established movement that had considerable resources and that was able to interface between formal and informal levels while generating substantial levels of public support. Equally importantly, whereas the purpose of contact had previously sometimes been unclear, it was now focused on defining Israel's territorial borders and removing illegal settlements.

During the initial years of this period, Israeli officials and PLO members also met in foreign countries. However, these meetings took place in the absence of real or meaningful support from the PLO leadership, who remained unconvinced about their value. The meetings also had to be held in secret, because mutual hostility remained deeply entrenched on both sides. However, a hugely significant development occurred in 1973, when Said Hammami[10] (the PLO's representative in Britain) published two articles in *The Times*, a British newspaper. The articles were significant because they represented the first occasion on which a member of the PLO had explicitly recognized the rights of Israelis. A number of Israelis responded positively to this initial gesture: Uri Avnery, the prominent Israeli peace activist and founder of Gush Shalom (the Peace Bloc), met Hammami in London during 1975 (Avnery, 1986). A number of other Israelis also approached Hammami with a view to setting up meetings with him.

Other Israelis who met with Hammami in an individual capacity played an important role in founding the Israeli Council for Israel-Palestine Peace (ICIPP). The council, which played an important role in establishing the basis for further contact during the 1970s and early 1980s, made an important contribution in both legitimizing dialogue and contributing to wider debates. Avnery (1986) notes that the signature of the ICIPP's founding document by one hundred Israeli leaders was particularly important because, at this point in time, many Israelis (including Golda Meir, the Israeli prime minister) denied the existence of Palestinians. The ICIPP sought to reconcile Zionist and Palestinian demands and thus demonstrate the potential contribution of dialogue between Zionists and PLO representatives (Keller, 1987: 164–5).

By the mid-1970s, a structured form of contact had become established at Harvard University, where academics had succeeded in establishing an unofficial third-party approach that sought to establish direct communication between representatives of parties that were in a state of conflict (Kelman, 1998: 310). Herbert Kelman, who helped to pioneer this approach, explained,

> What is essential to a joint process of analysis is that participants feel free to think out loud and to examine their reaction, without worrying that they will be held accountable for every word they utter: and free to listen to each other, without feeling obliged to counter every point to the other side. (1996: 108)

Because of wider sensitivities, its existence was not openly acknowledged or publicly advertised. Influential Israelis and Palestinians came together in a series of problem-solving workshops that sought to change attitudes through social interaction. Positive contact, Kelman maintained, would be conducive to friendly coexistence, cooperative relations and reconciliation. The workshops were grounded within the spirit of reciprocity ('only when the two sets of needs are on the table and have been understood do we move on to discuss the possible shapes of solution that might be responsive to them' (Kelman, 1996: 109)) and within theories of social psychology – this influence was clearly indicated within the belief that face-to-face contact would change attitudes and generate knowledge (see Allport, 1954; Brown, 1995).

Kelman applied the assumption that changes engendered at the micro level (individual) would automatically translate to the macro level (policies and political structures) (Kelman, 1979: 106). Kelman, claimed that these initial interactions helped to establish the basis for the Oslo Accords (see Kelman, 2005).

Issam Sartawi, a former heart surgeon, was a leading figure within the PLO who sought to establish contact with Israelis who were not committed to Zionist ideas or principles. In 1976, he met Matti Peled (a retired general who had become a Professor of Arabic literature at Tel Aviv University) in Paris. Despite the fact that this meeting had been approved by Arafat, Sartawi requested that it remain secret. During the course of subsequent meetings, which brought in other Palestinians and Israelis, the outlines of the two-state solution began to emerge.

Uri Avnery emphasizes that, at this point, contact was no longer conceived as an individual initiative that was conducted in isolation from, or even in opposition to, wider public opinion. He recalls publishing Palestinian contributions and reporting the details of contact – for him, 'Israeli readers were indirectly part of the contact'.[11] For him, this wider outreach provided an important justification and even rationale. He cites his meeting with Arafat in Beirut (at a time when the Lebanese capital was being subjected to sustained bombardment by the Israeli army) as a case in point. He notes that, in its aftermath, 'Israelis could not think of Arafat simply as the man who wanted to kill Israelis, and Palestinians could not see Israelis as monolithic'.[12] Yasser Arafat did not just approve these meetings but was actually a direct participant in them (he also met Avnery in 1983 and 1984). The approval of the Israeli authorities, meanwhile, was more indirect – it was indicated by the fact that they were debriefed after the initial meetings and allowed subsequent ones to take place (Bar-On, 1996; Kaminer, 1996).

In the aftermath of the meetings between Sartawi and Peled, the Parliamentary Association for Euro-Arab Co-operation in Britain arranged a seminar, which took place in London on 1 October 1977. Said Hammami, Issam Sartawi, Dr Nafez Nazzal (Birzeit University) and Karim Khalif (mayor of Ramallah) engaged with Israeli counterparts during the seminar (Avnery, 1986: 110). During a 2013 (21 October) telephone conversation with me, Uri Avnery emphasized the importance of this event. For him it had a human and political significance and contributed to the crystallization of his thinking on key issues. In addition, it also made it easier for him to align himself with his Palestinian counterparts. Avnery explained,

> I started to publish the Palestinian views and regularly reported the details of contacts when meetings were public and not secret. Israeli readers were indirectly part of the contact. Moreover, a hundred important Israeli leaders signed the founding document of the Israeli Council for Israel-Palestine Peace (ICIPP).[13]

However, the potential impact of these developments was substantially threatened when the Israeli Right came to power in 1977 with Menachem Begin's election victory. In 1977 the PNC had met, with a view to addressing the issue of contact with Israelis. The thirteenth session resolved 'to support contact with all the democratic movements that oppose Zionism in Israel' (the National Council reaffirmed this decision in 1981, 1982, 1988 and 1989). With Begin's election, Palestinians were confronted by the realization that this may be insufficient and that it may be necessary to proactively engage with Likud and the right of the Israeli political spectrum (Abbas, 1994: 62). For Abbas, this was necessary. However, this proposition was strongly opposed by both general and radical sentiment within the PLO (Abbas, 1994, 2001; interview in Ramallah). Ultimately, Abbas's position prevailed. During the late 1970s and early 1980s, the PLO engaged with Zionist political actors that were on the right of the political spectrum. Meetings were held both in the OPT and across a range of international locations.

This shift was also clearly demonstrated by Palestinian engagement with the Weizman Institute. The institute is widely viewed as right-wing, and it might therefore be assumed that Palestinians would be reluctant to engage with it. More 'liberal' institutions such as the Hebrew University or Tel Aviv University would provide, at first glance, a more obvious point of engagement (an expectation further enhanced by the fact that both institutions had contributed to contact-based initiatives).

However, this was not the case. During our interview, Taysir Aruri informed me of a 1981 meeting by a left-wing think tank. Those in attendance included Hanan Ashrawi, Khalil Mahshi and Nabil Qasis. The meeting addressed a communication from the institute, which invited its members to address an Israeli audience. Although this invitation precipitated a strong debate (in which PFLP and DFLP members expressed strong objections), it was ultimately decided to accept the proposal. In addition, the meeting also established that efforts would be made to engage Israelis who recognized the full rights of Palestinians and opposed the occupation.[14]

1982–6

Israel sought to tighten its grip on the OPT through the 'Iron Fist' policy which Yitzhak Rabin, Israel's then defence minister, had introduced in 1985. This policy sought to suppress Palestinian resistance through arbitrary incarceration, collective punishment, home demolitions and school and university closures – I myself was affected when I was a student at Bir Zeit University – the university was closed several times, resulting in my graduation being delayed by one year.

Heightened settlement activity in the years subsequent to 1977 also meant that Palestinians became increasingly subject to constraints and restrictions. For Palestinians whose homes infringed upon the settlements, water shortages, land confiscation and settler aggression became increasingly unavoidable features of everyday life. A deteriorating economic situation also meant that Palestinians were increasingly dependent on Israel (Tamari, 1988).

The prospect of a negotiated solution appeared remote and even non-existent. In the aftermath of the 1979 peace agreement with Egypt (Camp David I), Israeli politicians continued to reject the notion of a Palestinian nation, much less the proposition that they should negotiate with its representatives – both Shimon Peres and Yitzhak Rabin continued to view the 'Jordanian option' as the most viable option. The 1982 Reagan Plan similarly advanced the possibility of Palestinian autonomy (in association with Jordan), which the Palestinian leadership rejected outright.

The prospect of a negotiated settlement had been further undermined by Israel's 1982 invasion of Lebanon. At the regional level, the Iraq–Iran war overshadowed the Palestinian issue. At the Arab Summit in Amman in November 1987, the Palestinian issue was not, contrary to established convention, at the top of the agenda (Said, 1989). The failures of 'macro-politics' contributed to efforts to engineer change from below and influenced the emergence and development of the First *Intifada*. As this event progressed, the PLO sought to align itself with progressive elements within Israeli society – the eighteenth Palestinian National Council called for enhanced relations with democratic forces that supported the Palestinian people's struggle (Muslih, 1990: 23).

The declassification of Israeli state archives contributed to the emergence of a group of scholars who became known as the 'New Historians' (Pappé, 1997, 2009). They challenged the Zionist narrative about the foundation of Israel and its implications for the indigenous Arab population (Kimmerling, 1995; Shlaim, 1995, 2000) and also openly challenged the distortions and manipulations of the Israeli political elite (Pappé, 2009; Shlaim, 1995). But the 'New Historians' drew strong criticism from Left Zionists. Pappé explains,

[While Left Zionists] accep[t] criticism of post-1967 Israel, the period 1882–67 is off limits. Critics of post-Zionism could be heard in the past voicing strong opposition to the continued Israeli occupation of the territories seized in the 1967 war. This protest, however, far from being anti-Zionist, was based on a strong commitment to consensual Zionist positions; it was this commitment that kept the Zionist Left from accepting the fundamental Palestinian positions on central questions such as the fate of the 1948 refugees or the future of Jerusalem as long as the PLO remained faithful to its strategic concepts. (Pappé 1997: 39)

This was evidenced both during this period and the one following (see next section). While joint activities brought Palestinians and Israelis together in their struggle against the West Bank and Gaza Strip, issues pertaining to the pre-1967 period were frequently effectively 'off-limits'.

Israel's 1982 invasion of Lebanon resulted in a huge proliferation of peace groups; some were short-lived, whereas others persisted for a much longer period of time (Bar-On, 1996: 173) and actively contributed to the First *Intifada*. These groups were not single-issue (e.g. anti-war) but instead mobilized around a broad range of issues (predominantly Israeli settlement activities). At first glance, Peace Now's initial reluctance to come out against the war appears as something of a historical anomaly. However, this was not the case – the group's reluctance to openly criticize the government during this war reflected the fact that a large number of its members were serving in the Israeli army (Keller, 1987: 174).

Disillusioned members of Peace Now responded by forming the Committee Against War in Lebanon (CAWL). In acknowledging that its initial position had been an error, Peace Now came out in strong opposition against the war (the strength of the group's reversal was so compelling that Yasser Arafat, who was besieged in Beirut at the time, acknowledged its efforts) (Bar-On, 1996: 146). In recognizing Peace Now's potential contribution, the Palestinian leadership's 'peace offensives' began to directly target the group – by the mid-1980s, its meetings had begun to be openly announced in *Al-Fajr*,[15] a Palestinian newspaper. Oz ve Shalom and Yesh Gvul (an organization made up of army reservists) also mobilized against the war, and some of the latter's members were imprisoned for refusing to serve in the military. After the notorious Sabra and Shatila massacre, other groups, including Parents Against Silence, mobilized against the war.

Growing contact between Palestinians and Israelis in the aftermath of the war elicited considerable concern within the National Unity (Labor-Likud) government, which responded by proposing legislation (which the Knesset passed on 5 August 1986) that prohibited Israelis (an exception was made for journalists and academics attending international conferences) from meeting with PLO representatives outside of Israel. Israelis who defied this law faced the threat of up to three years in prison.

Israeli activists, in responding, adopted a range of different approaches and strategies. Some simply ignored the law. Latif Dori, an Israeli of Iraqi origin, established a committee that sought to improve relations between Mizrahi Jews and the Arab world. Dori also participated in a joint conference that took place in Romania during November 1986 – this was widely viewed as a direct challenge to the law (Massad, 1996). Abie Nathan (whose radio station has broadcasted from the 'Peace Ship' for two decades) went as far as it was possible to go when he met with Arafat on several occasions. He was later imprisoned for a total of two years (six months after being arrested the first time, eighteen months after the second arrest).

Other activists sought to honour the letter of the law while exploiting loopholes (Bar-On, 1996: 214). American and European activists made an important contribution to these efforts by providing the basis upon which third-party meetings could be arranged with PLO representatives and affiliates. Other activists established direct contact with Palestinians (such as Ghassan Al-Khatib, Hanan Ashrawi, Sari Nusseibeh, Sa'eb Erekat and Faisal Hussaini) who were resident in the Occupied Palestinian territories.

A considerable number of these activities were however vulnerable to the accusation that they had limited public impact or outreach. In part, this was a reflection of the fact that, at this stage, activists were predominantly concerned with establishing networks and working relationships. However, there was a legitimate suspicion – which is enhanced by the fact that activists share a common language, worldview and political purpose – that they were simply 'preaching to the converted'. Initiatives that sought to bring together individuals upon the basis of a shared professional background were similarly vulnerable to the accusation that they were elitist and had little or no relation to, or significance for, wider public opinion (Bar-On, 1996: 218).

Contact also continued to be undermined by strong Palestinian opposition. This was clearly illustrated on 10 April 1983, when Sartawi was assassinated while leading a Palestinian delegation to the International Socialist convention. Sa'id Hammami, Izz Al-Din Al-Qalaq, and Na'im Khader were also assassinated (Abbas, 1994). Contact with Israelis carried clear risks, and participants were aware that they could ultimately pay the cost of perceived betrayal with their own life.

Even when Palestinians willingly participated in contact initiatives, their engagement was brought into question by their predisposition to approach it as a strategic exercise that was concerned with challenging and altering the perceptions of the opposing side. Israeli participants, for their part, came with their own set of expectations and were no less forthcoming in informing their 'partners in peace' when they had fallen short. When the actual experience failed to closely approximate to either of the two models, then disillusion inevitably took root – by as early as 1986, clear questions were being raised about the benefits of dialogue (Touma, 1986).

Given this somewhat unstable foundation, it is perhaps unsurprising to learn that the general Palestinian appraisal of contact during this period was not universally positive. Even at this stage, it was clear that the act of contact was not in itself sufficient and that contact activities were situated within a wider set of interactions which substantially impacted, and even altered, their significance and potential contribution. For Ziad Abu-Zayyad, the Israeli education system (specifically its reproduction of prejudiced attitudes and predispositions) and the pervasive influence of the Israeli right were both foremost in this regard, structuring, orientating and even determining the act of contact (Touma, 1986; see also Peled-Elhanan, 2012).

4

Contact during the First *Intifada* (1987–93)

Contact peaked during the First *Intifada*. For purposes of comparison, it will be particularly instructive to compare the form of contact that emerged during this period against the contact that was envisaged and implemented in the P2PP. This is primarily instructive because of the differences between the two forms of contact and also the fact that contact in the First *Intifada* took place in the absence of financial or institutional support, which a number of contact theorists present as preconditions for effective contact. Contact during the First *Intifada*, which was focused on the ending of the occupation, is not therefore merely a historical question; rather, it has crucial implications for how contact is currently theorized and practiced. The First *Intifada*, which broke out on 9 December 1987, erupted in response to the repressive and humiliating policies that Israel had imposed on the OPT for two decades. The Israeli authorities had expropriated land, constructed settlements and actively undermined Palestinian development (Rishmawi, 1986; Tamari, 1988). Every aspect of Palestinian life was subject to the surveillance of the Israeli authorities (Pappe, 2013: 348). The occupation was a pernicious and pervasive form, forcibly imposing itself upon hearts, minds and communities.

The *Intifada* was a spontaneous popular uprising that broke out after an Israeli driver crashed into Palestinian labourers waiting to enter Israel from the Gaza Strip and caused four Palestinians deaths. A false rumour spread that the deaths had occurred in retribution for the death of an Israeli who had been stabbed to death in the Strip a few days previously. Although protests initially focused upon the four deaths, they rapidly escalated and took on a wider significance.

Palestinian notables and even the PLO leadership were initially bystanders as a younger generation of Palestinians seized the revolutionary impetus.

During the initial stages of the *Intifada*, the representatives of the main Palestinian political parties (Fatah, Popular Front for the Liberation of Palestine (PFLP), the Democratic Front for the Liberation of Palestine (DFLP) and the Communist Party) formed the Unified National Leadership of the Uprising (UNLU). In the initial stages of the *Intifada* it was local leaders, as opposed to Palestinian leaders in exile, who were at the forefront of the revolutionary struggle.

Abu Lughod noted the emergence of a new generation of Palestinians who were much more 'realistic' and who were possessed of a much clearer grasp of the 'adversary's intentions, policies, practices, and powers' (1990: 8). It should be noted that Lughod's use of the word 'realistic' is diametrically opposed to its conventional political usage. In political discourse, it is customary for the word to be deployed when idealists stray from the warm and familiar surroundings of realism. In order to guard against the danger that they will seek to impose their grand schemes upon an insubordinate reality, they are commanded to yield to the dictates of 'reality'.

However, in Lughod's usage, the word takes on exactly the opposite meaning. It is those who demand and assert Palestinian rights that are viewed to be 'realists', and those who yield to political expediency are deemed to be 'unrealistic'. The revolutionary leadership, the UNLU, made this clear when it spoke of 'clear and realistic objectives for the Palestinians in the occupied territories' (FACTS Information Committee, 1988: 5) – this implicitly served as an indictment of Palestinians who, whether for reasons of self-interest or expediency, had sought to elevate pragmatism as an end in itself. Thus, the UNLU approvingly observed that 'the uprising had placed new constraints upon certain prominent figures who previously showed signs of willingness to accept solutions which were unacceptable to the Palestinian people' (FACTS Information Committee, 1988: 10).

While the precise timing of the *Intifada* was contingent upon a set of random circumstances, a number of its key attributes could be traced back to the Israeli occupation. Hassassian observed that Palestinian civil society emerged in the absence of a political national authority in the 1970s to 1980s (2000). During this period, it established itself as a social and political actor that was responsive to the needs and requirements of the local population. Israel's neglect of the OPT over the previous two decades had created a vacuum that was filled by community organizations, who began to meet local needs by providing essential services. In responding to the popular uprising, these community organizations began to politically mobilize (see Hiltermann, 1991, chapter 4; King, 2007, chapters 5 and 6). Muslih confirmed,

> The Intifada [l]ed to the creation of relatively autonomous and organized social units with specific functional responsibilities, foremost among which were serving the population and shielding it from the shattering impact of the Israeli military measures. (1995: 255)

During the pre-Oslo period, Palestinian civil society played a hugely important role in helping to resist the Israeli occupation (Hammami, 1995; Hassassian, 2000). The occupying authorities were clearly uninterested in ensuring Palestinian economic, political and social development, and it was therefore incumbent upon Palestinians – and specifically Palestinian civil society – to rise to the challenge. (Hiltermann, 1991). However, this had political implications that extended beyond the immediate meeting of social need (Taraki, 1990).

Local resistance to the occupation therefore took a number of forms and was non-violent in character. While this was a matter of principle for the UNLU, it also had a certain tactical efficacy – images of Israeli tanks facing down Palestinian women and children forced many international observers to reconsider their view of the Palestinian–Israeli conflict (Jad, 1990). The commitment to non-violence was also important because it made it possible for Israelis to participate in the struggle against occupation. Contact no longer needed to be conducted in secret.

Positive collaboration was also made easier by the fact that there was now a clear consensus that Palestinians and Israelis should work together to challenge and undermine the occupation. This was the collaborative effort that Edward Said had in mind when he spoke of solidarity in seeking to end the occupation (1995: 20). During this period, the Israeli peace movement attained a renewed impetus and momentum. A number of peace groups reformed, while others broke with Peace Now's conservatism and sought to position themselves as radical alternatives (Bar-On, 1996: 237).

The Unified Leadership of the Intifada's (UNLU) communiques openly celebrated this consensus upon resisting the occupation. In 1988, its Fact Information Committee published *Towards a State of Independence*. The cover clearly depicted the West Bank and Gaza Strip, whose outlines were clearly indicated by red stripes (FACTS Information Committee, 1988). The document also invoked a joint treaty, which had been signed by Palestinian and Israeli artists, writers and academics, who supported the two-state solution (FACTS Information Committee, 1988: 261–3).

In contrast to previous contact-based initiatives, these activities also had a substantial impact upon mainstream political opinion in Israel. For the first time, peace became part of Israel's political agenda (Ashrawi, 1992: 12). Individual and joint actions produced a series of conferences, demonstrations, lectures, seminars, sit-ins and workshops which impacted, both individually and cumulatively, upon Israeli public opinion. Ghassan Khatib, in reflecting upon the significance of these developments, observed,

> The Intifada was a turning point in the dialogue experience. Dialogue and contact became massive and collective. Groups of Israelis came to show solidarity and support to Palestinians and at the same time to exchange ideas.[1]

The Palestinian acceptance of contact was strongly influenced by the fact that Israeli participants opposed the occupation. As Tayseer Aruri explained, this was the main purpose and rationale of contact for Palestinians – in their view, it would help to convey Palestinians experiences of life under occupation and would also directly influence Israeli public opinion.[2] Individual and joint contact activities during the *intifada* were generally directed against the occupation. In struggling against the occupation, Palestinian and Israeli activists focused upon Israeli public opinion, believing that this must be challenged if lasting change was to be brought about.

Some Israeli groups also emphasized the importance of the education system. Not all of these activities required direct contact with Palestinians, although Palestinians sometimes provided indirect guidance and advice. The activities of Yesh Gvul (There is a Limit), which was formed in 1985 by Israeli reservists in protest against Israel's military involvement in Lebanon, were a case in point. Its public statements and public education activities focused upon Israeli society and sought to persuade Israelis to refuse military service in the OPT.[3]

Palestinian groups also sought to target Israeli public opinion. These activities often overlapped with macro-level political activities. In the early 1990s, the Israeli government was under growing pressure from the Bush administration to participate in an international conference on the Middle East. These efforts were ultimately successful, and the Israeli government was one of the parties that participated in the Madrid Conference, which began on 30 October 1991. During this period, Palestinian organizations focused, with renewed intensity, on Israeli public opinion. Encouraged by these developments, Palestinians increasingly directed their activities towards Israeli public opinion (the respective leaders of Fatah, the People's Party and the Palestinian Democratic Union played an important role in these activities).

Cooperation with Israeli groups was made easier by the fact that they opposed the occupation. This established a firm foundation for contact-based activities. Rana Nashashibi observed,

> During the Intifada, the political bases and platforms for Palestinian-Israeli discussions were based on the right of self-determination and Palestinian rights, the PLO as sole Palestinian representative and the recognition of international resolutions.[4]

But while there was a common objective, approaches varied among different groups. Yesh Gvul was positioned at the outer edges of the spectrum. While its approach generated considerable disquiet, particularly among liberal groups (see Hall-Cathala, 1990), its integrity meant that it was widely respected (Kaminer, 1996: 72). 'The 21st Year' was another group which targeted Israeli society. It was formed just before the outbreak of the First *Intifada* (October 1987) by a group of intellectuals at Tel Aviv University. Adi Ofer, a philosophy lecturer, significantly influenced the group's emergence and development. It worked to establish an institutional boycott of the settlements and also challenged those aspects of the Israeli education system (a number of its members were teachers) which condoned or legitimized the occupation (Kaminer, 1996).

Peace Now substantially predated the First *Intifada*, having been established in 1978. Its caution and close adherence to legalism and non-violence (Bar-On, 1996: 230) meant that it was frequently criticized by more radical counterparts. While it was hugely successful in engaging broad sections of Israeli society, this success came at a cost – a number of separate offshoots were formed by disillusioned former members who sought to break with the group's apolitical approach and unwillingness to adopt specific ideological positions (Kaminer, 1996: 113).

However, these criticisms were perhaps unfair. After all, Peace Now did manage to provide a clear and unequivocal response to the PNC's acceptance of UN General Assembly Resolution 18. It called upon the Israeli government to enter into direct negotiations with the PLO and also sought to establish independent channels that would enable it to directly engage the PLO.

During the First *Intifada*, it also arranged joint activities that were held in a variety of locations across the OPT. Its commitment to legalism meant that it was well-placed to challenge, and ultimately overturn, arbitrary decisions by the Israeli authorities. The group also played an important role in helping to arrange meetings between Palestinians and Israelis.[5] While these meetings were generally initiated by Israelis, this was not always the case. Faisal Husseini, a Jerusalem-based Palestinian leader, frequently initiated meetings that took place at Jerusalem's Orient House.

While Peace Now's approach led a number of disaffected former members to form new groups, its work also contributed to groups that sought to imitate it or work alongside it. B'tselem ('in the image'), which was established by Dedi Zucker (one of the founders of Peace Now and a Knesset member), was an important example. B'tselem was founded in 1989 and it has since documented the human rights abuses of the Israeli army in painstaking detail. It is widely acknowledged as a reliable and authoritative source of information on the human rights situation in the OPT. 'Edei Kibush' (Witness of Occupation), which was formed by Adi Ofer (in 1988) after he refused to serve in the Occupied Territories in 1988, performs a similar investigative function.

Dia Lakibush (Enough with the Occupation) was one of the main Israeli peace groups that organized vigils and demonstrations in the Occupied Territories (although its activities within Israel also engaged Israelis and visiting tourists (Kaminer, 1996). Its committee was formed in 1987 by Israeli activists who were members of Matzpen (an anti-Zionist left-wing organization that was founded in 1962) and the Communist Party. A substantial part of Dia Lakibush's support base, however, did not identify with a political party. It recognized the PLO as the legitimate representative of the Palestinian people and sought to promote the two-state solution. Michel Warschawski, who was the most significant Israeli activist on the group's committee, observed that the group emerged in the context of a new desire to engage with Palestinians and Palestinian life experiences (1992: 94).

The group's activities were warmly received by Palestinians, who facilitated visits to Palestinian cities, refugee camps and villages. I helped to organize a number of these visits and personally witnessed the warmth with which Israeli visitors were greeted. For Palestinians, these visits were essential because they helped to educate Israelis about the realities of occupation. These beneficial consequences were further enhanced by the intensity and scope of Dia Lakibush's activities.

While this is generally true, it should also be acknowledged that a subset of these activities – specifically the attainment of permits that would enable Palestinians to enter Jerusalem and participate in legal demonstrations – proved to be more controversial. The proposition that Palestinians should apply for permits aroused particular opposition because it appeared to indirectly recognize Israel's authority over East Jerusalem.[6]

Women's groups also emerged during the *Intifada*. 'Women in Black' (WIB), which was formed in 1988, directly challenged the occupation through symbolic protest. Its members, who were dressed entirely in black, held silent vigils in Jerusalem and other Israeli cities. They also engaged with Palestinian counterparts, and joint activities were held throughout the OPT. The Women's Organization for Women Political Prisoners (WOFWPP) was formed in the same year as WIB. It worked with Palestinian women who had been incarcerated within Israeli prisons and focused upon day-to-day practicalities. Its members provided information upon prison conditions and the practices of the prison authorities. 'Women and Peace' was another coalition which sought to highlight how the occupation impacted upon Palestinian women.

Support committees also came to play an important role as the *Intifada* progressed. Members of 'The 21st Year' formed the 'Beita Affair' committee in order to assist villagers in Beita, which is located near to Nablus. Other committees, meanwhile, were formed with a view to assisting Qalqilya, which is close to the Green Line. In 1989, Israeli protestors who travelled to Qalqilya were arrested and imprisoned after confronting Israeli soldiers (Bar-On, 1996: 227).

In addition to these major shifts within Israeli society, Israeli politics was also experiencing a fundamental realignment. On 4 July 1987, shortly before the first *Intifada* broke out, Sari Nusseibeh and Salah Zhiza met with Moshe Amirav (a Likud member) and David Ish Shalom (a journalist and active member of the Mizrahi peace assembly). Faisal Husseini and Yitzhak Shamir, the Israeli prime minister, were also in attendance. After four meetings, the participants agreed on a 'Document of Principles' which was supposed to be presented to the Palestinian and Israeli leaderships at a later date. This hope evaporated when Husseini was arrested just three hours after the document was finalized. Shamir would later deny any knowledge of, or association with, the document, and Likud's opposition to dialogue and negotiation remained in place.

This meeting was however eclipsed by an even more incredible encounter that occurred five years later. Mahmoud Abbas (1994) alleged that Ariel Sharon, during the course of a meeting, affirmed that he would be willing to meet with the PLO. However, when the details were leaked, Sharon quickly backtracked (also see Bar-On, 1996).

In acknowledging the significance of these shifts, the PLO sought to reposition itself. In November 1988, the PNC formally accepted UN General Assembly Resolution 181, which informally recognized Israel. During the following month, Yasser Arafat convened a press conference during which he formally announced the PLO acceptance of UNSC Resolutions 242 and 338 – he also formally renounced violence and accepted that the 1967 Armistice Lines would form the outlines of a future Palestinian state. Israeli NGOs, in recognizing the significance of these developments, encouraged the Israeli government to engage in direct negotiations with the PLO (Bar-On, 1996: 254–5).

The PNC's momentous decision also encouraged a number of Israeli academics to initiate professional cooperation with their Palestinian counterparts. The Israeli–Palestinian Peace Project was established as a joint effort between the Palestinian Arab Studies Society (headed by Faisal Husseini) and the Harry S. Truman Institute for the Advancement of Peace, which was linked to the Hebrew University. However, while some Palestinians were enthusiastic about engaging with such initiatives (the Israeli/Palestinian Centre for Research and Information [IPCRI],[7] for instance, was formed after

Faisal Hussaini gave his approval), others were more cautious. During my interview with Dr Gershon Baskin, IPCRI's current co-director, he explained that Palestinians were reluctant to have their names published or to be formally recognized as partners. In their view, it was too soon for such a project and it was preferable to instead focus on solidarity activities.[8]

Similar issues were also encountered in 1988, when *American Nightline*, a television programme broadcast on ABC-TV, sought to recruit Palestinians and Israelis for a public debate. While Fatah and the Communist Party agreed to participate, the PFLP and the DFLP declined the offer. While the issue of contact remained contentious, it was widely acknowledged that participation – even of individuals independent of any political party – was subject to political approval.[9] When Sa'eb Erakat (Fatah), Hanan Ashrawi (Independent) and Haidar Abdel-Shafi (Independent) ultimately participated in the programme, they requested that they be separated from the Israeli participants by a barrier – this was intended to symbolize the two-state settlement.[10]

Hanan Ashrawi explains why contact-based initiatives were so problematic for many Palestinians:

> No Palestinian had ever addressed an Israeli in a public debate. As a matter of policy, Palestinians refrained from any official communication with the Israelis as a way of withholding recognition or legitimacy. Thus, the Israelis gained an exclusive access to the media, while the absent Palestinians were simultaneously blamed and misrepresented. (1992: 48)

By late 1990, it was instead Israelis who came to question the value of the activities that had hitherto been undertaken. Saddam Hussein's invasion of Kuwait on 2 August 1990 was supported by Yasser Arafat and a substantial part of Palestinian public opinion. This enthusiasm was not noticeably diminished by Iraq's occupation or its launching of Scud missiles at Israel – on the contrary, the latter was openly celebrated by Palestinians.

This placed Israeli leaders and activists in a difficult situation, and some were quick to express their disappointment. Others went further – Elazer Ganot and Yossi Sarid (the current leader of the Meretz coalition), both of whom were Knesset members, suspended their engagement with peace activities and accused the Palestinians of being 'untrustworthy'. Sarid then published an article in Ha'aretz (17 August 1990, entitled 'Until Further Notice the Palestinians Can Count Me Out') (cited in Bar-On, 1996: 273), in which he publicly announced his dissatisfaction with his Palestinian counterparts. This stance was by no means universally reproduced – Dedi Zucker, for example, argued that the war was a temporary diversion. This assessment was later proven to be correct, as contact-based activities resumed in the aftermath of the war.

Peace Now also remained committed to its previous political stance. In late September 1990, it invited Ghassan al-Khatib and Faisal Husseini to address an Israeli audience. Husseini was in no mood to apologize and actually sought to defend the position of the Palestinian leadership. He argued that the problem was primarily presentation, as opposed to actual content (1991: 100–1). He also noted that many Palestinians were disappointed by the fact that the international community militarily confronted occupation in Iraq and implicitly condoned it in the OPT.

Husseini also made a number of important observations on the subject of contact; first, he noted that many Israelis had internalized racist assumptions – this made it near-impossible for them to regard Palestinians as equals. Second, he observed that Israelis had made the mistake of viewing Palestinians as their friends. In his view, this was a fatal miscalculation, as the interests of the two sides ultimately led in opposite directions (Husseini, 1991: 100–1).

In the first instance, Husseini's claim of racism was not without basis. The outraged response of some Israeli activists to the Palestinians position betrayed an unfortunate belief that Palestinians should be grateful for what they had received. This suggested that they viewed peace as an act of generosity, in which benevolent Israelis granted Palestinians that which would otherwise be denied. Palestinians, upon this reading, had a clear obligation which they had infringed by openly siding with Husseini's act of aggression. In the second instance, Husseini correctly identified that Israelis engaged with contact on a personal level – this explained why they viewed it as being conducive to lasting friendships. Palestinians, meanwhile, viewed contact far more instrumentally – that is, as a means through which Israelis could be educated about the realities of life in the Occupied Territories. (This aim has not, it should be noted, been limited to Palestinian civil society. When the *Al-Aqsa Intifada* broke out, the Negotiations Affairs Department of the PLO developed an Israeli outreach programme.)[11]

It is important to recognize that Israelis engaged in joint activities for a number of reasons (see Kaufman, 1988: 70). Under certain circumstances, this could be viewed as a strength, which attested to the pluralism and breadth of the peace movement. However, in other instances, it could be viewed as a weakness, which limited the range of practical activities that could be undertaken (see Bar-On, 1996, chapter 11).

Internal divisions within Palestinian society similarly complicated Palestinian engagement with contact initiatives. While the *Intifada* could be accurately described as a popular uprising, there were also a number of sources of disunity and division, which became increasingly obvious over time. First, there were clear divides within the Palestinian national movement. During the initial decade of the occupation, the Palestinian Left (most notably the Communist Party) played an essential role in helping to sustain civil society against the challenges that it faced. However, by the late 1970s and early 1980s, this began to change, largely as a result of the PLO's increased financial support to civil society organizations (Sayigh, 2009). This funding enabled Fatah to expand the programmes that operated under its control, and this sparked a direct confrontation with civil society organizations that remained loyal to the Left. The so-called war of the institutions left behind bitter divisions that were still apparent when the *Intifada* broke out (Muslih, 1995: 251).

Rema Hammami, who has extensive experience of working with NGOs focused on improving the status of Palestinian women, referenced other internal divides within Palestinian civil society. She identifies that objectives (grass-roots development/political mobilization), organizational structures (hierarchy/community participation) and funding sources (political funding/donor funding) varied widely between organizations. In her view, these 'contradictions' produced tensions that were then evidenced as the *Intifada* progressed (Hammami, 1995: 55).

From 1991 onwards, a resolution of sorts began to be evidenced as Palestinian civil society underwent a fundamental readjustment. Hammami describes how the infusion of foreign funds established development centres which worked with clients rather than constituencies (1995: 55). The broader implications of this development, which can be broadly be described as the 'professionalization' of Palestinian civil society, was indicated by the discursive framing of 'empowerment', 'mobilization' and 'target groups' (1995: 57).

This development had important implications for contact because it shattered the organic links which had previously linked these organizations and the wider community. While their 'input' structures, processes and procedures were not representative, their 'output' nonetheless met local needs and requirements. Professionalization brought about a state of affairs in which local organizations became more accountable to external donors than the communities they ostensibly served.

This chapter has observed that the First *Intifada* was a hugely significant event which brought about a qualitative shift in relations between Palestinians and Israelis. In its aftermath, 'contact' took on a very different meaning and significance and became reconfigured as a broad-based practice that was directed towards the concrete realization of a shared agenda.

Conclusion

The main contribution of this chapter derives from the fact that it highlights a form of contact that is developed and which, in many respects, closely resembles the form of contact which the P2PP sought to 'create'. In resisting occupation, Palestinians and Israelis spoke a common language, learned and applied a range of techniques and directed their efforts towards a common purpose. In engaging both individually and collectively, Palestinian and Israelis evidenced hugely impressive organizational capacities, helping to arrange a wide variety of conferences, debates, demonstrations, presentations, protests and seminars.

In addition to highlighting the potential of contact, the First *Intifada* also drew attention to a number of its limitations and constraints. It is certainty the case that the consensus upon opposing the occupation concealed a number of underlying tensions and points of divergence. It was similarly apparent that underlying questions of historical justice remained unaddressed, and that the root causes of the Palestinian–Israeli conflict were rarely, if ever, touched upon.

It is also important to recognize that contact undertaken during the relevant period hinted at a number of the problems that would be subsequently encountered during the implementation of the P2PP. This was clearly indicated by the Israeli attitude towards contact; the recurrence of problematic attitudes and predispositions; and the incorporation of Palestinian civil society actors into externalized frameworks and priorities. Each of these themes will be expanded and examined in more depth and detail during the discussion of the P2PP.

This chapter has sought to situate the practice of contact within historical context. In tracing the development of contact during the period 1967–1993, it has been careful not to exaggerate its significance. The main point that needs to be inferred from the current chapter is that contact was evidenced prior to the onset of the formal peace process.

Contact has been an active consideration since 1968. It has taken numerous different forms and has varied enormously in terms of its scope and ambition. It has been undertaken by different actors with very different motivations; more often than not, it has not been conceived as an end in itself but has instead been viewed instrumentally – that is, as a means through which another end might be achieved. It has therefore frequently operated as a component of a wider strategy.

The fact that its history and development is infrequently appreciated is in large part attributable to the fact that it has been in the interest of different actors to conceal it from public view. Making peace has, in the context of the Palestinian–Israeli conflict, often proven to be almost as deadly as the act of making war. For this reason, the respective leadership refused to fully engage with the agenda of contact or to give it their full support. At particular points, they tentatively engaged before yielding to the pull of political expediency.

In this chapter, the roots of a more complete contact have been identified. It is possible to trace a clear progression beyond initial limitations. However, contact has also been presented as incomplete and somehow lacking, falling well short of the expectations that its sponsors had originally invested in it. In the following section, I will trace a qualitative change within the meaning of contact, a fundamental shift within its meaning and significance.

Contact between Palestinians and Israelis took on a different form and outline in the aftermath of the Oslo agreement. Oslo II put in place a P2PP, thus lending a clear structure to contact which would guide and frame interactions between Palestinians and Israelis. While this structure was apolitical, it had strong implications for Palestinian–Israeli relations, many of which extended into the future (Hermann, 2009).

5

The 'Oslo years' and 'facts on the ground'

Introduction

During this period contact became institutionalized and dependent on donor demands and criteria. Although many Israeli participants took the view that peace had been achieved, the reality was the P2PP took place in an environment of continued conflict. The division of Palestinian land did not just impact on the arrangement of P2PP meetings but also emerged as a topic of discussion during meetings. During the course of the P2PP, the gulf between Palestinian and Israeli participants, both in terms of their motivations for engaging and their ability to fully engage with the P2PP, became increasingly apparent. 'Final Status' issues and questions of historical justice were particular points of contention in interactions between Palestinians and Israelis. This had actually been a feature of the 'secret channel' Oslo negotiations. Ahmad Quray, the lead Palestinian negotiator, recalls that Savir, his Israeli counterpart, told him, 'If we keep arguing about the past, we will not reach an agreement, it is better for both of us to leave the past and focus on the future' (2005: 149).

While it subsequently encountered formidable obstacles (not least Yitzhak Rabin's 1993 decision to close the West Bank and Gaza Strip and Benjamin Netanyahu's 1996 election as Israel's prime minister), the initial stages of the peace process were characterized by a clear sense of progression. The Cairo Agreement (or Gaza-Jericho Agreement) of May 1994 put in place the foundation for the Israeli army's withdrawal from Jericho and parts of Gaza. The interim agreement (Oslo II), which was signed in September 1995, then established the basis for Israeli army withdrawal from Palestinian urban centres – by December of the same year this had, with the exception of

Hebron, been achieved. The Hebron Protocol[1,2] and Wye River Memorandum[3] followed later.

The P2PP, in contrast, found it difficult to progress, in large part due to the fact that it rested upon a number of deeply flawed premises that failed to grasp the historical context. From the outset, it was premised upon the understanding that interactions between the participants could be sealed off from the wider political context. This was reflected both in its conceptual foundations (which originated in theories of social psychology) and terms of engagement. Contact theory clearly establishes that contact should take place in a neutral or detached setting. This deliberate limitation of wider structural or societal influences is a clear precondition for the transfer or generalization of contact theory across different contexts. The insights of contact theory are, upon this reading, transferable and applicable to a wide range of conflict situations and scenarios.

In spite of these difficulties, joint projects continued to take place, and donors continued to provide generous support. Cooperation even appeared to be taking root within a broader context. Ma'oz[4] observes,

> By late 1995, there appeared to emerge a sense of cautious optimism regarding Oslo process among both Israelis and Palestinians, while various teams and sections among them were cooperating to advance common interests and mutual understanding in the fields of business enterprises, academic research, educational and cultural issues, and the like. (1999: 77)

Oliver Richmond has, in previously speaking of how the theory and practice of peacebuilding has converged upon a very specific set of priorities and predispositions, referred to the 'liberal peace'. For Richmond, the articulation and development of this 'peace' has been profoundly negative, for the reason that it has excluded alternative peacebuilding possibilities. He observed that international practice has converged upon a form of peace that is so 'ontologically solid' that it negates the need for further debate or discussion (Richmond, 2007: 250).

The current section instead inverts this starting assumption. Rather than understanding context as an item that is 'subsequently' incorporated, it instead insists that it should be the basis or foundation of any sustainable peace initiative. The programme's designers and donors instead began from precisely the opposite assumption and were therefore predisposed to focus on the ways in which the programme could change social realities.

The P2PP accordingly insufficiently acknowledged structural influences and instead strongly emphasized the potential contribution of attitudinal change and adjustment. Influence was therefore theorized unidirectionally and with reference to the ways in which the programme could alter or change deeply embedded social 'realities'. However, this overlooks the fact that issues which Palestinians consider to be integral to the conflict (Jerusalem, settlements and refugees) have essentially remained unchanged over time (Chomsky, 1999: 533–65; Usher, 1999).

This inattention to structural determinants is perhaps surprising given that both development and peacebuilding orthodoxy have converged upon a shared recognition of the importance of 'context'. This is why strategic framework documents, from across a range of international actors, now acknowledge the limitations of standardized 'one-size-fits-all' approaches. Meanwhile, heterogeneity and variation are emphasized and accentuated in these same documents.

Context of implementation

In this section, 'context' takes a number of different forms. First, it relates to the wider political, economic and security situation in the OPT (the West Bank (including Jerusalem) and Gaza Strip). Any analysis of one must incorporate the other two – for example, it is impossible to arrive at a sufficient understanding of the political situation in the OPT without first acknowledging underdevelopment and the ongoing occupation; to the same extent, underdevelopment can only be understood in relation to restrictions upon movement – of both people and goods – currently enforced by the Israeli army.

'Context' also relates to the wider peace process. The P2PP should therefore be conceptualized and theorized as a subset of a wider initiative that sought to promote positive interaction between Israelis and Palestinians. From its inception, it was therefore conceived as a 'bottom-up' accompaniment to formal negotiations between the PLO and the Israeli government. While the two levels were initially theorized to be mutually reinforcing, it was also possible to conceive of instances in which they could conflict. Under these circumstances, a lack of progress at the macro level would frustrate progress at the micro level and vice versa.

Third, the P2PP was situated in an international context. It was therefore subject to the influence of a range of international actors, whose objectives, resources and level of commitment varied widely. International actors played an important role in helping to design, implement and evaluate the programme. At each of these points, international influence was a significant influence which accompanied interactions between Palestinians and Israelis.

In the first sense, the P2PP was situated at the level of the OPT and interacted with a constellation of influences (political, economic and security-related); second, P2PP was situated in a wider process that brought together the PLO and the Israeli government in direct negotiations; finally, the programme was situated within a series of interactions between the domestic and international levels. This section will now proceed to set out each of these dimensions of 'context' in more depth and detail.

The Oslo Accords provided the framework within which the P2PP developed and consolidated. From the outset, they were marked by ambiguity. Uri Savir observes that (Yasir Arafat) 'misrepresented the agreement to his associates as a guarantee of a Palestinian state according to a fixed timetable' (Savir, 1998: 94). Israeli politicians and international sponsors viewed 'constructive ambiguity' as a means through which mutual commitment to the peace process could be sustained.

Far from establishing the basis for enhanced contact, the Accords actually reinforced divisions, most notably by creating isolated cantons and cutting Jerusalem off from the rest of the West Bank (Roy, 2004). Although Israel withdrew from densely populated Palestinian areas, it would be more accurate to describe this as a redeployment. The cantonization of Palestinian land and population had a hugely negative impact upon Palestinian economic and social indicators (United Nations, 2006). Land confiscations, the expansion of settlements and the construction of the so-called separation wall provided a broader context which imposed itself upon the programme. The Israeli government remained committed to the construction of settlements and the building of new housing units, both of which clearly violated Article XXXI of the Oslo Agreement.[5]

After 1993, settler housing projects increased by around 52 per cent (Peace Now, 2000; see also PASSIA, 2001). In the three-year period between 1996 and 1999, the number of West Bank settlers (excluding East Jerusalem)[6] increased from 145,000 to 193,000 (Tufakji, 2000: 55).[7] The Israeli government disrupted Palestinian communications (Roy 2004; Shehadeh, 1997: 7) and accelerated the construction of bypass roads in the period between 1994 and 1997 – these roads connected the Israeli settlements and also enabled the settlers to avoid populated Palestinian areas (Peace Now, 2000). Khalil Tufakji observed the encircling of Palestinians 'agglomerations' by settlements and bypass roads (2000: 54).[8] Israeli politicians openly spoke of creating 'facts on the ground' prior to formal peace negotiations, and Ehud Barak, the Labor prime minister, made it clear that Israel would not dismantle a single settlement within the occupied territories (Bishara, 2001: 119).[9]

Far from establishing the basis for Palestinian self-governance, the Accords instead established the basis for the division of Palestinian land into separate enclaves or 'Bantustanization' (Farsakh, 2008: 238). The Palestinian Authority was, by virtue of its dependence upon external funding (Khalidi, 2006, chapter 5; Haddad, 2016) and extensive donor oversight (Haddad, 2016), unable to challenge, much less alter, this situation.

As a result of expanded Israeli settlement construction, further restrictions on Palestinian movement were imposed and an extensive system of bypass roads was constructed. Apart from separating Israelis and Palestinians, these restrictions also separated Palestinians from their livelihoods, communities and land. Palestinian participants increasingly arrived at the conclusion that the Oslo Accords were a mechanism of control design to prevent the emergence of a contiguous Palestinian territory (Baskin, Qaq and Israel/Palestine Center for Research and Information 1997: 13). Even as it spoke the language of peace, the Israeli government was building more settlements, constructing more bypass roads and imposing internal closures that further entrenched rural–urban divides (Chazan, 2000).

These objective realities provided the soil in which the P2PP was supposed to take root. Far from altering material realities, the programme was instead deeply impacted by the occupation. Hilal observed that the practices of the

Israeli government impacted upon the attitudes of Palestinian participants, who became increasingly aggressive in their approach. This impacted negatively upon informal dialogue.[10] This insurmountable gulf between image and reality would later become a recurring feature of the formal peace process. Despite the fact that this external reality imposed itself upon almost every aspect of Palestinian life, donors continually evidenced a reluctance to factor it into their interventions and in some instances even refused to acknowledge it at all.

This was a significant oversight as my findings and overall experience suggested that this broader context was, in many respects, determining. Whereas contact theory emphasizes a process of change, the broader context instead more frequently presented itself as a totality that in many respects preceded the programme. Significantly, this broader context impacted upon the P2PP's preparation, implementation and evaluation.

In contrast to the expectations of contact theory, objective social and political conditions continually intruded on the P2PP. This was illustrated during ostensibly apolitical and neutral meetings, which brought professionals and students together. The initial expectation has been that both sets of participants would set aside 'divisive' political interests and would engage with each other on the basis of shared identities and professional commitments. However, this expectation was not realized. Instead, students spoke about how they had been personally impacted by restrictions; professionals, meanwhile, spoke about how their day-to-day work had been negatively impacted by the arbitrary whims and caprices of the occupying army.

Actions by the Israeli authorities during and after the *Al-Aqsa Intifada* both perpetuated a number of these constraints and introduced a number of novel impediments (Fact Sheet, 2011). Closures, checkpoints and roadblocks further impeded Palestinian freedom of movement within the West Bank (OCHA, 2008). Meanwhile, the construction of the so-called 'separation wall' further reinforced (already strong) tendencies towards economic, political and social fragmentation (World Bank, 2011).

This fragmentation means that it is no longer appropriate to speak of Palestinians in the singular: that is, as a people conjoined by a common political identity and a shared history and culture; rather, it is more accurate, in the contemporary context, to define Palestinians with reference to their immediate location. Gazans, West Bank Palestinians and Palestinian refugee communities therefore present themselves as the disaggregated components of the Palestinian national community. This feature clearly recalls Fanon's assertion that the colonial world is 'a world divided into compartments' (1963: 37; see also Makdisi, 2010).

Israeli and Palestinian NGOs: Power imbalances and asymmetries

Power imbalances imposed themselves at each stage of the P2PP but were most obviously evidenced during the implementation phase. As previously noted, this development was in large part attributable to the fact that the broader context imposed itself upon participants. This subverted the formal commitment to equal terms of engagement and participation and ensured that the programme mirrored, rather than altered, wider interactions.

The first main inequality was evidenced in the funding arrangements that were put in place for both sides. The Palestinian Planning Group was represented by the Palestinian Centre for Peace (PCP), which was established by Fafo funding as an accompaniment to the P2PP. In contrast, the Israeli Planning Group, which was established by CRB, already existed as a funding foundation. The CRB committed to provide half of funding to Israeli NGOs, and it also operated as a planning group: there was no Palestinian counterpart in place. This imbalance had significant implications, as Israeli NGOs frequently felt that they could impose their own interests and priorities.

At times the contrast between the logic of contact and actual material practices bordered upon the Kafkaesque – to take one example, a number of Palestinians who were denied access to Israel were granted special permits that enabled them to travel to Europe (from Israel) in order to participate in programme activities – a substantial number of programme activities were hosted in Europe. Even while participant travel was limited and restricted, the programme still claimed to uphold formal equality. As Rouhana explained, any engagement with reconciliation that does not take into account power relations, or which erroneously assumes symmetrical power relations, will invariably lead to flawed conclusions (2004: 41–2).

Even when Israelis and Palestinians with shared professional backgrounds were brought together, politicization inevitably arose – this was contrary to the expectations of Social Categorization Theory (Brewer and Miller, 1984; Hewstone and Brown, 1986; Marilynn and Norman, 1996; Tajfel et al., 1971). This was the case even in ostensibly apolitical health projects. While Israelis used to tell their Palestinian counterparts, 'let's cooperate and then separate', Palestinians used to tell Israeli counterpart, 'let's separate and then cooperate' (Barnea and Abden, 2002: 300). Even in apolitical contexts, Palestinians were predisposed to think and act in political terms (Sussman et al., 2002).

Advantages and privileges created by the occupation significantly impacted interactions between programme participants. For instance, some Palestinian participants were quite candid about the fact that their main reason for participating was to gain entry permits to Jerusalem and Israel. Even in those (largely hypothetical) instances where positive effects were produced, it was clear that they would largely accrue to the privileged group.

In contrast to contact theory, which appeared as a flawed and insufficient theoretical framework, social identity theory (SIT) appeared to correspond more closely to the different dimensions of the programme's development (Tajfel, 1974; Tajfel and Turner, 1979). SIT clearly establishes that the goals of privileged social actors may differ radically from those of underprivileged groups. The reason is simple – the key priority of the former is to sustain the status quo as it is synonymous with existing advantages.

In addition to providing an insight into the attitude of Israeli participants, this theoretical framework also helps to explain why Palestinian participants orientated towards action-based activities (a broad category which encompasses advocacy and solidarity activities), which were viewed as a basis for social change. It also calls into question the programme's underpinning theoretical assumptions: it appeared just as likely that contact under the established conditions would reproduce, in subsequent effect, prior distortions.

It is to be expected that Israeli and Palestinian NGOs will differ in a number of respects – this could conceivably apply to the relationship with formal political actors, the development of the civil society sector and the internal level of professionalization. While none of these differences are inherently problematic, they can present clear challenges when they are reproduced within the context of a working relationship – when they present themselves in this form they can complicate and substantially impact on interactions between project partners.

Israeli NGOs, in general, have a number of advantages over their Palestinian counterparts – they tend to have a stronger resource base (financial, material and human), are professionalized and are invariably more fluent in the vernacular of 'donor-speak'. In the context of the programme, Israeli NGOs tended to be better organized than their Palestinian counterparts. They were better prepared for joint meetings and frequently took the lead in producing proposals and conducting evaluations. This also applied to participant selection. Whereas Israelis were selected through a process of advertisements and interviews, their Palestinian counterparts were more frequently identified and selected through social connections and acquaintances. The Norwegian P2PP coordinator observed that Israelis dominance of the dialogue was reflected at a number of points, which included the number of participating organizations, organizational efficiency and willingness to enter into dialogue (Endresen, 2001: 22).

In one Palestinian evaluation meeting that I attended at the PCP in Ramallah, a number of participants accused the Centre of not having access to information on workshop updates. Their efforts and capacities were then negatively compared to the Israeli Economic Co-operation Foundation. One participant claimed that he had to telephone the Israeli side if he required any administrative information because the Palestinians were never able to answer his questions.

Palestinian NGOs also had to contend with the occupation, along with its associated restrictions upon movement. It was not merely that these restrictions impacted upon the programme; quite often, they became topics of discussions within workshops. Ifat Maoz,[11] an Israeli academic who has carried out a considerable amount of research on joint projects, observes,

> Inequality between Palestinian and Israeli NGOs manifests itself in several ways. Examples include asymmetry in terms of location of meetings (Palestinians mostly come to meet Israelis in Israel and not vice-versa, and Israeli organizations may refuse activities being held in East Jerusalem for political reasons). (2000: 66)[12]

By 1998, Palestinian discontent had accumulated to the point where Palestinian grass-roots organizations, committees and unions argued that any future contact within the context of the programme should be preceded by the establishment of a Palestinian national framework. Collective organization along these lines was conceived as a response to the power imbalances that adhered within the programme framework. This was the start of a process which extended over the following two years, in the course of which generalized discontent solidified into a more purposeful conduct. Increasingly, Palestinians were predisposed to question the principle, as opposed to practice, of P2PP diplomacy. However, even leaders as prominent as Marwan Al-Barghouti continued to stress that instrumental engagement remained a viable course of action.[13]

Over time, Palestinian priorities converged upon capacity-building. The programme's administrators also increasingly acknowledged the importance of this goal. Jon Hanssen-Bauer, Fafo's managing director, observes,

> We make provisions for creating equality between the partners. The budget is split into two halves and support is given to each of the partners individually. [Our] explicit aim is to strengthen the Palestinian NGO sector through the program, and the Palestinian Center for Peace will provide capacity building for Palestinian NGOs. (2000: 38)

This appeared to indicate that Palestinian priorities were being acknowledged and assimilated into the programme's structures and procedures. Despite this, participants continued to voice criticisms of the donor agenda. A joint 1999 conference that discussed NGO contributions to peacebuilding notes,

> Although the cumulative experience of an NGO might indicate that it should test a new direction, funders would insist that it continue as before. Many NGOs are totally dependent on external funding agencies that are not always sensitive to the developments in the field and often have different agendas. (Adwan and Bar-On, 2000: 70)

This provides one explanation of why established frameworks, in spite of the fact that they are manifestly not adapted to the requirements of the working context, donors still insist in imposing their understanding of the meaning of contact process and structure. The preferences of donors, in addition with a limited capacity for innovation and adaptation, militate against the possibility that programme structures and procedures will be adapted to the demands and requirements of the local working context. Donor exigencies also resulted in a situation in which NGOs received funding support from different donors, often in support of very similar projects. This resulted in project duplication and associated inefficiencies which were exacerbated by a lack of donor coordination, donor strategy and a division of labour grounded within comparative advantage (Qutaineh, 2000: 45).

During an international conference organized by the Welfare Association Consortium, which was held in Ramallah a few months before the *Al-Aqsa Intifada* broke out, Palestinian participants expressed their concern that the P2PP was insufficiently focused upon organizational development (Shadid and Qutteneh, 2000: 93), inequalities between Israeli and Palestinian organizations and ongoing developments on the ground (ibid., 80–3). Despite this ostensible recognition of Palestinian needs and requirements, continued donor insistence upon joint projects made it very difficult for Palestinian organizations to obtain the funds that would enable them to enhance existing capacities. Palestinian, and a number of Israeli participants, increasingly arrived at the conclusion that the joint projects were primarily motivated by financial interests.[14]

Uri Avnery, the veteran Israeli peace activist, observes,

> Dialogue and meetings became an industry and were not genuine. Organizations were paid to do the job. There is an element of corruption in these projects. The real peace activists hold such projects in contempt because there are no real aims. (telephone conversation, 21 October 2003)

Samir Saif[15] referred to one instance in which a Palestinian Centre suspended cooperation, withdrew and declared its strong opposition to the programme. While a number of Israelis were responsive to these criticisms, Palestinian NGOs more frequently tended to prioritize continued funding. During the 1999 Helsinki conference, which evaluated P2PP activities, Israeli and Palestinian participants put forward a number of recommendations to donors (KATU, 2000).

However, these suggestions failed to engage with the issue of neutrality and did not question whether the donor agenda was realistic or workable. The drafting parties instead encouraged donors to focus on the development of a 'fast-track' fund that would enable NGOs to rapidly respond to developments on the ground, thus lending further impetus to the wider peace process (KATU, 2000: 71). While all Israeli participants signed the final document, a number of their Palestinian counterparts refused to provide their assent.

The processes and procedures through which funding was dispersed were also deeply unequal. Palestinian and Israeli observers frequently remarked upon the donor tendency to give more money or even all joint money to the Israeli NGO. Philip Veerman observed that these arrangements often complicated relations with Palestinian NGOs and further compounded pre-existing inequalities (Adwan and Veerman, 2000: 123). This also resulted in perverse arrangements – in one instance, an EU-funded empowerment course that engaged with Palestinians from the northern West Bank was run and administered by an Israeli NGO.[16] The US state department also deducted money from funding that had already been allocated to Palestinians; no comparable arrangement was made for the Israeli government.[17]

Conclusion

The P2PP was focused upon attitudinal change, and it accordingly sought to change the way/s in which participants related to themselves and the world around them. This was a key feature that escaped Palestinian participants from the outset, who instead engaged with the profound misconception that the programme provided a means through which their personal perspectives and life experiences could be directly conveyed to Israeli counterparts. It was a profound mistake to believe that the programme was a 'blank slate' that could be inscribed with Palestinian political meaning. P2PP, in stressing adherence to established parameters of engagement, delegitimized Palestinian narratives of resistance and struggle, thereby forcing Palestinians to engage upon terms that were unfamiliar to them.

The P2PP could therefore be traced back to the belief that the conflict arose within mutual misunderstandings that could be corrected through sustained contact and interaction. This framework of reference – which was predisposed to engage at a psychosocial level – was poorly placed to engage with the material dimensions of the conflict.

It was therefore scarcely surprising that Palestinian expressed strong discontent or even withdrew from the programme – in actual fact, it would have been a greater surprise had this not been the case. Even so, in the aftermath of 2000 participants still continued to engage with joint projects, although Palestinians increasingly sought to ground their participation in clear preconditions. In the aftermath of the outbreak of the *Al-Aqsa Intifada*, there was also a heightened emphasis upon action-intensive activities. In the next chapter I will explain the dynamics of Palestinian and Israeli interaction in P2PP through a case study.

6

'From Both Sides': A case study of the programme

This chapter provides insight into work that was carried out in the post-Oslo era by engaging with a specific initiative that was implemented between 1997 and 1998. 'From Both Sides' (FBS) brought together a total of 180 Palestinians and Israelis, who included university students, educators (formal and informal), professionals (social workers, municipality workers and health workers) and 'opinion formers' (artists, electronic media workers and journalists). FBS, whose operational language was English, sought to establish the basis for professional cooperation and constructive dialogue.

This chapter will touch upon all aspects of the FBS (administrative, logistical and evaluative) with a view to bringing out its wider significance and contribution. Even though FBS ostensibly achieved its goals and objectives, there were a number of underlying tensions and issues that were not fully appreciated or engaged by those that engaged with it.

FBS was instructive because it highlighted a number of themes that we will discuss in more depth at a later stage. First, it reinforced wider power relations and rendered Palestinians and Israelis in very different roles. Second, it reiterated that Palestinians and Israelis were predisposed to engage on very different terms. Whereas the former sought to engage on a political basis, the latter instead engaged as individuals, with a view to building social relationships, often to the extent of extending invitations to social gatherings, picnics and even weddings.[1]

But Palestinians almost always failed to respond to these invitations. One of the Israeli administrators invited me and my family to his house. I apologized and told him I would be unable to attend. I then told Lee Perlman, the Israeli coordinator, 'You participate in these meetings to be able to sleep, but we participate so that you are unable to sleep.' This was one illustration of how Israeli participants came to these meetings with the intention of convincing themselves that peace had been achieved and there was no longer any need to feel guilt. Palestinian participants had the exact opposite intention – to come to the meetings and explain what was happening in the OPT.

In reflecting on Palestinian–Israeli encounters, Abu-Nimer offered a similar observation. He observes, 'The apolitical approach frustrates Arab members because it reflects their inability to influence outside reality and structure' (1999: 52). The Palestinian insistence on political engagement resulted in a series of internal evaluations, which donors also attended. These will be discussed in more detail in this chapter's final section.

FBS provides an ideal means through which to access the programme's broader dynamics because I was closely engaged with the project as a coordinator; this experience provided me with a close insight into its dimensions and dynamics and also gave me an opportunity to engage with individual participants. Al-Jiser (also known as the 'The Palestinian Peace Information Centre', which was established by a group of Palestinians in 1994), the NGO that I worked for, was closely involved with undertaking joint evaluations with Israeli NGOs. The first meeting of this kind was held on 23 June 1995.

As an organization, Al-Jiser's stated intention was to contribute to 'the process of promoting dialogue, understanding, and co-existence between the peoples of Palestine and Israel on the basis of mutual recognition of national rights, including the right of each people to determine their own future in their own state'. With a view to achieving these ends, Al-Jiser arranged a series of lectures[2] (in universities and educational and academic centres), seminars, workshops and (local and international) conferences. Al-Jiser's staffing arrangements were project-based – apart from an executive director (I filled this role at the time) and secretary, its staff were employed on a project-by-project basis.

The Israeli partner was an organization called Melitz,[3] which was first established in 1973. As a non-partisan Jewish education agency, its main goal is to provide education about democracy in Israeli society. It sets up programmes around the world to educate Jews about Israel with a view to establishing constructive relationships. In 1997, it decided to participate in joint Palestinian–Israeli projects. According to Melitz, this development was a 'natural' outgrowth of its belief 'in the promotion of an open, tolerant society'.

One of the most intriguing features of the FBS project derived from the fact that the participants were not Israeli peace activists, and many had no experience of contact or contact-based initiatives. This was intended as the project had developed in response to the criticism that previous contact initiatives had engaged with a very small number of like-minded participants – in these terms, Adwan and Veerman had condemned joint projects on the grounds that they were 'usually limited to a small group of believers from both sides, a sort of preaching to the converted' (2000: 121). This criticism however overlooked the fact that, as noted earlier, many parts of Israel's peace constituency remained deeply conflicted.

For Palestinian participants, this was a clear benefit – one of the main reasons for engaging in contact was to reach out to sections of Israeli public opinion that remained unconscious of Palestinian suffering under occupation. In the understanding of FBS, engagement would proceed through stages that began with cultural exchange and concluded with political interaction.[4]

FBS took place during the so-called 'honeymoon period' (as one Israeli named it), when generous funding was available to support a wide number of initiatives. This was significant precisely because financial initiatives were sometimes the sole incentive for some projects, with salaries even being paid from these contributions. Other non-pecuniary incentives, such as entry or security-related priorities, also sometimes motivated participation.

Al-Jiser experienced great difficulty in recruiting Palestinian participants and decided to hire a recruitment coordinator who would be responsible for each single track. When circumstances allowed, an individual was recruited from the same profession or category (e.g. an architect for a meeting of architects). However, this was not always possible, and it was sometimes necessary to recruit on the basis of educational background (e.g. sociology or psychology graduates for the social worker track). One Palestinian participant was highly critical of this approach and maintained that Palestinians were recruited in order to meet pre-established quotas. This was a legitimate criticism – many Palestinian participants came from Jenin because this was where the Palestinian coordinator responsible for recruitment was based.[5] Israeli participants, in contrast, were recruited on a much more selective basis.

Advertisements were prepared and displayed in advance, and the personal and professional qualities of participants were assessed beforehand.

In 1997, when Melitz took the decision to participate in joint Palestinian–Israeli projects, it justified this participation as an extension of its ongoing work. It works mostly within Israel, in the educational system in elementary, junior and high schools. It primarily engages with teachers, students and sometimes parents through seminars and other activities. It develops curricula that are used in schools and other educational settings and also tutors informal educators. It works with municipalities, the Israeli police and Jewish and Christian groups that visit Israel.

Melitz employs thirty full-time staff and around eighty freelance facilitators and coordinators, who work from offices in Jerusalem, Tel Aviv and Haifa. It does not have fixed funding but receives revenues from donations and also contracts out (to ministries and education, social integration and welfare service providers).

Most joint projects in the post-Oslo period were initiated by the Israeli side or by a funding agency. When the idea of the project had been accepted in principle by the two sides, representatives of both sides would meet to discuss details. The Palestinian coordinator would meet with his or her Israeli counterpart to discuss the general guidelines of the project, and drafts of the project proposal would usually be produced by both coordinators – however it was normally the case that the Israeli side would, because of greater experience in writing proposals and identifying funding sources, usually take the initiative. This was a further reiteration of the fact that Israeli organizations were more professionalized and well-resourced.

Israeli NGOs enjoyed a number of clear advantages, which were in part attributable to the way that the FBS functioned. But Israeli counterparts rarely acknowledged this fact or considered the implications which extended from it. Even now, I remember how, during one evaluation meeting with a donor, an Israeli counterpart saw fit to complain that Palestinians never initiated contact, having apparently never paused to consider why this might be the case.

Melitz had little or no experience of working with Palestinian organizations, and they were introduced to Al-Jiser by the Economic Co-operation Foundation (ECF), an Israeli organization that had extensive experience of working with Palestinian organizations. Melitz's lack of experience in the people-to-people field was actually an asset. Lee Perlman, an Israeli project coordinator, observes,

> The ECF's thinking was that by 'mainstreaming' the peace process with organizations like Melitz, the Society for the Protection of Nature (also non-partisan) and others, they could help break the monotonous cycle of the same peace camps supporters.[6]

Whereas Al-Jiser favoured a more independent approach, Melitz viewed ECF's engagement positively. Perlman observes,

> Melitz preferred ECF involvement, because ECF was very supportive in helping find funding, work with the military authorities to get permits, give general guidance, open doors, and give general background on political developments in Palestine etc.[7]

The ECF also approached the Arab Studies Society (ASS), a prestigious Jerusalem-based centre directed by Faisal Al-Husseini, a prominent Palestinian leader. The EU was the main funder of FBS, and ECF and ASS were responsible for dispersing funding to Al-Jiser and Melitz. The project agreement was signed by ECF and ASS; if either of the implementing partners (Al-Jiser and Melitz) wished to alter the initial terms, they were required to submit a formal request to the EU – this was done at the beginning of the project, when both partners requested the rescheduling and condensing of meetings and greater budgetary flexibility. ECF and ASS were also responsible for supervising project implementation and were tasked with evaluating technical and financial reports submitted by Al-Jiser and Melitz.

FBS benefitted from the input of a core team of Israelis and Palestinians, whose twenty members had extensive experience and knowledge of fields such as curriculum design and teacher training. This core team essentially functioned as a think tank, and their contributions fed into the work of the project coordinators. The core team, who were paid, was also tasked with mapping out an overall strategy and developing a methodology and evaluation system for the programme. Although the core team had a significant impact during the initial stages of the project, this influence gradually diminished as the practicalities of the project, most notably the meeting of donor deadlines, were prioritized.

FBS also invested considerable time and effort (one month of training) into building the skills and capacities of facilitators. Sixteen facilitators, who were equally divided between Palestinians and Israelis, were trained to guide joint meetings. Particular emphasis was placed on the development of skills relating to cross-cultural contact. Feedback on the facilitators varied, often in accordance with whether the respondent was Palestinian or Israeli. This generally reflected the fact that, for Israelis, facilitation was a question of professional competence, whereas for Palestinians it was a means through which the Palestinian experience and narrative could be more completely conveyed. Palestinian participants therefore often observed that one of the main contributions of Palestinian facilitators was to enable them to express their views or perspectives more completely.

An Israeli participant told me on one occasion that Palestinian facilitators were trying to intimidate Palestinian participants who did not speak English well and that they sometimes changed what they had been saying through translation. Facilitation was thus a professional matter for the Israeli side, while for the Palestinians facilitation was one of their political tools. The Palestinian facilitators themselves admitted that the Israeli facilitators were more professional. A Palestinian facilitator remarked, 'Facilitators need more training, especially the Palestinian ones.' Another commented, 'Israeli facilitators are more professional.'

Participant views on the role of the facilitators are helpful in examining the Palestinian position more closely. Many Palestinian participants thought that facilitators were important for leading and organizing sessions, an opinion that is similar to the Israeli view. What is different, however, is that most Palestinian participants emphasized the significant role that the facilitators played in strengthening their political position. One Palestinian participant, for example, considered the facilitator to be 'a leading model that gives me support and confidence in discussion'. But this participant acknowledged that the Israeli side was more professional and experienced. Israeli participants also expressed the view that Israeli facilitators were more professional. One Israeli facilitator observes,

> Facilitators were important, but co-facilitation was more important to me. It was hard for me to work with another facilitator who had little group experience. (Interview, 9 August 2001, Tel Aviv)

Another Israeli participant was however more critical:

> There were one or two activities where we were supposed to talk about where we came from. The person with whom I was paired, in one case the Palestinian facilitator, talked for most of the very limited time we had been allotted, leaving no chance for me to say anything. It was like a political harangue. (Interview, 9 August 2001, Tel Aviv)

This perfectly encapsulates how Palestinians approached Israelis within the P2PP. Palestinians generally took little or no interest in the person whom they were speaking to and instead viewed Israelis as an undifferentiated mass. It was no coincidence that few personal relationships extended beyond the end of the project. In most instances, it was more appropriate to speak of 'encounters' that occurred within the confides of the P2PP.

But the Palestinian facilitator emphasized the political benefits of facilitation. For him, facilitation had an important role in raising group spirit and gave support to Palestinian participants while helping inexperienced participants to prepare for the joint encounters and encourage them to 'speak'. In his view, 'inexperienced participants' needed to strengthen their political position so as to better present the Palestinian view.

Palestinians were also deeply resistant to the proposition of interpersonal contact (an important pre-requirement for the contact hypothesis) and instead insisted upon meeting in groups. This was shown when Palestinian architecture students met with their Israeli counterparts who had been framed around shared professional interests. Palestinians refused to engage on this basis and instead sought to enlighten their Israeli counterparts about the checkpoints, refugee camps and settlements in the West Bank. It should be noted that this approach was not without clear benefits – a number of Israeli participants openly admitted that FBS had provided them with greater insight into the realities of occupation.

Two coordinators from each side were tasked with supervising the overall development of FBS. This entailed an assessment of both the content and logistics. Oversight and evaluation were originally understood to be a joint commitment and undertaking. The likelihood this would be the case was substantially enhanced by the fact that the coordinators were usually directors of their organizations: they therefore had extensive experience of the requirements and time demands which these conditions imposed.

Relations between coordinators were positive, and clear efforts were made to acknowledge, engage and incorporate the priorities of the opposing side. However, even here there was evidence of continued mutual suspicion and distrust. I found an anecdote from Lee Perlman to be particularly telling in this respect:

> Before arriving at Ramallah, I made sure to call the Israeli army and inform them that we would be there and give them a list of the names and identity numbers of all the participants. This was for two reasons: one psychological and one organisational as part of our responsibility and policy.[8]

Here it is particularly important to note that, for Perlman, this was not simply a case of upholding and honouring conditions that had been imposed by the Israeli 'security' forces. Rather, he felt that this was necessary for his own *psychological well-being*. Compliance was clearly not just imposed from without but had been internalized to a considerable degree.

Upon assisting with the development of FBS, I went to great lengths to ensure that the importance and centrality of political contact was fully acknowledged. I insisted that contact activities should include political content, and that social interaction should be superimposed upon political context. With a view to achieving this end, I helped to plan visits to both refugee camps and settlement areas, with the intention of showing how close they were to Palestinian homes.[9] In addition, I also ensured that staff with political affiliations were directly engaged with FBS.

Nisreen Abu-Zayyad, a Palestinian facilitator with extensive experience of working on joint projects, informed me that she disapproved of the Israeli insistence on focusing upon social or cultural engagement. She observes,

> They (the Israelis) do not want to talk politics; they think it is useless because we cannot change the political situation. For us (Palestinians) it is impossible to establish interpersonal relations and friendship without the recognition of our rights.[10]

However, the Israeli perspective was almost diametrically opposed. One Israeli participant complains,

> At the time of the meeting I was disappointed by the fact that the meetings did not have a more focused goal. I was hoping that the idea of meeting

on a professional basis would make this more than the usual encounter of Palestinians complaining and the Israelis apologising. All along I was trying to push towards a common project. (Interview, 9 August 2001, Tel Aviv)

This 'project' was, of course, very different to the one Palestinians had in mind. For Palestinians, the essential 'project' was to educate both participants and wider Israeli about the realities of occupation. Furthermore, they sought to achieve a clear and unconditional acknowledgement of historical injustices. I found an anecdote from Haseeb Ali, who participated in a joint educational project, to be particularly telling in this respect. He recalls,

> In one case a Palestinian brought along a manual coffee grinder as an example of Palestinian culture. One Israeli participant commented that he had seen this mill before. The Palestinian answered that he (the Israeli) must have seen it abandoned in one of the houses taken over by Israelis in 1948.[11]

It should be noted that it was impractical to expect Palestinians to engage on an entirely professional basis. This may have been possible had the operating language been Arabic, as this would have enabled them to discuss relevant concepts, theories and practices to a high level of sophistication. Professional engagement presupposed a level of English language proficiency that was not always evidenced.

FBS was a one-year project.[12] Preparatory meetings between the Palestinian and Israeli coordinators took place between June and September 1997. The project was divided into two stages – the first lasted from September 1997 to March 1998 and the second from April 1998 to June 1998. This division was deliberate as it was anticipated that this would establish the basis for the transfer of lessons (relating to programming, recruiting and general progress) between the two phases.

Throughout September and October 1997, Palestinian and Israeli coordinators met once a week in order to identify the number of project tracks, the target population and recruitment methods. A total of twelve tracks were finally identified, and it was envisaged that this would bring together Palestinians and Israelis with shared professional interests. In addition to the facilitator training track, other tracks brought together university students and educators (this broad category included experienced teachers, social workers and Ministry of Education employees). Each track included twenty participants (ten Palestinian and ten Israelis). Each joint meeting lasted for a single day and included a sleepover (Thursday afternoon to Friday afternoon). Over a two-week period, each group participated in a total of four meetings. In the intervening period between each joint meeting, Palestinians and Israelis also held separate national meetings. For Palestinians, these meetings were particularly useful because they helped to clarify arguments to establish a common evaluative framework for joint meetings and, perhaps most importantly of all, establish a *unified* position. Abu-Nimer suggests that these preparatory meetings (which were also debriefs of the preceding joint meeting) were also useful for Israeli participants (1999: 74).

The project also encountered a number of logistical problems that were related to the occupation. At particular points, these obstacles became the focus of workshop discussions. Palestinian participants encountered particular difficulties in obtaining permits to enter Israel and Jerusalem. The applications of several Palestinian applicants were frequently turned down by the Israeli authorities. Even when permits were issued, they were frequently provided at the last minute.[13] Lee Perlman observes,

> I believe that the issue of permits was very dehumanising for the Palestinians and it certainly had a terrible impact on the dignity of the Palestinians. A Palestinian who had spent from two to six hours to obtain the permit would come very angry to the meeting. Thus, [the] first activity was always connected to what happened with the permits.[14]

This example clearly illustrates that inequality of status was embedded within the programme from the outset and therefore preceded interaction between participants. A number of these inequalities derived directly from the occupation (e.g. freedom of movement), whereas others were more indirect in character (e.g. institutional underdevelopment deriving from the occupation). I asked Muhammad Shahin, who directed a joint health project, if he could expand on this point. He notes,

> We try to achieve equality, but Israelis have institutional support and diversity of qualifications; they are empowered … We sometimes feel stronger because of our belief in our cause – we have nothing to lose. One Israeli once told me 'you have the power as Arabs. Israelis feel vulnerable'

... Israelis learn from us about community work and social support, which they lack.[15]

Perlman rationalized this advantage by persuading himself that he was, in securing security permits for Palestinians, assuming the role once described by Moshe Dayan – that of the 'enlightened occupier'. He felt that when he secured permits he came to be appreciated as a human, as opposed to an occupier.[16] This is consistent with the general Israeli predisposition to engage on an individual basis.

However, it is also significant because it highlights another feature which all too frequently evidenced during the course of joint meetings, specifically the belief that Palestinians should be 'grateful' for the 'sacrifices' which enlightened and progressive Israelis had made and the 'concessions' which they now extended in their open hand. This of course overlooked the Palestinian objection that these 'concessions' and 'sacrifices' were the very least that could be expected.

Palestinians sought to challenge the terms of engagement by refusing to apply for permits. On one occasion, a group of Palestinian students refused to apply to enter East Jerusalem on the grounds that it was internationally recognized as Palestinian territory. Samir Saif, the Palestinian facilitator, notes that contact was, for many Palestinians, part of their wider struggle against occupation – this applied both to participation within the programme's frameworks and participation that sought to challenge or subvert from within.

FBS is an instructive example because it highlights a number of key issues that pertain to the wider programme. It functions, in effect, as the P2PP in microcosm and leads into themes that will be further addressed over the course of the following two chapters. The weaknesses and defects of the project also provide an instructive reference point for future contact-based initiatives.

Both before and during implementation, it became clear that Palestinians and Israelis engaged with the project for very different reasons. Whereas Israelis sought to establish personal relations, Palestinians instead sought to convey aspects or dimensions of their collective experience. While this was in many respects an a priori divergence, it only became fully manifested during the course of project implementation.

The project also highlighted a lack of mutual comprehension on the part of Israeli participants. While inequalities were deeply embedded within the project and subsequently emerged as a core feature, Israeli coordinators failed to grasp the implications which extended from these resource and capacity imbalances. As a consequence, these inequalities were manifested in the form of unequal power relations. A lack of self-reflection (an inability to fully disengage from a position or privilege) on the part of Israeli coordinators further reinforced this feature.

FBS raised profound questions about both the practice and the purpose of contact. In the first respect, it touched upon a number of problems and challenges which could conceivably be addressed. Even in those instances where they cannot be removed entirely, they can nonetheless be mitigated. In the second respect, the project touches upon questions which relate to the anticipated end goals and final contribution of contact. This is a much more challenging question that requires a sustained engagement with underpinning assumptions along with the surmounting of established parameters.

Divergences during FBS

From the outset of FBS, it was clear that the participation of Palestinians and Israelis was guided by very different motivations. Any assessment of participant engagement would therefore need to begin by acknowledging that Palestinian participants engaged for reasons that had little or nothing to do with FBS's goals and objectives. Divergences were also evidenced at and across different points.

For a number of Palestinian participants, FBS confirmed that Israelis approached the question of 'peace' with a very different mindset.[17] This, of course, was one of the main lessons of the peace process – 'peace' is an empty signifier which assumes different meanings and implications in separate contexts. 'Peace' is, to put it differently, an open question that must be explored and developed.

This insight notwithstanding, it is somewhat curious that the form of contact produced within FBS should prove to be so unsatisfactory; after all, as has already been noted, preceding contact initiatives were considerably more productive and self-sustaining. In these instances, dialogue (the expression of mutually opposed views) gave way to negotiation and compromise.[18] It is also particularly instructive to note that these encounters produced a consensus around the establishment of a Palestinian state in the OPT and an arrangement where Jerusalem would simultaneously operate as the capital of two states (West Jerusalem as the capital of Israel; East Jerusalem as the capital of Palestine) (Keller, 1987: 164–5).

Contact initiatives during the 1980s therefore strengthened a consensus that had begun to develop during the preceding decade, when elements within the PLO began to move towards *de facto* recognition of Israel. This development complemented an international consensus that had begun to emerge around UNSC Resolutions 242 and 338. Palestinian–Israeli Solidarity initiatives during the First *Intifada* explicitly called for the implementation of this framework and the establishment of a Palestinian state within the 1967 'borders'. However, international actors, in seeking to put in place a programme that would feed into wider peacebuilding activities, entirely failed to acknowledge this history of contact or to incorporate it into the programme.

Even so, workshop sessions ultimately converged on a very similar solution. Samir Saif, a Palestinian freelance facilitator, therefore observed that a *number of workable agreements were reached on Jerusalem* (ranging from 'two capitals for two states' to one capital with joint administrations)[19] and settlements; predictably, the Right of Return proved to be considerably more problematic, and compensation was most frequently proffered as a compromise solution.

Despite progress in each of these respects, Palestinian participants remained disenchanted with FBS. This disillusion had been evidenced since 1995, when the P2PP was founded. As a Palestinian coordinator, I frequently encountered the objection that the P2PP effectively legitimized the occupation and provided a covert means for the advancement of Israeli state interests. The ostensible appearance of a peace process therefore gave the impression that peace had been achieved, and the sole remaining challenge was to establish precisely how this peace should be defined and moved forward. This, of course, was an illusion – the occupation actually intensified during the 'Oslo years'.[20]

In addition, divergence was also a consequence of the fact that Palestinians had engaged with the programme without first agreeing a clear agenda or strategy. From the outset, the Palestinian position had therefore been defined by clear divisions – significantly, Palestinian participants only began to move towards a shared agenda and framework of action towards the end of the 1990s. Hassan Abu-Libedeh[21] notes that Palestinian leaders had sought to establish a plan that would set out the goals and objectives of P2PP.[22] Even in those instances where a common position was subsequently established, there was still considerable room for equivocation and deviation.[23] Mahmoud Abbas (Abu Mazen), who had been one of the original advocates of contact-based initiatives, criticized the P2PP because he felt it did not have a clear 'vision or strategy'.[24]

Evaluating the lack of a 'common goal'

On this point, it is also instructive to note that the Palestinian–Israeli movement which emerged during the course of the First *Intifada* had also lacked clearly defined goals and objectives. While opposition to the occupation provided an important unifying influence, it could never function as a sufficient political goal in and of itself. This is one reason why, during the First *Intifada*, strategy and tactics appeared as overriding and preponderant preoccupations. Interestingly, however, Palestinian and Israeli participants in P2PP do not hold generalized negative views about each other. When I interviewed participants from the FBS project and asked about their perception of the other side, the majority did not provide any prejudiced view. One Israeli participant summarized the general sentiment when he told me, 'Palestinian people are like any nation – some are good, some are bad.' This suggests that, in contrast to the contact hypothesis, it is the political context rather than a lack of knowledge of the 'other' that needs to be overcome.

The preceding discussion might be presumed to imply that it was incumbent upon Palestinians, whether as direct participants or associated political actors, to clearly define their common position. The manifest failure to achieve this suggests that Palestinians should be held responsible. However, it is also important to recognize that the P2PP was predicated upon a clear understanding that all participants would converge upon a shared agenda – it is no coincidence that all theories of contact agree that the 'common goal' variable is the most crucial determinant of success. Jon Hanssen-Bauer, the managing director of Fafo, explicitly advocated projects that 'pursue a common interest or solve a common problem' on precisely this basis (2000: 38).

However, from the outset there was no clear sense of a common problem or goal. Palestinians tended to engage for political reasons, whereas their Israeli counterparts sought to establish and strengthen personal relations. Palestinians generally sought to 'educate' Israelis about ongoing political realities (PPIC-Al-Jiser and Melitz, 1999a: 2). Israeli motivations were much more closely aligned with the P2PP's terms of engagement, and Israeli participants were more comfortable with a situation in which 'political' issues such as settlements, refugees and Jerusalem were off limits (Al-Khatib, 1995; Usher, 1999: 34).

A study of twelve Israeli organizations, in contrast, found that each one adopted a personal/social approach to their programming (Perlman and Schwartz, 1999: 22). Far from being contingent, this personal/social orientation was a structural attribute. Through engaging with FBS, Israeli participants sought to engage at a human level and learn more about Palestinian culture and society. In other instances, Israelis sought to develop a personal relationship through a shared professional interests and commitment.

Lonning's research on dialogue and cooperative projects provides support for this inference. He concludes,

> While Israelis to a large extent come to dialogue as individuals with no positive sanctions from their respective political organizations, Palestinians often join with the aim of accomplishing political results. (Lonning 1995: 107; also see Gawerc, 2012, chapter 9)

Lee Perlman, an Israeli coordinator who assisted in the development of many joint projects, confirms,

> When final status issues were presented, Palestinian participants seemed to know a lot more and push for more concrete discussions, while Israeli participants either resisted discussions or discussed the issues in more general terms.[25]

Israeli coordinators, in attempting to uphold the apolitical programme framework, also frequently adopted positions that were clearly political. This was shown when Israeli coordinators attempted to prevent Palestinian NGOs that were based in Jerusalem from participating in the programme. However, as Sufian Abu Zaida, in his capacity as the Palestinian director general of P2PP, observes that Palestinian coordinators insisted that participants from Jerusalem should be allowed to engage with the P2PP (Interview, Exeter, 28 November 2002). Most Palestinians active in P2PP projects also expressed the view that joint projects should be held in East Jerusalem.

While Palestinian grievances were sometimes rooted within a general sense of discontent, they gradually converged upon a more precise agenda focused on inequalities in reporting and grant-writing capacities and programme goals and objectives. In the aftermath of the *Al-Aqsa Intifada*, Palestinian participants (significantly reduced in scale) sought to advance this agenda.

However, this aspiration was frustrated by ongoing tensions between the NGOs, which were discussed at a 1999 Beit Jala conference.[26] The conference was attended by thirty-one (Palestinian and Israeli) representatives.[27] The possibility of establishing a coherent shared agenda was further complicated by the fact that many NGOs did not concentrate their activities on a specific problem area.[28] This had clear internal (Palestinian NGOs) and external (relations between Palestinian and Israeli NGOs) implications.

This appears to have been part of a deliberate policy rather than an accidental oversight – the lack of a precise agenda made it easier for NGOs to align themselves with donor requirements. During this conference, most participants knew very little about their fellow participants and made little or no effort to engage them (Adwan and Bar-On, 2000: 68). This was also true more generally – during the Oslo years, most Israeli and Palestinian NGOs made little effort to ensure that they were not pursuing and developing identical projects (although it should be acknowledged that Palestinians NGOs did attempt to establish common objectives for joint projects).

Towards the end of 1999, a qualitative shift within relations between Palestinian and Israeli NGOs had begun to emerge. The Finnish Citizens' Security Council (KATU), in cooperation with the Palestinian Centre for Peace (PCP) and the ECF, took the decision to organize an evaluative workshop. The 'Workshop on the Israeli-Palestinian Civil Society Co-operative Activities' took place in Helsinki in late November 1999. It brought together a range of NGO representatives (European, Israeli, Palestinian) with the donors who financed

P2PP activities – fourteen Palestinian NGO representatives, fifteen of their Israeli counterparts and twenty donor representatives attended this event.

The meeting concluded with the following joint declaration:

> We emphasize the need to enable the expansion of the people-to-people activities to reach a critical mass of Israelis and Palestinian citizens, particularly those who are not fully supportive of the peace process and those who are moderately opposed to it. (KATU, 2000: 71)

The declaration inverted the assumption that the primary objective was to transform Palestinian society. Rather, it proposed that the main aim of contact should be to inform Israeli public opinion about the realities of occupation. This clearly moved the terms of discussion beyond the apolitical and narrow terms of engagement which had previously characterized the programme. Despite these important concessions, a number of Palestinian participants felt that the final Declaration was too closely aligned with Israeli interests and refused to sign it.

A few months later, Palestinian NGOs were invited to a meeting with the Palestinian Ministry of NGO Affairs, which was attended by twenty Palestinian NGO representatives and five ministry officials. The meeting attempted to establish a framework for the future engagement of Israeli NGOs[29] and also put in place a schedule for future meetings of a newly established committee.[30] It was henceforth established that relations between the PA and Palestinian NGOs should be governed by partnership and transparency; it also established that interactions with Israeli NGOs should be undertaken from a unified position. It also proposed that a constitution should govern these interactions and maintained that all interactions (pertaining to administration, funding and implementation) should uphold the principle of equality. The role of Orient House[31] in Jerusalem-based projects was also clarified, and it was established that joint meetings should be conducted on an institutional, as opposed to individual, basis (Palestinian Ministry of NGOs, 2000).

Once the *Al-Aqsa Intifada* broke out, it became apparent that any consensus was fragile and prone to fracture. Israeli participants evidenced a pronounced inability to engage with the underlying causes of the uprising or its political significance. Hermann observed that many Israeli participants, under the force of these political developments, began to adopt more hawkish political positions (2009: 188). They also disengaged from those who they had previously sought to contact. One Palestinian participant from FBS told me, 'When the Israeli army shelled and occupied our cities, not one Israeli, from those who participated with us called to check on me or my family.'

As the *Intifada* progressed, it became increasingly clear – and here the contrast with the First *Intifada* was transparent – that only a small number of Israelis were, by virtue of the fact that the uprising was viewed as a struggle against Israeli itself, willing to support the Palestinian struggle for national rights (Carey and Shainin, 2002). Pappé suggests that only a small number of Israeli were genuinely opposed to the occupation (Pappé, 2002: 113).

This contributed to a clear divide among Palestinian NGOs, which was clearly evidenced in newspaper articles and unpublished journal articles. While one group (including the Popular Cultural Centre) rejected any contact with Israelis, another group (which included the Palestinian Working Women's Society) continued to be engaged with the programme, despite a clear and ongoing dissatisfaction.[32] However, Akram Attalla, speaking in 2004, questioned whether it would be possible to find sufficient numbers of participants,[33] even in instances where a willingness to work together was clearly indicated.[34]

Divergences were clearly evidenced at the start of the P2PP and were subsequently evidenced in fundamental divides which related to core tenets and key elements of the programme. A number of wider disputes related not just to the content of past history but also its significance within the wider context of the conflict. The terms of dispute were 'essentially contested' to the extent that the respective participants did not even agree on what should be the subject of debate. Far from reconciling these points of divergence, P2PP itself became subject to debate and contestation, and this was reflected both in passive disengagement and in the emergence of an agenda that sought to establish a firmer foundation for contact.

Conclusion

This chapter has shown that Palestinian and Israeli participants engaged with the P2PP with very different motivations and expectations. It is important to recognize that Palestinian participants were sceptical from the outset, and that this was reflected both in the difficulties encountered in engaging both individual and institutional participants. In the initial stages of the P2PP, this disillusionment was somewhat inchoate and lacked a clear direction and purpose. Over time, Palestinian participants began to develop a clear agenda that was focused on both the P2PP itself and the NGOs through which it was implemented. In some instances, the P2PP actually succeeded in bringing Israeli and Palestinian participants in *opposition to* its frameworks and procedures. The next chapter, which will focus on critical assessments of P2PP, will examine these developments in more detail.

7

The P2PP – a critical assessment

Introduction

Most of the criticism of the P2PP focuses upon contact conditions and donor criteria. Lina Endresen emphasizes differences between Palestinian and Israeli NGOs (Endresen, 2001: 22), while others instead highlight divergent donor and NGO agendas (see Adwan and Bar-On, 2000; Shadid and Qutteneh, 2000: 93). But it should also be acknowledged that an embedded donor bias privileged Israeli NGOs (Adwan and Veerman, 2000).

The P2PP operates within established parameters that attribute the Palestinian–Israeli conflict to negative attitudes. It did not take material realities as pregiven but instead asked how they could be transformed. By virtue of this feature, it lacked an analysis of materiality and failed to critically engage its own theory of change or to place it within wider social perspective.

As I will demonstrate, this prior predisposition forecloses a number of important questions. This mental enclosure immunizes the two-state solution from critical scrutiny; it also blurs or occludes the relationship between 'peace' and wider strategic interests. Furthermore, it takes the good intentions of the international community as an article of faith and places the process itself outside of critical scrutiny. As Oliver Richmond has previously observed, this overlooks the danger 'that top-level actors will instil in the system their own biases and interests, while arguing that they are constructing a universal system. Any universal peace system is therefore open to being hijacked by hegemonic actors' (2007: 258).

It is therefore important to note that, from the outset, the P2PP lacked public support or engagement on both sides of the divide. The majority of

Palestinians that I spoke to felt that there was no strong support from their family, friends or neighbours for the programme.

The impact of narrative and historical context

The closest that the P2PP came to a 'structural' analysis was to acknowledge mindsets, thought patterns and schemas that had accumulated over time. John Kerry, the former US secretary of state, implicitly acknowledged the influence of interpersonal and attitudinal approaches when he claimed that 'mistrust' and 'narrative' lie at the heart of the conflict (Ravid, 2014). In addition to failing to acknowledge the conflict's structural foundations, Kerry therefore failed to acknowledge that it is as much a question of justice.

In advancing contact as an instrument of social change, the P2PP's designers sought to engage and break down deeply rooted hostilities and animosities. The concept of contact was conceived at an interpersonal, as opposed to societal or political, level. The terms of engagement were strikingly apolitical and explicitly encouraged participants to engage on the basis of shared personal interests.

The workshops evidenced a degree of success in this regard. Participants manged to establish practical frameworks that could be taken forward, particularly on issues such as Jerusalem and settlements. Questions of historical responsibility, which rest on a prior conception of justice, proved to be considerably more problematic. One Palestinian participant observed that even 'liberal' Israelis failed to acknowledge the 'Israeli crime in 1948'. Another noted that the Palestinian and Israeli narratives on the 1948 war and subsequent history clearly diverged. In his view, it was 'impossible' for Israelis to accept the Palestinian position on refugees and the right of return. The views of Israeli participants tended to align with their own government's claim that the refugee issue is a humanitarian question. Although it has recognized that a limited number of returns will be permitted, primarily for purposes of family reunification,[1] it has made it clear that this 'recognition' is contingent on Israel's political and social 'integrity' (Zureik, 1994: 16).

In acknowledging the centrality of the refugee issue, the director of the Jerusalem Centre developed a joint project that would create dialogue through video training. Palestinian and Israeli participants were tasked with creating films that would then be shown to a joint audience. After watching a film about a village that had been taken over by the Israeli army in 1948, one Palestinian audience member enquired why the film had omitted the history of the Palestinians who had previously lived in the village. She was informed that this was 'in the past' and 'we shouldn't bother with it'.[2] This reflected the common Israeli complaint that far too much discussion tended to be 'backward looking' – that is, focused on past history. One Israeli participant, in reacting to the raising of the refugee issue, observes,

> I react strongly to both Palestinians and Israelis who go on and on discussing what the other has done. To me, the only way to proceed is to start with a clean slate rather focusing on past injustice. The past does not help with the future. (Interview, 9 August 2001, Tel Aviv)

Similar issues also arose in interactions between Israeli and Palestinian women's organizations. The director of the Jerusalem Centre for Women[3] recalls how Israeli women always objected to the raising of political issues and sought to ground any discussions in gender-related concepts and themes. One Palestinian participant recalls how a film on the First *Intifada* aroused strong objections from Israeli participants.

Other Israeli participants argued that it was not appropriate for them to make further 'concessions' or 'compromises' as their government had already done this on their behalf. This strongly recalled Hermann's (2009) discussion of the Israeli peace movement, which noted that most groups evidenced a clear reluctance to depart from the state narrative or Zionist ideology. Many groups therefore appear to believe that the conflict began in 1967 and consequently overlook the colonial attributes of the conflict. Some Israeli participants called on Palestinians to take responsibility for their own political situation and strongly objected to the proposition that they should condemn their own society and military.

The question of historical responsibility was a key priority for Palestinians, as the Zionist project was predicated on the denial of Palestinian history, culture and identity. For them, it was only possible to move towards the future when past wrongs and injustices had been acknowledged. Mahdi Abdul-Hadi, head of the Palestinian Academic Society for the Study of International Affairs, has previously argued that the pervasive Israeli denial of historical responsibility and the centrality of the refugee issue is at the heart of the ongoing conflict.[4] Rachid highlights the huge symbolic significance of UN General Assembly Resolution 194(III) (which was declared on 11 December 1948)[5] and argues that the Palestinian leadership's insistence on a right of return was one of the main reasons why the Camp David negotiations collapsed[6] (see Hanieh, 2000).

Given these clear divergences between Palestinian and Israeli participants it is scarcely surprising that, by as early as 1995, Palestinian participants had begun to criticize the programme. In registering this discontent, Al-Jiser, a Palestinian NGO, provided Palestinian participants with the opportunity to engage in an evaluation of the P2PP. Thirty-five Palestinians, representing twenty different NGOs, attended the event, which took place in July 1995. This produced a clear set of key activities, which centred upon a strategic framework, public engagement, capacity-building and strategic reforms such as the establishment of a Palestinian organization that would put in place a strategic framework that would guide NGO interactions with donors. Training was highlighted as the foremost priority by Palestinian participants.

The ability of donors to respond to these complaints was limited by the fact that donors, coordinators and participants clearly diverged on the question of what should be taken to constitute 'success'. Fafo maintained that the ultimate measurement of 'success' was the number of participants who engaged with each project. Yolla Haddadin criticized this assertion and instead argued that impact was the key unit of assessment. Janet Aviad, who was CRB's director at the time, also maintained that Fafo was concerned with the quantity rather than the quality of joint projects.[7]

The need for an event of this nature had become clear – as the Al-Jiser coordinator for joint projects, I continually encountered the complaint that the lack of a coherent Palestinian strategy on joint projects meant that Israeli partners were frequently able to impose their own agenda. This was reflected, for instance, in the fact that a number of the projects appeared to be focused upon changing Palestinian, as opposed to Israeli, society. One project, which was entitled 'Education for Peace', quite clearly had this objective.

From the outset, the terms of engagement were therefore strikingly artificial and removed from 'real-world' reference points. Palestinian participants found it difficult to relate to a framework that failed to acknowledge, much less engage, political and social realities. This was a particularly important oversight because these political realities (their experience of the occupation and desire to share it with Israeli participants) usually provided their reason for participating in the first instance.

It was significant that few, if any, Israeli participants sought to engage with the political demands or conditions that Palestinians attached to contact. They began from the misconception that their political beliefs and perspectives could be detached from personal or social engagements. The 'political', in many respects, appeared as an unwanted and unwelcome intrusion. Tellingly, the expression of personal regret or solidarity rarely translated into a specific political position or commitment.[8] The Palestinian position was frequently the exact opposite.

In many cases, it was near impossible to disassociate Israelis from their position of privilege or from the militarized society that was the source and incubator of this privilege. During one session, an Israeli participant informed me of her disappointment when a Palestinian told her, during the course of one workshop, 'When I look at you I can only see a solider at the checkpoint.'

The P2PP also failed to acknowledge the forces and influences that pulled participants in both directions. In retrospect, it was profoundly unrealistic – especially taking into account solidarities forged through conflict and residual collectivist influences – to expect the individual to break with social influence and to engage on a personal level. Here it is instructive to take into account the contribution of Bar-On and Adwan, who observe,

> The Palestinians are often under attack by their own people for their willingness to cooperate with the 'enemy'. This causes some of them to take a more extreme stand toward the Israelis in general, which may in turn become an additional obstacle to open communication and activities. (Adwan and Bar-On, 2000: 69)

The detachment and artificiality that Palestinian participants encountered in the workshops was not an unfortunate or accidental feature. It is no coincidence that contact theory stresses the need for participants to interact within a closed and confined setting. What might in one instance be taken as a strength (enabling participants to engage within a neutral setting) is, in another context, a defect (an insufficient acknowledgement of the wider context).

This brings to mind Jabri's (2006) critique of 'generic' conflict resolution frameworks. As she explains, these frameworks present a

> language that is managerial to the core, aiming to solve the problem at hand, and hence not implicated. However, we know that the language of analysis is not simply a mirror-image of the world 'out there', but actively constructs the world, in its choice of parties to a conflict, its understanding of the issues, the historical trajectory to a conflict, and its conception of desirable interventions and outcomes. (Jabri 2006: 73)

Far from enabling Palestinians to express their own views and perspectives, the P2PP instead sought to subtly guide and reformulate them. Through engaging with the P2PP, participants 'learned' to express themselves in a way which was more closely aligned with programme requirements and objectives. When conceived in this framework, the programme can be theorized as part of a wider project that sought to reconfigure Palestinian society (Bouillon, 2004; Bouris, 2010; Haddad, 2016; Khalidi and Samour, 2011).

This was, of course, fundamentally opposed to the vision that Palestinian participants had of the P2PP, which more closely resembled a political vehicle through which Israelis could be encouraged to take responsibility for events such as the Nakba, something which its official leaders even failed to do during the Camp David negotiations (Hanieh, 2000: 82). This was resisted by Israelis at all levels, who viewed this as an imposition on the practicalities of peacebuilding.

This reflected very divergent priorities. Whereas for Palestinians the conflict is synonymous with the refugee issue, the P2PP's terms of engagement instead shifted the terms of reference to the OPT; even here, there was still a deeply ingrained predisposition to neglect the day-to-day reality of occupation.

Hegemony and consent

Gramscian concepts have a particular relevance to the P2PP as they help to explain practices that seek – to borrow a phrase of Foucault's – to 'govern through the social'. In expanding this theme, Buchanan examines how international actors engage with civil society actors with the intention of further perpetuating a particular model of economic governance (2000: 117).

Gramsci also enables an analysis that shifts attention away from direct coercion towards more subtle forms of indirect influence. While direct force is clearly evidenced in military occupation, power also takes more subtle and indirect forms. Naser-Najjab and Pappé (2016) demonstrate this by considering the convoluted question of Palestinian school textbooks. The authors analysed reports of Israeli textbooks that had been published with the intention of disassembling claims by the Israeli/Palestinian Centre for Research and Information (IPCRI) that the Palestinian curriculum incited hatred against Israel.

Despite the fact that the supporting evidence was, at best, questionable, a number of important donors felt that it was appropriate to redirect funding. Hilary Clinton argued that any future funding to the PA should be made contingent upon changes to the textbooks (Henry, 2000). Both Sharon and Netanyahu repeatedly called for incitement to end and even sought to make it a precondition for negotiation (*Haaretz*, 2003; Keinon, 2014; Mualem and Benn, 2004). In 2008, the Israeli Committee Against House Demolition (ICAHD) was subject to extensive pressure after the NGO monitor, a pro-Israel organization, accused it of supporting the one-state solution. It quoted Jeff Halper, ICAHD's director, of having voiced explicit support for the imposition of sanctions against the Israeli government. As a consequence, the EU withdrew funding for the organization (NGO Monitor, 2016).

Gramscian concepts also have a clear contribution to make because they also enable an analysis of hegemony, a concept which, as Robert Cox reminds us, applies at both the national and international level (1996b: 56; 1996c: 9).

But in addition to providing insights into the extension of hegemony, the history of the P2PP also provides insight into its points of limitation and denial. While incentives were important in attracting participants to the programme in the first place, their influence gradually waned. In addition, over time, Palestinians also came to identify means through which the P2PP could be subverted and aligned with their own interests.

However, the Palestinian belief that P2PP could be politicized was quite clearly misconceived. This point is further reiterated by Janet Aviad, the director of CRB, an Israeli NGO, who observes,

> The Israeli reading of P2P was in accord with the spirit of P2P aims and goals, which were in the social realm. The problem was with the Palestinian reading of P2P. The Palestinians were looking for politics, and I agree with them because they were still living under Israeli occupation, and P2PP did not bring about changes in their daily lives, which continued to get worse.[9]

This closely corresponds to the Gramscian concept of hegemony, where power is indirect and conveyed through subtle means. Gramsci observes that this concept relates to

> the entire complex of practical and theoretical activities with which the ruling class not only justifies and maintains its dominance, but [also] manages to win the active consent of those over whom it rules. (Gramsci, Hoare and Nowell-Smith, 1971: 244)

This subtle influence was clearly evidenced by the way that some NGOs took the decision to operate within the P2PP's framework of reference and restrict themselves to non-political projects (Adwan and Bar On, 2000: 71). Here it should, however, be noted that most Palestinian NGOs managed to resist this 'normalizing' influence and remained committed to the furtherance of national struggle (Hassassian, 2000: 29).

In addition, capacity limitations also made it difficult for Palestinian NGOs to fully engage with their Israeli counterparts. This was also a factor in their disengagement. Yolla Haddadin, the PCP representative, makes this important point when she clearly distinguishes instances in which Palestinian NGOs did not want to engage from instances in which they were – by virtue of capacity, knowledge or material limitations – unable to engage.[10] Haddadin therefore stresses that, in all too many instances, Palestinians lacked an 'institutional mentality'.[11]

The P2PP also transparently lacked any analysis of the established history of contact between Palestinians and Israelis. The proposition that contact needed to be created therefore reflected a profound oversight on the part of the programme's designers. To put it differently, the programme transparently lacked an analysis of the specificity of the Palestinian–Israeli conflict. It also lacked a clear theory of change – contact is not in itself transformative and it is just as likely that it will reinforce established predispositions.

It is also important to recognize that the Palestinian–Israeli experience challenged the core grounding tenets of contact theory. Over the course of the First *Intifada*, contact took place in the absence of the preconditions which contact theory advances as preconditions for successful contact. Contact theory also fails to recognize the various joint strategies that Palestinians and Israelis have developed in response to the *absence* of these conditions. These initiatives problematize claims previously advanced by Allport (1954), Amir (1969) and Pettigrew (1971).

For instance, contact theory takes institutional support to be one of the key preconditions of successful contact (see Allport, 1954; Brown, 1995). Despite the fact that this was manifestly lacking in the Palestinian–Israeli context, successful contact – or at the very least relatively successful – could be said to have occurred.

There was no social support, let alone laws and legislations, on either side to support contact. The official stance on both sides was, in the absence of meaningful public support, cautious and reticent. When news of the contacts spread in the Israeli media, both the PLO and the Israeli government denied any interest, let alone association (Avnery, 1986; Bar-On, 1996).

But despite these challenging circumstances, contact expanded to encompass a wider range of social actors; in addition, those initiating contact became increasingly influential within both communities. Rather than being a condition, it instead appears that institutional support is a 'situation-specific' (Tajfel, 1981) variable that adjusts in accordance with the individual context.

Second, it is important to note that the contact between the respective parties was both interpersonal and intergroup. The literature on contact has yet to reach a clear consensus on which of the two is more effective (Brewer, 1997; Brown, 1995; Tajfel, 1981). In advancing the former, some observers have claimed that personal meetings establish the basis for personal encounters, while enabling participants to bypass political interests. It should nonetheless be observed that debate continues as to whether it is possible to generalize contact experiences across different contexts (Hewstone and Brown, 1986; Pettigrew, 1986).

The P2PP's predisposition to engage at the level of generality was clearly set out in its stated intention to

> promote initiatives in areas which are likely to have an impact on people's everyday lives and welfare, including practical activities which will promote communication and understanding by demonstrating the advantages of working together for mutual benefit and tangible results. (Partnership for peace, 2014: 1)

I would therefore suggest that the oversight of context was not accidental. On the contrary there was, by virtue of the fact that this position corresponded much more closely to donor priorities and prejudices, a clear preference to begin from the assumption that the conflict is psychological in character. For donors, this position had a clear expediency.

But analysis should also consider the P2PP in context and engage with the contradictions and tensions that affected the wider peace process. It should specifically attend to gaps between language and material reality, along with intent and outcome. Contact theory fails to provide a clear purchase or contribution at any of these points.

Contact experience from South Africa (Foster and Finchilescu, 1986) provides further empirical support for this claim. Closer reflection upon contact experiences frequently elicited the sense that integration and reconciliation would only be possible when political settlement was achieved; in the absence of such a settlement, contact would only appear legitimate to the extent that it provided a basis for the discussion of strategies, techniques and methods orientated towards the change of the status quo. This argument was also frequently advanced by Palestinian participants during the P2PP.

A critical analysis should consciously and deliberately engage with the assumptions that underpin the programme. In the absence of such an engagement, it is likely that the programme will continue its own internal contradictions in subsequent effect – the same observation can be made in relation to the Oslo Accords and liberal peacebuilding more generally.

It is therefore significant that external donors have continued to fund P2PP-related activities. The EU 'Partnership for Peace Program' (2002)[12] therefore functioned as part of the organization's Neighbourhood Policy until it was replaced by the EU Peacebuilding Initiative (EU PI) in 2007.[13] The latter now disburses an annual total of between €5 and €10 million. EU PI is currently aligned with other initiatives such as the Arab Peace Initiative[14] and the Road Map.[15] The United States, for its part, after founding Conflict Management and Mitigation (CMM) in 2002,[16] has committed an annual total of around $10 million (USD) to P2PP activities. In 2004, the US Congress legislated for the establishment of the Reconciliation Funds Program. USAID and the US Consulate in Tel Aviv also continue to invest in the CMM programme with a view to encouraging reconciliation.[17] In 2011, CMM published a programme guide which further affirmed its ongoing commitment to P2PP. It asserts,

> Projects in this arena address the prejudice and demonizing that reinforces the perceived differences between groups and hinders the development of relationships between conflict parties. (People-to-People Peacebuilding: A Program Guide, 2011: 6)

This continued commitment highlights a clear lack of critical engagement on the part of each of these international actors. Despite the fact that the benefits are, at best, deeply questionable, funds continue to be committed and political commitment remains in place. Although it appeals to a body of empirical research, the programme appears to be sustained, to a considerable extent, by normative value judgements and institutional priorities.

Indeed, it was all too telling that, in instances where joint projects were successful, this was largely achieved by working around the programme. A joint proposal submitted by PPIC and Givat Haviva, which focused on educational cooperation therefore asserted – in direct opposition to the underpinning logic of the programme – that political discussion should be regarded as an integral component of a 'constructive dialogue' that would establish the basis for cooperative activities. As if directly speaking to the P2PP's inherent limitations, the applicants asserted,

> The real problem – the Israel/Palestinian conflict – must be confronted and discussed honestly if there is to be progress in the communication between the two sides. Any attempt to go around the issue is only counterproductive because it denies the reality of the situation and the people who live it. (Palestinian Peace Information Centre (PPIC)-Al-Jiser and Givat Haviva, 1999b: 4)

Donor evaluation of P2PP

P2PP activities that took place in the aftermath of the *Al-Aqsa Intifada* combined the following features: (1) they were low-profile and were not announced; (2) they were generally held outside Palestine/Israel; (3) they only included a limited number of participants; (4) they mostly addressed political issues and facts on the ground; and (5) relations between Palestinian and Israeli NGOs that were characterized by a degree of equality.

The final two developments do suggest that, to a relatively limited extent, the lessons of past experience have been acknowledged and incorporated. The Canadian International Development Agency (CIDA) has attempted to adjust its funding criteria to Palestinian needs. Meanwhile, Ra'id Malki suggests that the Palestinian prioritization of equality has resulted in a new donor emphasis on Palestinian capacity-building.[18]

However, joint activities that bring together Palestinians and Israelis are not currently on the agenda. Issa Rabadi, the co-director of the Peace Education Department-IPCRI, a joint Israeli/Palestinian centre,[19] observes,

> Joint student encounters are not possible, at the present time. Palestinian schools (administration) and parents of students do not accept the idea of joint encounters. Students also refuse to participate in such encounters. [A]t present, we have separate projects on peace education. When I approach Palestinian schools to talk about the Palestinian peace education package, they initially refuse because they think it has to do with joint ventures.[20]

The ongoing limitations of P2PP activities are further underlined by the fact that it is mainly Palestinians from elite groups, such as intellectuals. Furthermore, these activities are often only made possible by technology, which enables participants to work around logistical restrictions such as permits.[21]

Given this continued and ongoing support, it is also important to note that some observers have questioned the ongoing contribution of P2PP activities. For example, in 2006 the Labour MP Joan Ryan asked the British Foreign Office (FCO) how much money had been committed to Palestinian and Israeli NGOs through the relevant funds (FCO, 2016). Tobias Ellwood, the FCO's parliamentary undersecretary, provided a detailed answer (ibid.), which was primarily of interest because it highlighted a substantial discrepancy. Over the course of 2015–16, the FCO dispersed £851,000 to Israeli organizations and £141,000 to a single Palestinian organization.

This support fails to acknowledge that the very concept of P2PP is regarded with widespread scepticism by Palestinians to the extent that some have even suggested entirely dispensing with the term. Signe Gilen, a counsellor in the Norwegian Representative Office, acknowledged, during a 2005 workshop, 'We have to work to creating a consensus for the P2P. We need to re-evaluate the whole concept of P2P to enable us include wider sectors to participate in joint activities.'[22]

In 2000, the Palestinian NGO Network (PNGO), in response to the outbreak of the *Al-Aqsa Intifada*, issued a press release that set out a number of key decisions. It called for the cessation of joint projects, argued that further participation should be made conditional upon a clear acknowledgement of international law and suggested that Arab and Palestinian organizations that did not abide by these conditions should be clearly identified on a public register. None of these conditions, it should be recognized, ruled out cooperation with Israeli organizations that acknowledged Palestinian national rights (PNGO, 2000).

A two-day workshop was held in Oslo in June 2000. This workshop had been arranged in response to complaints that had submitted to the Norwegian Secretariat by Palestinians NGOs. It was noted that limited wider social impact had impacted negatively upon the programme itself; both the attitudes of Israeli NGOs and clear variations in internal capacity were also acknowledged as important limiting points. Unilateral initiatives, in particular those focused upon lobbying, were also recommended by participants.[23]

Ghassan Al-Khatib, who headed the Palestinian committee for P2PP in the Abu Mazen government, suggested precisely this course of action. In his view, P2PP increasingly appeared as an elitist activity that had become too closely associated with personal benefits (travel, accommodation, etc.). Aside from raising questions of sustainability, this feature also brings the wider social impact of P2PP into clear question and suggests that P2PP should be adapted to the purposes of solidarity-based activities.[24] It should come as no surprise that al-Khatib upholds contact during the First *Intifada* as a model of imitation and emulation.[25]

In the aftermath of the *Al-Aqsa Intifada*, this sentiment became increasingly influential within Palestinian society. Whereas Palestinians had previously requested solidarity from Israeli participants, they now demanded it as a precondition. Dr Hanna Nasir,[26] in writing an open letter that replied to the members of a Jerusalem synagogue, clearly expressed this view (also see Dalsheim, 2005). He called on his correspondents to

> direct your pens towards your own people. Ask them to declare their acceptance of international and legitimate resolutions without ambiguity or misinterpretations and their willingness to completely withdraw from the territories occupied in 1967 including east Jerusalem. Ask them to find a just solution to the refugee problem.[27]

A 2005 workshop that was organized by the Canadian Representative Office found that the apolitical terms of reference and deeply embedded inequalities had acted to the detriment of the P2PP. Dominique Rosetti, the deputy representative and head of aid in Canada's Representative Office, admits, 'In general, the Israeli partners were better funded, more experienced and enjoyed superior technical and administrative capacities' (Rosetti, 2005/6). This was certainly consistent with my own experiences – during P2PP activities, Israelis were always better prepared. This frustrated me and substantially motivated my research on P2P.

The workshop also highlighted the lack of consensus within both societies and acknowledged the importance of context.[28] Ron Rundak, the director general of the Peres Center for Peace, clearly failed to acknowledge the full centrality of context in asserting that 'P2P activities should be carried on regardless of the macro-level political changes as the P2P programme is supposed to create an environment of co-existence' (Pundak, 2005/6).

Previous initiatives have also suggested that P2PP could provide further impetus to separate initiatives. The Israeli–Palestinian Peace Committee (IPPC) was a significant development in this regard. After initially developing as a P2PP initiative, it has since emerged as a quasi-official organization that is actively engaged in attempts to engineer a peace coalition. Even after it took on this role, many of its activities (most notably those focused on attitudinal change) could still be categorized under the P2PP heading.

In 2006, Norway's Representative Office to the PA organized a public debate on P2PP that was coordinated by the Jerusalem Media & Communications Center (JMCC).[29] (The Evans Program for Conflict Resolution and Mediation at Tel Aviv University conducted the evaluation on the Israeli side.) A broad cross-section of Palestinian and Israeli society participated in the debate; however, only one joint meeting took place in Jerusalem. During the debate, it was noted that the P2PP had failed to engage with broad sections of public opinion. Many of the themes had been engaged before (asymmetries between NGOs, the clear need for capacity-building), although an important additional insight was provided when it was noted that the P2P had helped to improve Israel's international image.

Conclusion

In this chapter, criticism has predominantly been conceived within an established framework of reference and with reference to the P2PP's implementation. The discussion has primarily focused on the question of how Palestinians related to the programme and their attitudes towards the terms of engagement and emerging agendas. These agendas were part of a broader discussion with donors about how the P2PP could be improved and developed.

The disconnect between the terms of engagement and Palestinian participants was reflected in the latter's orientation towards action-based activities, a category that includes solidarity activities and initiatives directed towards influencing public opinion. Action-oriented activities appear, in this instance, to be privileged by the subordinate group (Palestinians) precisely because they seek to fundamentally alter existing social conditions.

The insistence of donors on working within a conflict resolution framework that sought to encourage cooperation and change negative attitudes failed for two main reasons. First, this framework is apolitical and focuses on psychological questions and themes (Mu'allem, 1999). Second, it ignores the power dynamics of the conflict (Hanafi, 2007) by attempting to create superficial conditions of equality.

There was accordingly something of a divergence between my engagement as a practitioner and as a researcher. In direct opposition to the contact hypothesis that was foregrounded within the P2PP, my research findings suggest that the difficulties did not arise in attitudes but rather from objective social and political conditions. This is problematic precisely because P2PP endowed attitudinal change with a transformative potential and significance. However, this was quite clearly unwarranted: even in those (limited) instances where positive effects were evidenced, it was clear that they would accrue to the privileged group. This clearly recalls Social Identity Theory (SIT), which makes it clear that the goals of privileged social actors may be different radically from those of underprivileged groups. This divergence originates within the fact that the former orientates towards the preservation and perpetuation of the status quo.

Even if the hypothesis is hypothetically accepted on its own terms, its relation to the Israeli–Palestinian conflict is questionable. Israelis and Palestinians undertook, and continue to undertake, solidarity initiatives, even in the absence of most of the aforementioned conditions (it is striking to reflect that the First *Intifada*'s peace movement does not appear to closely approximate to *any* of the four conditions). It should also be recognized that Palestinians and Israelis have initiated cooperation in response to the *denial* of these conditions. This is consistent with research that openly contradicts Allport (1954), Amir (1969) and Pettigrew (1971) by claiming that conditions for optimal contact do not necessarily produce positive relations.

The Palestinian–Israeli case therefore raises clear questions about the general applicability of these research findings. This appears to reiterate that the Palestinian–Israeli conflict is not reducible to the negative views that Israeli individuals have of Palestinians and vice versa. This suggests an alternative hypothesis: when negative attitudes stem from an ongoing political conflict between groups or states, they will not necessarily be transformed by interpersonal contact; even when they are, this will not necessarily culminate in cooperative behaviour.

8

The P2PP during and after the *Al-Aqsa Intifada*

Introduction

The failure of the P2PP raises the question of precisely how cooperation can be conceived, theorized and practically implemented. The scale of the challenge is highlighted by the signs which stand at the entrance of the roads that lead to Palestinian Authority-administered areas. Written in Arabic, English and Hebrew, they render a stark warning that 'this Road leads to Area "A" under the Palestinian Authority. Entrance for Israeli citizens is forbidden, dangerous to your lives and is against the Israeli law.' The so-called 'separation wall' serves as an equally stark reiteration of the challenges that confront those who seek to imagine and apply alternative forms of cooperation.

The preceding discussion has repeatedly argued that the P2PP was poorly adjusted to the wider context, and that many of its key weaknesses can be conceptualized and theorized in relation to the negative interaction. However, it is also important to note that similar initiatives were also called into question by previous research. Robinson and Preston's 1976 study of racial prejudice, which engaged with black and white participants, found significant attitudinal differences between the two sets of participants. This had important implications for attitudinal change in the context of equal-status contact, and significant differences were accordingly observed at this point (Robinson and Preston, 1976: 921).

This raises the question of how contact can be reconfigured. In seeking to revive a stalled process, these actors operate in a past history of abortive attempts to engineer a peace settlement.[1] In addition, they should also acknowledge the centrality of context and take into account the fact that, for Palestinians, the P2PP concept is discredited currency. Although P2PP projects continued in the aftermath of the *Al-Aqsa Intifada*, it is important to recognize that they only persisted in very limited form. While the Norwegians no longer provided support, a number of Palestinians and Israelis continued to implement joint projects and to apply to international agencies for support. P2P initiatives have also continued to be developed within the wider framework of neo-liberal state-building (Bouillon, 2004; Bouris, 2010; Haddad, 2016; Khalidi and Samour, 2011).

Both the United States and the EU have made it clear that they intend to continue to support P2PP-based activities (Hanafi, 2007; Scham, 2000). This was despite the fact that, in the aftermath of the *Al-Aqsa Intifada*, they aroused no real enthusiasm within either society. In fact, P2PP projects became subject to an increased re-evaluation when the *Al-Aqsa Intifada* erupted. Even in instances where Palestinian and Israeli participants expressed a willingness to meet, the political situation complicated face-to-face contact. In some instances, it was only possible to hold meetings abroad.

Nonetheless, the *Al-Aqsa Intifada* did not lead the relevant actors to dispose of the principle of P2PP; rather, it was instead the practice of P2PP, as implemented within the internal context of the programme, which was increasingly challenged and subject to critical scrutiny. A clear Palestinian agenda has emerged, which directly addresses the flaws and weaknesses of the P2PP. Palestinians have also explicitly requested changes in the agenda and implementation of P2PP.

In this chapter I will engage with the contributions of donors, Israelis and Palestinians, with a view to identifying how donors sought to engage with an emerging agenda. In many respects, as will be noted, this emerging agenda extended from Palestinian responses during the process of programme implementation. In addition to political education and the engagement of Israeli public opinion, an engagement with the political dimensions of the conflict was also highlighted as a key priority for Palestinian participants (JMCC, 2006).

The different perspectives of Palestinians and Israelis could be summarized in the follow quotes from the participants in the workshops. A Palestinian recalls,

One time, we were in one of the villages [as part of the P2P Programme], and they were distributing a publication on how to use water and economize in use of water, and one woman asked me a question: I cannot imagine how an Israeli is coming here to educate me on how to use water while I still use the bucket and close to me there is a settlement where they have swimming pools, so how an Israeli comes to educate me on how to use water and they are occupying our land? The Israeli institution working with you should work inside the Israeli society and not to educate me. . (JMCC, 2006: 21)

Limits of cooperation

As has already been noted, this vision of contact was often diametrically opposed to Israeli readings. Taking this fact into account, it is nonetheless necessary to acknowledge that the *Al-Aqsa Intifada* had fundamentally altered the parameters within which the P2PP was engaged. In contrast to its predecessor, this *Intifada* was both militarized and violent (Hammami and Tamari, 2001). Palestinian suicide bombs targeted both Israeli civilians and military personnel. In this environment, political opinion increasingly hardened and both sides were reluctant to make compromises. As one Israeli activist noted, peace projects were now widely viewed as a 'dream' or 'honeymoon' (Hermann, 2009).

Israeli public opinion generally showed limited sympathy with the Palestinian struggle (Svirsky, 2001). Hermann observes,

> For many who, during the Oslo years, had been torn between support for the idea and ongoing scepticism regarding Palestinian intentions, the *intifada* resolved this cognitive dissonance and pushed them to the hawkish right. It did not cause a majority of Israeli Jews to ponder whether Israel itself had contributed in any way to the gathering Palestinian anger that led to its eruption. (2009: 188)

In large part, this was attributable to the active campaign of distortion that had been launched by the Israeli government in the aftermath of the failed Camp David negotiations. In following their government's lead, many Israelis – including a significant proportion of the Israeli Left – arrived at the conclusion that there was 'nobody to talk to'. Only a small minority of

Israelis now supported Palestinian national rights (Carey and Shainin, 2002; Pappé, 2002: 113). The media's coverage of the bombings also distorted Israeli public opinion. Most Israelis came to believe that they were confronted with an existential threat rather than a more specific threat to the occupation. As Ophir explains,

> When the Oslo process collapsed at the end of summer 2000 and the Intifada erupted, the Israeli public underwent a rapid shift to the right. Many perceived the failure of Camp David talks and the subsequent violent outburst as a sign of the Palestinian pretence that had characterized the negotiation from the start, or of the Palestinian insistence on principles that endanger the very existence of the State of Israel – an insistence that proved, in retrospect, that there was never anyone to talk with in the first place. (2002: 52–3)

Neve Gordon, an Israeli peace activist, maintains that the Israeli media legitimized the actions of the Israeli government. She observes, 'For Israeli television viewers, Palestinian suffering is virtually non-existent, while attacks on Jews are graphically portrayed, replayed time and again, thus rendering victimhood the existential condition of the Israeli Jew' (2002: 102). Gideon Levy, an Israeli journalist and regular *Haaretz* columnist, notes that because the Israeli media did not depict the daily struggles of the Palestinians, most Israelis were ignorant of the realities of the occupation. In his view, this 'filtering' was intentional. He observes, 'Rare shots of the suffering that Palestinians are enduring were broadcast on Channel 2 and led the defence minister to temporarily close the territories to the Israeli media' (Levy 2002: 179).

The Israeli reaction to the *Al-Aqsa Intifada* affected every aspect of Palestinian life (Fact Sheet, 2011). Closure, checkpoints and roadblocks restricted Palestinian movement within the West Bank (OCHA, 2008). Jerusalem was closed and the so called 'separation wall' sealed the city off from the rest of the West Bank and hindered Palestinian freedom of movement more generally (OCHA, 2011a). Israeli activities within Area C, including the use of violence, forced displacement and settlement activity, further exacerbated the fragmentation of Palestinian land (B'Tselem, 2010: 5; OCHAb, 2011; World Bank, 2007, 2011).

After September 2000, the Israeli army imposed curfews upon Palestinian cities and also entered to conduct 'security operations'. Populated areas were bombed, homes were demolished and the West Bank was transformed into a series of enclaves.[2] This had clear implications for the P2PP. Samir Saif observes,

> Recruiting Palestinian participants has been always difficult, but in 1999 when Palestinians had lost hope in political change, there was one case where Palestinian participants were paid a hundred and fifty dollars each to encourage them to participate.[3]

By September 2000, P2P was largely discredited currency for Palestinian. This applied to the extent that Ghassan al-Khatib recommended that the very term should be dropped. He recalls,

> As the head of the Palestinian committee for P2PP during the Abu Mazen government, I suggested to the Norwegians that we should change the title of the Programme. P2P is more related now to elites who obtain material benefits, either in the form of salaries or expenses when travelling abroad and staying in hotels and places that are removed from the reality of the situation. Although such a form of contact still exists, it involves very few people.[4]

As the *Intifada* progressed, Israeli and Palestinian coordinators tended to focus on arranging uni-national meetings – this addressed the Palestinian scepticism about joint meetings and also offset the logistics of movement. Akram Attalla recalls,

> In 2003 we received more than 50 proposals. The set-up of these proposals was different. Most joint proposals considered similar topics that could be discussed in parallel uni-national meetings with a minimum number of joint meetings. Even though Palestinian and Israeli co-ordinators and directors of organisations have been willing to work together, I doubt whether they can recruit participants.[5]

The Palestinian loss of faith in political change was further exacerbated by the stance of Israeli participants, whose acknowledgement of Palestinian grievances was invariably always conditional and contingent. One Israeli participant reflects,

> I feel angry for what we, the Israelis, did to Palestinians, but as I told the Palestinians, it is because of the Palestinian terror that Netanyahu was elected. I blame the Palestinians for the political situation here. (Interview, 9 august 2001, Tel Aviv)

In January 2004, the P2PP administrators decided to freeze all activities. Ghassan Al-Khatib provided further insight into the context of this decision. He notes,

> When Mahmoud Abbas (Abu Mazen) became Prime Minister in 2003 he was interested in reactivating P2P, and formed a Palestinian committee that included ministers and deputy ministers to follow up the matter. I was the head of the committee and we held several internal meetings to discuss P2PP in a new spirit and a set-up that would be closer to reality. We spoke to the Norwegians and presented our view. The Norwegians spoke to the Israeli Foreign Ministry and asked them to form a parallel committee to the Palestinian one. I also spoke to the Israeli side, who showed willingness about P2P. In practice, however, the Israeli side never came back to us and never formed a committee.[6]

One of the main problems with P2PP is that it is premised upon official involvement. At different points throughout the programme's development, this 'official' dimension proved to be a complicating factor, as it became clear that political actors did not necessarily share the contact agenda. But external donors addressed this by seeking to align with was significantly enhanced by the fact that external donors sought to recognize and engage local needs. The Canadian International Development Agency (CIDA), for example, sought to adapt its funding criteria to Palestinian needs. Ra'id Malki reflects,

> The main concern for Palestinians is the equality aspect in terms of their roles as partners in joint projects. The partnership includes decision-making and leadership. Therefore, and based on our own assessment, we are now considering a new phase for Palestinian capacity building.[7]

While it was clear that the *Al-Aqsa Intifada* did not bring the P2PP to an end, it did nonetheless provide renewed impetus to attempts to develop alternative approaches. A series of donor evaluations were an important development in this respect. Local actors also sought to take contact in a very different direction, with the consequence that it came to increasingly resemble the form evidenced during the First *Intifada*. Ghassan Al-Khatib has therefore noted that 'the most influential form [of contact] now is the solidarity-based type of contact, which develops more of a genuine dialogue'.[8]

But Fafo insisted on continuing to fund P2PP, albeit with some modifications. The Geneva Initiative (which has since become institutionalized as the Peace Coalition) was an important offshoot of the IPPC's work that was declared on 1 December 2003. This is a quasi-official organization that includes governmental and NGO members. It includes two counterpart organizations (Palestinian and Israeli) that functioned as a peace coalition, and each one engaged with its respective public to promote peace through various actions and programmes. It initially received funding from Fafo and is therefore a P2P project.

The coalition moved beyond seeking to change attitudes through dialogue and actively sought to contribute to a political agreement, and this feature distinguished it from traditional P2PP activity. When the core members of IPPC developed a proposed peace agreement, they sought to create an institution that would work to develop a political proposal and that would provide an official declaration signed by official leaders. These efforts, which were led by Abed Rabbo and Yossi Beilen, were supported by Palestinian and Israeli public figures and activists. The first joint action of the IPCC was a joint protest at the Al-Ram checkpoint that protested against the Israeli occupation and called for dialogue and negotiation.

Its work is focused on the organization and implementation of forums, seminars and workshops. It has separated Palestinian and Israeli branches, and some members are employed staff who work on initiating programmes. It is part of the wider state/peacebuilding project (Haddad, 2016). It presents its vision in the following terms:

> We are committed to exposing each side's public to the message of the other – despite the technical and psychological barriers.[9] [The initiative] provides realistic and achievable solutions on all issues, based on previous official negotiations, international resolutions, the Quartet Roadmap, Clinton Parameters, Bush Vision, and Arab Peace Initiative.[10]

After the founders of the IPPC announced a 'Joint Call for Peace', many Palestinian and Israeli intellectuals, academics and politicians signed the call, which outlined a detailed draft proposal for an agreement on unresolved issues including Palestinian refugees, Jerusalem and Israeli settlements. While the initiative was focused on very specific target groups (academics and public figures – see Kelman, 1996), it should nonetheless be recognized that it still continues to be strongly opposed by elements within both societies. In addition, while the initiative (which is action-based and therefore similar to a number of initiatives undertaken during the First *Intifada*) made progress in each of the aforementioned respects, it still continued to be confronted by a number of the procedural problems that impacted the P2PP (access to information, inequality of power relations, etc.).[11] In this case, efforts to establish joint activities were also unsuccessful.[12]

While the initiative is often cited as the most sustainable offshoot of the P2PP, it is important to recognize that it is impacted by many of the same issues and challenges. The issue of access to technical information has, for example, been cited by Palestinian participants. Nabil Kassis, a member of the Palestinian team in Geneva, notes that 'in general Israeli members have access to wider circle of expertise in greater number of areas. This is related to the fact that Israelis have an establishment that provides all information needed. Palestinians made efforts but needed additional expertise.'[13]

Although the initiative has worked towards terms that are likely to be close to those that will eventually be accepted, interactions between Palestinians and Israelis, as Kassis notes, continue to be by power relations. The initiative's belief that reality can be changed through dialogue also continues to be frustrated by ongoing realities on the ground, and public support continues to be limited, as reflected by the fact that difficulties continue to be encountered in the recruitment of Palestinian participants.[14,15] Samir Rantisi, coordinator of the Palestinian Peace Coalition, affirms,

> It has been difficult to recruit Palestinian participants for joint activities. In cases where we succeed in bringing participants, we then face a problem of drop-off. Palestinians might participate once, but many do not show up again.[16]

But Israelis continue to fail to grasp the importance of this feature – for instance, Ron Pundak, director general of the Peres Center for Peace, argues that 'P2P activities should be carried on regardless of the macro-level political changes as the P2PP is supposed to create an environment of co-existence'. It should also be recognized that the activities of the Peace Coalition are not publicly announced and only include a limited number of intellectuals and political leaders. Despite this, those engaged with the initiative believe that associated academics and public figures can exert influence within their respective societies (Kelman, 1996).

I previously received an invitation from the Geneva Initiative to join the newly formed (February 2004) Women's Intellectual Forum, which brings together political leaders, NGO directors and public figures. During the few meetings that I attended, the terms of discussion were very similar to those that characterized the P2PP: Palestinian participants again reiterated the importance of confronting the occupation and made it clear that any assessment of their engagement would ultimately be measured against this yardstick. As before, there was a clear prior expectation that Israelis should assist the Palestinian struggle against occupation.[17] Salim Tamari explains,

> As all colonial conflicts have shown, reconciliation is a slow process that comes much later than the ending of the conflict. To impose reconciliation while the wounds of domination are fresh would be contrived and could undermine the agreement itself. Better to leave healing as consequence of concord than a condition for it. (2004)

In the current context, contact has not necessarily been rejected outright; rather, it has given rise to different modes and the exploration of alternative possibilities. Insofar as contact has sought to engage within the same framework of reference, it has invariably evidenced the same weaknesses as the preceding P2PP. In some respects, it would be appropriate to speak of a reversion, within clear limitations, back to the form of solidarity-based contact that was evidenced during the First *Intifada*.

Outside of the programme popular resistance activities did bring Israelis and Palestinians together, even if to a much more limited extent than had been the case during the First *Intifada*. The separation wall was a focal point for joint activities that sought to limit or challenge its construction (see Darweish and Rigby, 2015).

Palestinians who had supported contact with the Israelis from the outset continued to work to influence Israeli public opinion. In this respect, there was no clear distinction between contact activities in the Oslo and post-Oslo periods. In both instances, Palestinian activists engaged with the intention of 'educating' or 'enlightening' Israeli public opinion about the realities of occupation and the legitimacy of the Palestinian national struggle.

Palestinian non-violent resistance and the 'war of position'

After the *Al-Aqsa Intifada* broke out, Palestinians who had previously been involved in P2PP and joint projects were forced to distance themselves from their previous commitment. The P2PP had, after all, been controversial prior to the outbreak of the popular uprising. The General Assembly of the Palestinian NGO Network (PNGO) issued a press release that clearly clarified its position. It called for an immediate disengagement from joint P2PP activities; the cessation of any cooperation until the Israeli military fully withdrew from territories occupied since 1967; the cessation of any transaction with any Israeli NGO until the latter fully recognized Palestinian national rights (a Palestinian state in East Jerusalem, West Bank and Gaza Strip) and the Right of Return of Palestinian refugees; and to publicly identify Palestinian and Arab NGOs which failed to recognize these conditions. The same press release establishes that

> these decisions do not conflict with the principle of cooperation with any activity held by the Israeli Human Rights Associations to support the Palestinian nation in its struggle for liberation and the establishment of a Palestinian state, and to declare their support for a fair and durable peace. (PNGO, 2000: www.pngo.net)

This statement reiterated the widespread Palestinian position that holds that any cooperation needs to be grounded within Palestinian rights and directed towards the occupation. This implies preconditions for dialogue, as opposed to a wholesale rejection of the principle of dialogue. For some Palestinians, dialogue is important because it has a strategic value – this is the basis on which Marwan Al-Barghouti advocates continued contact with Israel.[18] He clarifies,

> Not all Israelis are ignorant of the Palestinian suffering. There are Israelis from different political parties and other intellectuals who are fully aware

of what is going on, but their position is weak and fragile in supporting our struggle.¹⁹

For Al-Barghouti, dialogue is an instrument and not an end in and of itself. This is consistent with the general Palestinian belief that contact is an instrument that can be used to influence Israeli public opinion. This is also the view of the PLO which, when the *Al-Aqsa Intifada* broke out, established an Israeli outreach programme that operated from within its Communication Department. In addition to functioning as an independent source of information, the department sought to directly challenge the distortions of Israeli official discourse.²⁰

Some Israeli organizations responded to these initial gestures. Bat Shalom, the feminist organization, drafted a letter to the Palestinian people that was published in *Al-Quds* newspaper on 25 March 2001. Some of the points in the letter include the following:

- We believe that Israel's recognition of its responsibility in the creation of the Palestinian refugees in 1948 is a prerequisite to finding a just and lasting resolution of the refugee problem in accordance with relevant UN resolutions.
- We pledge to do our utmost to influence the Israeli government to dismantle the apparatus of occupation and oppression.
- We Israeli women, Jewish and Palestinian, in the name of all progressive Israelis, join hands in solidarity with those Palestinians and Palestinian organizations in the Occupied Territories who continue to struggle for our common vision of peace, coexistence and cooperation in the Middle East.²¹

This letter acknowledged historic responsibility for the creation of the refugee crisis, committed the group to dismantle the apparatus of occupation and committed the group to work with Palestinians in a spirit of solidarity. Significantly, the group also accepted the Right of Return, which was significant as this had proven to be one of the most divisive topics that had been addressed during joint meetings.

During the *Intifada*, the 'compartmentalization' (Fanon, 1963) of Palestinian land proceeded when, in 2002, the Israeli government began to construct the so-called 'separation wall'. This had profound implications for both Palestinian–Israeli interaction and Palestinian struggle and resistance.[22] In 2004, the International Court of Justice (ICJ) declared the wall to be illegal. In 2005, a total of 170 Palestinian civil society representatives appealed to international civil society to support boycott, divestment and sanctions against Israel. This is the point at which the BDS movement emerged and became part of the global political vocabulary (Qumsiyeh, 2016). In an open letter, in 2005, these Palestinian civil society representatives explained that this course of action had been initiated in response to the following fact:

> All forms of international intervention and peace-making have until now failed to convince or force Israel to comply with humanitarian law, to respect fundamental human rights and to end its occupation and oppression of the people of Palestine. (BDS, 2005)

BDS's three main demands were to end the occupation, establish equal rights for Palestinian citizens of Israel and implement the Palestinian right of return (BDS, 2016; also see Qumsiyeh, 2012, 2016). Sara Roy previously reflected upon the movement's significance. She observes,

> In the civil society sphere, the widespread adoption of peaceful, nonviolent resistance as the dominant strategy for dealing with the Israeli-Palestinian conflict is highly significant, and has as its main component nonviolent mass mobilization around a rights-based agenda that solicits support from the international community, including Israel. This includes a renewed campaign around the refugee right of return, which has reasserted itself after years of absence during the Oslo period; a boycott and divestment movement; and a strengthened relationship between Palestinians in the occupied territories and the Palestinian citizens of Israel. (Roy, 2012: 87)

It could also be argued that BDS emerged as a form of resistance to the emerging reality of land fragmentation and the ongoing creation of 'facts on the ground' (Lloyd, 2012: 66). From this perspective, BDS appeared as a creative response to the fact that fragmentation has 'rendered Palestinian communities – inside historic Palestine and outside – very vulnerable, and made collective action against collective colonial repression (including a third intifada) more difficult' (Hilal, 2015: 1).

BDS can also be conceptualized as a counter-hegemonic form of struggle that is sustained through the active engagement and commitment of international civil society (Buchanan 2000; Lloyd and Wolfe, 2016). The *Al-Aqsa Intifada*, and the clear and ongoing need for new means of struggle and resistance, is also important in this regard. Hilal observes,

> Cumulative conditions pushing for collective popular action, leading to organized popular resistance against the Israeli colonial occupation, should not be excluded, given the entrenchment of the political deadlock and the policy of collective repression and punishment, as well as the ongoing intensification of colonization and national humiliation, and an extremely right-wing Israeli government. (2015: 9)

BDS has also provided a framework in which other political and social actors have been able to articulate the precise terms of resistance. Members of the Health Sector, for example, published 'An Open Letter to the Palestinian and International Community Regarding Palestinian-Israeli Cooperation in Health', which listed their ongoing objections to joint projects (Palestinian Health Sector Signatories, 2005). The letter voiced a strong objection to the fact that international donors had exerted strong pressure, with a view to forcing members to 'enter into Palestinian-Israeli cooperation schemes in the sphere of health' (ibid.). The letter states,

> [Conditions] are imposed largely from the outside, either luring professionals and academics with funds, facilities and opportunities for personal advancement in a resource starved environment, or bringing them solutions to individual medical and systemic problems that the Israeli military occupation of Palestinian land has created and maintained. (ibid.)

Antonio Gramsci once spoke of how consent to power correlates to the benefits that are extracted (Gramsci, Hoare and Nowell-Smith, 1971). The neo-liberal state-building project (Bouillon, 2004; Bouris, 2010; Haddad, 2016) reiterates that, in the Palestinian context, these benefits have frequently applied at a personal level – after all, the collective benefits have been so scarce that they hardly merit further consideration. Closer inspection reveals that it is Israel that benefits, while the occupation remains in place. But this hegemonic order is now vulnerable. Buchanan observes,

> Absent mass consent at the level of global civil society, international hegemony has not obtained. This opens the possibility of engaging in counter hegemonic wars of position using notions of good sense to force a

change in the terms of the hegemonic debate in favour of subaltern groups. (2000: 117)

Contact in the contemporary context

Having learnt the lesson of the *Al-Aqsa Intifada*, and the futility of attempting to attack Israeli at its strongest point, Palestinians have now come to adopt a 'war of position' that resists through non-violent means[23] (see Gramsci, Hoare and Nowell-Smith, 1971: 495). This course of action is necessitated by the fact that power is widely dispersed across Israeli and international society. Gramsci explains,

> The superstructures of civil society are like the trench systems of modern warfare. In war it would sometimes happen that a fierce artillery attack seemed to have destroyed the enemy's entire defensive system, whereas in fact it had only destroyed the outer perimeter; and at the moment of their advance and attack the assailants would find themselves confronted by a line of defence which was still effective. (Gramsci, Hoare and Nowell-Smith, 1971: 498)

In November 2007, the Palestinian BDS movement held a conference in Ramallah, which resulted in the formation of the BDS National Committee (BNC). This committee would henceforth play an important role in helping to coordinate international BDS campaigns. It also clarified the concept of normalization, which it defines in the following terms:

> The participation in any project, initiative or activity, in Palestine or internationally, that aims (implicitly or explicitly) to bring together Palestinians (and/or Arabs) and Israelis (people or institutions) without placing as its goal resistance to and exposure of the Israeli occupation and all forms of discrimination and oppression against the Palestinian people. (PACBI Statement, 2011)

Here it will be noted that this definition (which also applies to projects organized by a third party with a view to promoting cooperation, dialogue and understanding) (Palestinian Campaign for the Academic & Cultural Boycott of Israel, 2017) is an exact inversion of the one provided by the P2PP. This definition of normalization clearly encompasses PLO attempts to engage with Israeli society. In December 2012, the PLO's Central Committee established the Committee for Interaction with Israeli Society, which included many Fatah leaders, including Muhammad al-Madani. The committee's activities have been strongly criticized by many Palestinians, who have accused it of undertaking activities that normalize occupation (Melhem, 2016). In October 2017, the committee, in cooperation with 'Women Wage Peace', organized a march in Jericho and invited Israeli women to attend.[24] In response, BDS issued a call for a boycott and also called for the Committee to be dissolved.[25] The Union of Palestinian Women's Committees strongly condemned the march and stated,

> We affirm that we will stand strong and confront this rhetoric and these malicious conspiracies in the name of Palestinian women and the so-called 'peace' deception, which in reality only reflects the will of a monopolistic sector that wants to impose its interests and decision by force against the Palestinian national consensus of women and men. (UPWC, 2017)

Al-Madani's efforts were also resisted by more extreme elements of the Israeli government. In June 2016, Avigdor Lieberman, who was then Israel's defence minister, revoked Al-Madani's authorization to enter Israel. Lieberman accused Al-Madani of 'subversive activities' and justified his decision on the grounds that 'a foreign diplomatic official who is trying to intervene in political life in Israel is illegitimate' (Staff, 2016).

For Jeff Halper, this is essentially a question of leadership, a leadership that the PA has manifestly failed to provide. He observes, ' "End the Occupation" is a beginning, but end it for what? The many Israelis and internationals mobilized to support Palestine must be empowered and led by Palestinians' (Halper, 2017). The website of Women Wage Peace does not provide any firm guidance in this regard. It simply asserts that 'we will not stop until there is a peace agreement'. Here 'peace' is rendered as a general imperative rather than as a focused or disciplined strategy (Hasson, 2017).

The Palestinian position on the march can also be traced back to the *Al-Aqsa Intifada*, when PNGO issued a statement that called for the regulation of Palestinian–Israeli joint projects. Clarity was one of the main preconditions, and it was made clear that terms of reference must not be ambiguous but should instead be clearly and precisely defined. This is clearly exemplified by

Halper's observation that the 'just peace' demanded by the women activists should incorporate the Palestinian right of return.

The *Al-Aqsa Intifada* established a different foundation for cooperation. For Palestinians, it was clearly preferable to engage with organizations that directly supported the Palestinian struggle – however to some extent, it could be argued that this was not a matter of conscious intent or will: rather, by imposing itself on Palestinians, the wider context effectively demanded this course of action. In addition, it also implied certain courses of action – the influencing of Israeli public opinion and providing information about Palestinian circumstances (Darweish, 2016) were necessitated by the circumstances in which Palestinians found themselves.

The Coalition of Women for Peace was established just after the *Al-Aqsa Intifada* broke out. The coalition brought together women's peace groups and organizations, many of which had been in existence since the First *Intifada*, which supported Palestinians rights (including the Right of Return). The coalition, in working with Palestinians and Israelis, organized solidarity activities in Israel and the West Bank (Darweish, 2016; Svirsky, 2001).

These activities are arranged in the expectation that they will contribute to fundamental changes within both societies. In Israel, concrete experience of the occupation will establish the basis for social engagement with the realities of the occupation (something that is transparently absent in contemporary Israeli); Palestinians, meanwhile, will (even if only temporarily and on an individual basis) have the opportunity to regard Israelis as something other than soldiers and occupiers.

Other action-based initiatives continue to be conducted in Israeli society. One example is a movement called 'Courage to Refuse', which was founded in 2002 when a small number of Israeli officers and soldiers refused to serve in the OPT. Even though the Israeli media has not extensively covered this story (it has actually been covered more extensively within the Palestinian media), it has undoubtedly contributed to debates within Israeli society that question the nature of military service and the political priorities of the Israeli government (see Chacham, 2003). In 2004, soldiers who served in Hebron founded 'Breaking the Silence'. Former troops compile testimonies and contribute to public events, with the intention of educating the Israeli public about the realities of life in the OPT.[26]

It is instructive to note that subjects which Israeli participants were reluctant to address within P2PP encounters were increasingly engaged in the aftermath of the *Al-Aqsa Intifada*. Zochrot ('remembering' in Hebrew) was founded in 2002 with the intention of situating the Palestinian Nakba at the centre of resistance. Zochrot attempts to enlighten Israeli public opinion on the origins of the Palestinian–Israeli conflict with a view to increasing Israeli awareness of the Nakba.[27] Zochrot arranges free tours, for both Arabs and Jews, to destroyed Palestinian village and cities. It also engages with schools, teachers and students with the aim of enhancing understanding of the Nakba.

Israeli solidarity activists also accompany and protect Palestinians (Darweish, 2016). The Israeli Ta'ayush group[28] mainly focuses on organizing solidarity activities that prevent Israeli military operations (closures, curfews and land confiscation) that are conducted against Palestinians. Ta'ayush is focused on tangible activities that support Palestinians and work to build peace between the two societies. It anticipates,

> A future of equality, justice and peace begins today, between us, through concrete, daily actions of solidarity to end the Israeli occupation of the Palestinian territories and to achieve full civil equality for all Israeli citizens.[29]

Machsom Watch[30] is an Israeli organization that operates in a similar manner, although its activities are more focused. It is a feminist initiative that aims to monitor human rights violations at Israeli checkpoints. It states that it seeks to report its observations 'to the widest possible audience, from the decision-making level to that of the general public'.[31] Israeli religious groups also campaign against occupation and human rights violations in the OPT. The most prominent is 'Rabbis for Human Rights', which seeks to educate Israeli public opinion about Palestinian life under occupation.[32] The Israeli Committee Against Demolishing Houses (ICADH), which describes itself as 'a non-violent, direct-action group originally established to oppose and resist Israeli demolition of Palestinian houses in the Occupied Territories' is another important organization.[33]

In the aftermath of the *Intifada*, a Culture of Peace committee (COP), a US-sponsored reform project, was formed. Tellingly, its interpretation of cooperation was largely consistent with that of the P2PP and was focused either on apolitical topics (culture, media, science, sport) or subjects that covertly reflected Israeli priorities (education, incitement and racism) (Palestine Papers,

2008, Document 2352). The committee meetings show how Israeli members focused on Palestinian incitement and favoured apolitical cooperation, while Palestinian members sought to resist the terms of engagement by raising political questions (see Hanafi, 2007, for insight into how this mirrored the Palestinian position on P2PP). This is a further reiteration of how 'peace' has been discursively reconstructed and diverted away from Palestinian concerns and priorities (Badarin, 2015).

Some Israeli activists adopted 'non-violent direct action' as a strategy during the *Al-Aqsa Intifada* (Svirsky, 2002). Gila Svirsky, an Israeli peace activist, argues that this strategy was increasingly applied by Israeli peace groups for two reasons. She references,

> The dramatic increase in violence in the territories, heightening the desire of activists to respond dramatically, and also the lack of public response by Peace Now, the large, mainstream peace organization. (ibid.)

Svirsky proceeded to describe, 'In one particularly dramatic action, two women activists (an Israeli and a Palestinian) chained themselves to olive trees to prevent them from being razed by army bulldozers' (ibid.). These groups cooperated with Palestinians in organizing protests and demonstrations (Qumsiyeh, 2011, chapter 12), and many Israeli activists participated in protests at Budrus, Bil'in and other areas affected by the wall (ibid.: 184–95). In these instances, Palestinian, Israeli and international activists were arrested, beaten and shot.

Anarchists against the Wall (AATW), an Israeli peace group that was established in 2003, coordinated activities with Palestinian local popular committees.[34] In distancing themselves from mainstream Israeli activities, they present their contribution in the following terms:

> We are aware of the fact that for many, the participation of Israelis in a Palestinian struggle serves as a stamp of approval, but in our eyes, this partnership is not about granting legitimacy. The Palestinian struggle is legitimate with or without us. Instead, the struggle is an opportunity for us to cross, in action rather than words, the barriers of national allegiance. (Gordon and Ohal, 2013: 31)

These action-oriented activities are complemented by dialogue-oriented counterparts. One example is the Parents' Circle: The Families Forum[35] – this is an organization that was founded in 1994 which works with both Palestinian and Israelis who have lost a family member to the conflict. The members work together to promote reconciliation, change attitudes and influence public opinion. Their objectives are (i) to end occupation, terminate hostility and achieve a peace settlement agreed upon by all sides; (ii) to educate towards peace, reconciliation and democracy; (iii) to prevent bereavement from being used as a means of deepening hostility between peoples; and (iv) to provide mutual support among the forum's members.

The forum adopts various methods to achieve its goals. It organizes seminars and conferences and also seeks to influence policymakers and the educational system. Members give lectures in schools and reflect upon their personal experiences of losing relatives. In 2004, I attended a conference that had been arranged by the Parents' Circle-Families Forum in Jerusalem.[36] I personally saw how Palestinian and Israeli participants guided the interaction. On several occasions, Israeli participants stated their belief that the Israeli occupation was the underlying cause of suffering on both sides. Adel Misk, the Palestinian co-chairperson of Parents' Circle, reflects,

> Palestinians and Israelis in this Forum have on-going discussions. The Israeli members agree that the Israeli occupation is immoral and should end. We are equal in our right to live in peace. In this forum we try to understand each other and to talk about what we have suffered through the loss of relatives, caused by the occupation. We want people to understand that peace is the only way to put an end to suffering.[37]

I also interviewed the Israeli co-chairperson of the forum, Yitzhak Fankenthal,[38] and asked him for his opinion on Palestinian suicide bombings (most Israeli members of the forum are relatives of Israelis killed in these bombings). He told me,

> Talking to Palestinians helped us to understand their position. I believe that all Palestinians are freedom fighters. The occupation should end so we can all live in peace. Through this Forum I want to send a message to the Israeli public. I want the Israeli public to know that when the occupation ends violence will stop.[39]

In his opening remarks to the conference, Frankenthal said, 'We as families can engage in dialogue. If a Palestinian mother tells me "an Israeli soldier killed my son and I want peace", this is a genuine dialogue.' This comment reflects the atmosphere of understanding among participants (both Palestinians and Israelis) in the forum – this prevailed despite the fact that participants did not engage on an equal basis (many Palestinian participants were unable to get to Jerusalem because they were refused permits by the Israeli authorities).

Practices of conflict resolution necessitate close scrutiny and attention, in large part due to their complicity in producing pacification (of the weaker side), exclusionary practices and the legitimization of discourses and institutions that are the root cause of violence. Conflict resolution practices are always distinctly political and are therefore always open to contestation (Jabri, 2006: 75).

Given the shift within Palestinian–Israeli cooperative projects and activities, P2PP project should be conceptualized and theorized as part of a neo-liberal peacebuilding and state-building project. However, closer examination reveals the limits of this hegemonic order and the points at which it can be challenged and contested. Joint activities that are undertaken in opposition to the occupation are a rejection of both colonial conditions and the means through which these conditions are sustained and embodied (e.g. the P2PP). Importantly, this approach is comprehensive, something which clearly sets it apart from the more compartmentalized Oslo peace process. It is also important to recognize that some Israeli Jews support BDS and view it as a non-violent means through which prevailing political conditions can be challenged and subverted (Gordon, 2009). The Jewish Voice for Peace (JVP) goes as far as to suggest that the freedom of Jews is contingent upon the freedom of Palestinians. It states,

> In the long and varied history of Jewish experience, we are inspired by those who have resisted injustice and fought for freedom. We strive to live up to those values and extend that history. By endorsing the call, we make our hope real and our love visible and we claim our own liberation as bound with the liberation of all.[40]

Nonetheless, it is important to also acknowledge the limits of this cooperation. There are a number of challenges that clearly confront Palestinians and Israelis who seek to engage in joint activities (Darweish and Rigby, 2015, chapters 6 and 7). In the contemporary period, the Palestinian resistance is restricted by a clear lack of leadership. Israeli peace groups are also confronted by challenges that derive from their position within Israeli society (ibid., chapter 7). Despite this, it is possible to identify the outlines of a reversion, in which the emphasis has shifted back to action-based initiatives.

Resisting colonialism

The application of the settler colonial paradigm to the Israeli–Palestinian conflict helps to explain both the policies that Israel has applied and the forms of Palestinian resistance that have emerged in response to these policies. Palestinian resistance has taken different forms since the Balfour Declaration of 1917, extending through British Mandate, the 1948 partition of Palestine and the dispossession of Palestinians in 1948, the 1967 occupation of the West Bank and Gaza and the post-Oslo period.

Settler colonial theories discuss the different methods the colonizer employ against natives, which include, but which not synonymous with, the use of force. In adapting to the political reality, Palestinians have developed methods of non-violent resistance. Up until the Oslo Agreement, popular resistance had also been an important part of the national liberation movement. In responding to the intensification of colonization and the fragmentation of land during the post-Oslo period, Palestinians have changed their tactics (Alazzeh, 2015; Qumsiyeh, 2012, 2016).

As Alazzeh observes, the formation of the PA established a new modality of control in which nativist authority and indirect control created obstacles to Palestinian mass participation (2015: 252). Fragmentation of the land, closures and restriction on movement imposed additional restrictions on Palestinian collective organization and mobilization (Hilal, 2015).

There are clear parallels between other colonial struggles, such as those waged in Canada and the United States, and the Palestinian situation. Bi'lin Popular Committee Against the Wall provides a clear example of a popular struggle against a colonial structure. In 2007, the Israeli Supreme Court responded to its activities by ruling that the path of the wall should be changed (Ma'an News Agency, 2010). This is mirrored by the native American struggle against the Dakota Access Pipeline (DAPL) that resulted in a court ordering its construction to be delayed in 2017 (Stand with Standing Rock, 2017).

The struggle against colonization in Palestine, Canada and the United States targets both the policies on the ground and the neo-liberal projects that seek to co-opt resistance, for instance by calling for divestment from businesses and partners (Stand with Standing Rock, 2017). BDS is far from an isolated example in this respect.

Resistance has sought to challenge the colonial structure along with the colonial distortion of the meaning of rights and self-determination (Coulthard, 2014). Natives seek to 'create a new reality' (Alfred, 2005: 19) on their own terms (Simpson, 2011: 17) – and also seek to 'negotiate a relation of nondomination with a structure of domination like the colonial nation-state' (Coulthard, 2014: 159). This approach clearly contrasts with Palestinian leaders who have engaged in negotiations that have effectively perpetuated the colonial structure (interviews I previously conducted with Palestinian leaders clearly reveal that they endorsed the Israeli vision of peace) (Naser-Najjab, 2014).

Viewing Israeli practices from a settler colonial perspective enables us to understand its ongoing practices. Laws and legislations are colonial tactics that situate and arrange resistance. The Nationality Law, which was passed in July 2018, and which defines Israel as a home for Jews with an exclusive right to self-determination is a case in point. In addition, it also institutes Hebrew as a state official language with a 'special status' for Arabic (Omer-Man, 2018). This law is not an exception but is instead a continuation of Israel's racist and eliminatory policies that it has initiated since it was established (Cook, 2017). In protesting it, Palestinians and Israelis held a large Arabic class in Tel-Aviv that called for equal partnership between Arabs and Jews (Zieve, 2018).

A similar pattern of dispossession is ongoing within the colonial context in Canada and the United States. For example, in 2012 Canada passed bill C-45 (or the 'Jobs and Growth Act'), which enables the state to access native land and resources. Four native women organized a protest in response and used a Facebook page (entitled 'Idle No More') to advertise the event (CBC News, 2013). This protest mobilized thousands of supporters from different constituencies who use different peaceful activities to protest. The use of social media helps activists in colonial states where natives are fragmented and enables them to communicate and publicize their activities (Barkar, 2015).

Both Palestinians and natives are not protesting against individual events but are instead seeking to resist the colonial structure itself and to situate it within the historical context of their dispossession. Idle No More therefore contends that '[our resistance] lies in a centuries old resistance as Indigenous nations and their lands suffered the impacts of exploration, invasion and colonization' (Idle No More, 2018). Palestinians also place the Nationality Law in the historical context of discriminatory Israeli policies that have been implemented since the 1948 Nakba (Adala, 2018). Resistance over this time has taken different forms. In the words of Foucault,

> Where there is power, there is resistance, and yet, or rather consequently, this resistance is never in a position of exteriority in relation to power. [There is] *a multiplicity of points of resistance*: these play the role of adversary, target, support, or handle in power relations. These points of resistance are present everywhere in the power network. Hence there is no single locus of great Refusal, no soul of revolt, source of all rebellions, or pure law of the revolutionary. Instead there is a *plurality of resistances*, each of them a special case. (Foucault, 1990: 95–6)

International solidarity can also contribute to anti-colonial struggle by enabling it to more effectively challenge the domination of capital (Coulthard, 2014). There is a clear rationale for aligning the Palestinian collective effort with other struggles. As Salamanca et al. observe,

> Such an alignment would expand the tools available to Palestinians and their solidarity movement, and reconnect the struggle to its own history of anti-colonial internationalism. At its core, this internationalist approach asserts that the Palestinian struggle against Zionist settler colonialism can only be won when it is embedded within, and empowered by, broader struggles – all anti-imperial, all anti-racist, and all struggling to make another world possible. (2012: 5)

Resistance will also be more effective if it disrupts the colonial structure (Coulthard, 2014: 166). Coulthard explains how 'disruptive' 'direct actions' are more effective than negotiation in challenging the colonial order. BDS also justifies its actions in similar terms, citing the fact that 'all forms of international intervention and peace-making have until now failed to convince or force Israel to comply with humanitarian law, to respect fundamental human rights and to end its occupation and oppression of the people of Palestine' (BDS, 2005).

As Coulthard notes, this can lead to activists being branded as disruptive, militant or violent (2014: 166). He notes that this ascribed confrontation can also impact relations with the non-indigenous (Barkar, 2015: 55) but maintains that this criticism is unavoidable. But this raises the question of how such relations should be conducted and also brings to mind Memmi's analysis of the 'colonizer who accepts' and the 'colonizer who refuses'. He observes,

> The colonizer who accepts his role tries in vain to adjust his life to his ideology. The colonizer who refuses, tries in vain to adjust his ideology to his life, thereby unifying and justifying his conduct. (Memmi 1974: 89)

Memmi notes that it is disturbing for the colonizer to recognize him or herself in their true form and, as such, he or she is predisposed to be disturbed by the very proposition of decolonization and self-determination (Simpson, 2013). The insistence of Palestinian activists on the right of return and Israeli recognition of ethnic cleansing in 1948 was, for example, one factor in the disengagement of Israeli activists from joint peace initiatives in the aftermath of the *Al-Aqsa Intifada*. As Trouillot observes,

> Built into any system of domination is the tendency to proclaim its own normalcy. To acknowledge resistance as a mass phenomenon is to acknowledge the possibility that something is wrong with the system. (2015: 84)

Barker, in addressing himself to colonizers, observes that they

> at times represen[t] themselves as staunch allies while in fact embodying practices that further Indigenous transfer and displacement. Social movement scholars have increasingly engaged in criticism of activists. (2015: 55)

In raising these points, I do not intend to question the contribution of Israelis and Jews who unconditionally support the Palestinian struggle. They have, to take two examples, contributed significantly to solidarity actions in Bil'in and the BDS campaign. I instead argue that it is essential to view relations between Palestinians and Israelis from within the overarching colonial structure as this is what ultimately lends meaning and significance to their interactions.

Waziyatawin's visit to Palestine is also instructive as it highlights a number of similarities with US settler colonialism. One of her key points is that the loss of hope preceded the ethnic cleansing of indigenous populations (Waziyatawin, 2012). Jabotinsky, a revisionist Zionist who broke away from mainstream Zionism, anticipated this observation when he observed that Palestinians will resist 'as long as there remains a solitary spark of hope' (Jabotinsky, 1923).

Netanyahu and his ministers are followers of Jabotinsky and work to implement his vision through a variety of different methods with the intention of frustrating Palestinian resistance and the aspiration of ending occupation. Waziyatawin however draws inspiration from the fact that resistance continues to occur and the end goal of liberation remains in sight (2012: 182).

Angela Davis, meanwhile, emphasizes how 'international solidarities' can help to produce hope and inspiration and provide a basis for moving forward (2016: 53). She further insists that there is a clear analogy between the international dimension of historical anti-colonial struggles in South Africa and Vietnam and the international component of the contemporary Palestinian struggle.

Conclusion

The political reality had overshadowed P2PP since it began. The *Al-Aqsa Intifada* marked a watershed as it represented the point at which Palestinian, inspired by shifts in his environment, sought to take action and impose their own terms and conditions on contact with Israelis. Although P2PP had produced limited benefits, these fell some way short of the anti-colonial struggle that Palestinians now sought to force on to the agenda. Although Palestinian scepticism about the P2PP had always been evidenced, it was in this context that it began to be viewed as an impediment, with the consequence that the very existence of the P2PP began to be threatened by a lack of participants.

It is something of an irony that although the P2PP was founded on the idea of promoting Palestinian participation, it ultimately succeeded in mobilizing Palestinians in opposition to its guiding tenets and implementation. A clear agenda began to emerge which was rooted in a clear understanding of the limitations of contact and which assumed form within a broad-based popular uprising. Israeli objections to contact also began to gather more strength during this period, although different motivations and factors informed this opposition. Whereas Palestinians had been largely disengaged from the P2PP from the outset, Israelis instead gravitated towards it, in no small part due to the fact that it reflected their priorities and interests. But as Palestinian adherence to the norm of non-violence began to disintegrate, the credibility of Israeli peace activism steadily decreased in due proportion.

But even as the conceptual foundations of the P2PP were challenged and its implementation became increasingly impractical, prominent sponsors still entertained the proposition that the P2PP could subvert and ultimately reconfigure material realities. As in so many other instances, it was difficult to escape the view that this attested to the P2PP's essentially ideological character. Given the magnitude of the changes occurring on the ground, which had profound implications for Palestinian–Israeli relations, it appeared legitimate to question if these certainties could ever be entirely evaporated.

Although contact-based initiatives continued on a limited basis, they were increasingly surpassed by the emergence of the BDS movement which appeared, in diametric opposition to the P2PP, as an organic movement rooted in Palestinian agendas, interests and priorities. In addition to appearing as an abstraction removed from the wider context, the P2PP increasingly took the form of an anachronistic irrelevance removed from ongoing developments and the momentum of events within Palestinian society.

Conclusion

Antonio Gramsci once depicted a situation where the 'old is dead and the new not yet born'. The peace process and the P2PP were both consistent with this state. There is now a widespread acknowledgement that they are insufficient to achieve the ends to which they are ostensibly addressed. The two-state solution is now, by virtue of the creation of 'facts on the ground', little more than a convenient fiction that exists within the imagination of international statesmen.

Given that the P2PP was conceived and originated within the wider context of the peace process, it is strange that international donors, in apparent defiance of the fact that there is no peace process to support, continue to fund P2PP initiatives. This is all the more surprising because Palestinian public opinion, which was far from receptive to the initiative in the first place, has hardened in the years since. In the current circumstances, it is difficult to understand what the P2PP can achieve. Strong and ongoing public opposition implies that any contact will be limited, and its broader significance will be open to question.

Perhaps it is the case that international donors view contact as an achievement in itself. Needless to say, this is precisely the opposite of the view which Palestinian participants consistently advanced during the course of the programme; on numerous instances, they reiterated that contact must always be undertaken with a clear purpose in mind and on the basis of a shared consensus. Furthermore, these initiatives are fundamentally opposed to the broad-based consensus within Palestinian society which remains strongly opposed to normalization.

This opposition, contrary to widespread misconception, is not grounded within a rejection of compromise or negotiation; still less is it grounded within an exclusionary or rejectionist logic. Rather, it can instead be traced back to previous Palestinian experience of contact-based initiatives which reinforced established power relations. In advancing their own normative preference, international observers therefore simultaneously reject a substantial body of empirical evidence.

Einstein once observed that madness consists of 'doing the same thing over and over again and expecting different results'. This observation could clearly be applied to contemporary P2PP initiatives. Failure, it seems, only reinforces the determination to continue to operate within the established terms of reference. Quite clearly, it does not contribute to a sustained critical questioning of underpinning assumptions. On the contrary, the P2PP persists in the absence of such an engagement.

In retrospect, it is equally clear that P2PP should be anticipated by such an engagement. First of all, it should have been questioned whether the programme was sufficiently aligned with local context and local political conditions. A closer engagement at each of these points would have provided considerable insight into deeply imbedded inequalities, many of which originate within the occupation. Measures could then have been introduced, with a view to reducing their impact on the P2PP.

While the P2PP was ostensibly justified and advanced on the basis that it would bring about a fundamental transformation of political conditions, it actually came to function as a conservative instrument through which the status quo was sustained. Its apolitical terms of reference disqualified Palestinian narratives of struggle and resistance. Its transformative intent was therefore all too frequently belied by an inherent conservatism. That this should be the case was not coincidence. 'Peace', in the Palestinian–Israeli context, has invariably derived from external sources. The first Camp David agreement between Anwar Sadat and Menachem Begin envisaged that the Palestinian territories would be autonomous; various abortive US initiatives followed over the course of the 1980s before an exiled Palestinian leadership negotiated the Oslo Accords. In each instance, 'peace' was imposed from without and the inhabitants of the OPT appeared, at best, as an afterthought.

The peace envisaged by Palestinians when the Oslo Accords were established in 1993 was of a very different order and significance. This 'peace' would not be the termination of hostilities (negative peace); rather, it would acknowledge Palestinian demands for justice, human rights and a basic level of dignity. This 'positive peace' was, however, not what was on offer. The US and Israeli governments envisaged from the outset that Arafat would function in the lineage of a long line of Arab 'strongmen' who would exert control over their own society. The Palestinian–Israeli peace was deeply 'securitized', and by implication compromised, from the outset.

It was therefore far from coincidental that the P2PP should overlook a tradition of contact, in which Palestinians and Israelis united in opposition to the occupation. This tradition was deeply problematic by virtue of the fact that it was rooted within the principles of solidarity and opposition to the ongoing occupation. The unstated purpose of the 'peace process' was precisely the opposite – namely to perpetuate the occupation by presenting it in a more sanitized form. In many respects, the peace process appeared as a dark farce that was conducted for the benefit of international audiences. As long as each of the local actors played their part (Israelis as benevolent and enlightened emissaries of peace; Palestinians as grateful supplicants who would accept all that was on offer, including their own moral redemption), the performance could proceed as planned.

The internationalization of the P2PP and the wider peace process was therefore, to all intents and purposes, an externalization, in which external priorities were preponderant. This originated something of a paradox, as the P2PP was originally conceived as the local-level 'track' which would complement its macro-level counterpart. However, local-level participation in the formulation of the programme was limited by the fact that it functioned in accordance with a generic conflict resolution framework which applied across individual contexts.

Taking these different factors into account, it would perhaps be more accurate to observe that the Americans and Israelis envisaged 'pacification', as opposed to the establishment of a positive peace. 'Peace' was an instrument of strategic intent, which would be applied with the view of furthering the interests of the powerful and consolidating the status quo. Edward Said was one of the very few Palestinians with the insight and perspective to fully register this point. At the time, I strongly criticized Said for his position and maintained that his perspective largely derived from his position of privilege and detachment from the political realities of the OPT.

During my participation in the P2PP, I repeatedly experienced difficulties that were shared by my fellow Palestinians. Relative distributions of power – or more specifically the advantaged position of Israeli participants – was a particular grievance. Any attempt to challenge this and other grievances was ultimately frustrated by the criteria and conditions put in place by international donors.

In common with many other Palestinians, my initial engagement with the P2PP was preceded by an inability to see that the wider peace process was part of an innovation within methods of control and coercion. In common with past colonial projects, it envisaged a form of indirect rule that would be exerted through local agents whose loyalty would be purchased through assorted financial and political inducements. The Oslo Accords instituted a situation in which the occupied territories would become the 'disputed' territories and the costs and burdens of occupation, but crucially not the benefits, would be lifted from Israel's soldiers. No longer subject to the dictates of international law, the present and future of the OPT would be governed and regulated by (grossly unequal) power relations.

The P2PP functioned as a subset of these wider relations. It was, to borrow a phrase of Michel Foucault's, a 'technology of government' that operated through the condition of freedom. While ostensibly predicated upon local-level 'ownership' and 'empowerment', it sought to reframe the terms of engagement in ways that were often subtle or insidious. Participation within the terms established by the P2PP therefore served to further consolidate pre-established priorities. The P2PP was therefore highly prescriptive, and it was arranged in a way that essentially prefigured or structured participation.

This corresponds closely to a Gramscian analysis, in which power is reinforced through consent rather than direct imposition. Values, principles and beliefs are subtly inculcated through iteration and a shared culture. Power, as Foucault asserted, is only exerted over free agents. While the P2PP provides considerable insight into the exertion of this power (both its form and the technologies through which it is rendered), it also highlights its points of refusal, which were manifested in both direct and indirect acts of resistance.

In the preceding chapter, I argued that the P2PP should be conceptualized as part of a broader Palestinian refusal which is rooted within past experience of ill-conceived and abortive contact initiatives. The P2PP, I suggest, should be conceptualized and conceived in this wider context. An analysis that takes the P2PP to be a power relation therefore logically precedes an intellectual and practical project which seeks to achieve its inversion and overhaul. This point, I suggest, is underlined by the contemporary emergence and development of the BDS movement.

In engaging within the P2PP, Palestinian participants sought to advance aims that are in many respects synonymous with those of the BDS movement. They therefore sought to engage 'enlightened' Israeli political opinion, with a view to establishing the basis for a common struggle against the occupation. Furthermore, they sought to 'educate' Israeli society about the fact that 'peace' was prefigured, and substantially anticipated, by justice. However, this ambitious agenda was ultimately frustrated, both by the P2PP's terms of references and the 'limitations' of Israeli counterparts.

Palestinians engaged with the P2PP with the profound misconception that Israelis could 'step outside' of their position of privilege. This was a profound error precisely because privilege impacted upon almost every feature of the P2PP. Far from acknowledging or directly addressing this privilege, Israeli NGOs more frequently sought to rationalize or justify it. The fact that a benevolent occupier is an occupier nonetheless escaped close critical attention and engagement. Accordingly, in the worst instances, Israelis came to view their 'compromises' and 'concessions' as an act of generosity that affirmed their progressive credentials. For Palestinians, of course, these obligations were not intelligible at the level of interpersonal relations.

These encounters with 'enlightened' Israeli political opinion clearly recalled Memmi's depiction of the 'colonizer who refuses'. Memmi clearly described the cognitive dissonance of this deeply conflicted individual and depicted their fruitless attempts to navigate beyond two positions. Just as the colonizer was unable to reconcile with the experience of the colonized in its entirety, Israeli participants often sought to engage with Palestinians on a personal or professional basis. It was scarcely surprising that expressions of personal regret rarely expended to the acceptance of particular political positions.

Far from forcing Israeli participants to question or confront the contradictions of their own positions, the P2PP actually legitimized them – it was no coincidence that Israeli participants felt more comfortable with the P2PP's terms of engagement. In this sense, P2PP came to function as a conduit through which settler colonial relations were embodied and sustained. Its ostensible neutrality served to legitimize, and even sustain, an inequitable status quo.

For their part, the P2PP's designers were clearly naïve to expect that it would be possibly to uphold and perpetuate the principle of neutrality within such a deeply politicized context. This is aside from the fact that the very concept of 'neutrality' requires a more sustained critical interrogation. As a further case in point, the belief that international law is a neutral instrument through which power can be held to account is similarly in need of a comparable engagement. Is it not after all conceivable that neutrality may come to function as a means through which power is circulated, as opposed to the point at which it is denied or refused?

In the absence of such a critical engagement it is conceivable that powerful international actors will try to impose their own interpretation of 'peace'. Had history taken a different course, with the vision expounded during the First *Intifada* instead prevailing, then it is possible that 'peace' may well have taken on a different meaning and implication. As it was, the concept became inseparable from strategic interests and priorities. Ultimately, the Oslo Accords became an abject demonstration of the limits of securitized peace.

In the absence of any analysis of power, Palestinian participation was liable to reproduce this hegemonic power in subsequent effect. Palestinian opposition was, at least in the initial phases, too localized and atomized to substantially impact the programme. Although this opposition later assumed more coherent and cohesive form, it remains questionable whether the terms of P2PP reference are sufficiently amenable to Palestinian concerns and priorities. The likelihood that this agenda will be pursued to the point of completion is further drawn into question by the fact that Palestinian NGOs have, in a manner which all too closely resembles their political masters, evidenced a willingness to be 'brought off' by financial incentives.

This brings in a separate set of questions which relate to the underpinning rationale of the P2PP. It was questionable from the outset whether the P2PP was sustainable upon its own terms – the fact that participants engaged for such a wide range of reasons (many of which had little or no relation to the formal P2PP objectives) clearly attested to this. Had financial incentives been discontinued, then it is extremely questionable whether P2PP could have continued, even in considerably diminished form. There is a separate discussion here, which this book has barely engaged, which relates to the largely pernicious influence of professionalization and the creation of vested interests within the NGO sector.

During the First *Intifada*, Palestinians and Israelis had united with the intention of confronting the occupation. This was an organic and dynamic form of contact, which was characterized by a shared purpose. Palestinian organizations were generally deeply rooted within local needs and requirements, and participation was not therefore driven by financial motivations. The term 'civil society' is inappropriate in this context as this presupposes associations of individuals who are driven by personal or economic interest; in contrast, many of the Palestinian organizations were explicitly political, both in their approach and their end objectives.

The P2PP sought, to this extent, to import an externalized vision of 'civil society', whose lack of political vision strongly resonated with the project of neo-liberal state-building. It tied in, to this extent, with a broader project that did not just deny Palestinian political priorities but politics more generally (see Haddad, 2016). However, this vision of a fundamentally altered Palestinian politics was not self-sustaining but was instead reinforced through the (largely indirect) exertion of hegemonic influence.

The P2PP was therefore founded upon an essential dichotomy. In the first instance, it sought to establish the basis under which Palestinians could actively engage and participate. However, in the second instance it sought to reformulate the terms of this participation and subtly guide it towards predetermined goals and objectives. Far from representing the limitation or denial of external influence, 'empowerment' or 'participation' instead represents the points at which this influence is more completely embodied.

Critical contributions to the development literature have similarly noted how 'empowerment' and 'participation' function as means through which social actors become inculcated within more 'appropriate' forms of conduct. Engagement under these conditions is an essential means through which 'discipline' and 'regulation' are rendered. However, rather than acting directly upon individual participants, this influence is rendered through the 'social'. This also clearly recalls Gramsci's depiction of civil society, which he presents as an essential accompaniment of hegemony.

In retrospect, I argue that P2PP, along with the broader peace process, can be viewed as an innovation within methods and techniques of control. Far from addressing colonial conditions, as Palestinian participants had originally anticipated, it came to function as a means through which established relations of power were reproduced. The original criticism that the P2PP had no clear purpose was, from a Palestinian perspective, proven to be correct.

It is unclear if the P2PP's international designers and sponsors fully intended its political consequences. However, this is to miss the point – as both Gramsci and Foucault identified, power does not operate at the level of conscious intent; to the same extent, it cannot be simplified into clear cause–effect relationships. Power is embodied within structures, cultures and discourses and therefore operates above the level of conscious intent and often consciousness more generally.

In operating within a wider hegemonic culture, international actors therefore came to conceive the peace process as part of an incremental progression, in which Palestinian society would be subtly inculcated within hegemonic norms and standards of conduct. The state-building project is therefore advanced in the belief that the international community possesses the requisite capacity and knowledge to guide Palestinian society to the point where it embodies and reproduces the benign axioms of 'good governance'.

This intention cannot be relayed in its full meaning or implication, for that would violate the development axiom which establishes that local-level participation is an essential precondition of, and accompaniment to, successful intervention. In addition, if this intervention was comprehended in its true significance, it would inevitably elicit resistance, which would ultimately act to the detriment of the overall enterprise. The 'disciplinary' and 'regulatory' intent of external intervention – and this applies to state-building, the P2PP and the peace process more generally – must therefore be concealed by discursive obfuscations such as 'empowerment', 'participation' and 'ownership'.

Each of these discursive innovations operates within a wider context and is therefore framed by relations and practices that seek to reform or reconfigure a society that is deemed to be defective or insufficiently adjusted to the grand realization of the Enlightenment project. However, rather than producing this progression, external intervention in support of the peace process instead produces a range of contradictions, which are operationalized at the level of the interaction between internal and external and the interaction between the project's internal components (state-building and peacebuilding). While peacebuilding theory suggests a unification of opposites, the actual reality is considerably more fractured and internally incoherent than this benign vision suggests.

The P2PP's history and development lend further support to this reading. One of the few instances in which the P2PP succeeded in its ends was when it brought Palestinians and Israelis in opposition to a number of its operating procedures. In all other respects, the P2PP was essentially contested (e.g. there was no agreement upon the object itself as opposed to its application) and it frequently served as a point of division and dispute. Far from functioning as an ameliorative or unifying force, external influence therefore *originates* contradiction and tension.

Those who continue to counsel the benefits of contact would do well to address themselves to the fact that the 'peace' project has become inextricably interwoven with strategic interests, to the point where they appear to be inseparable. The meaning of this 'peace' does not present itself as an objective reality but must instead be critically interrogated and probed. To the same extent contact, the 'midwife' of peace, must also be subject to closer examination and justified with reference to past experience in the given working context. All too often, it is the exact opposite, and 'contact' and 'peace' are accordingly invoked as generalized imperatives.

There is a broader question here which relates to the role of international actors within the conflict and the essential contribution which they can make. BDS is a significant development because it is rooted with Palestinian society and it is rooted within local priorities. It should also be recognized that BDS is not a solution in and of itself. I believe that BDS has an essential role to play in mobilizing Palestinian society and opening up new opportunities for political engagement. This is why the BDS has sought to draw upon sources of international support and sustenance.

In the current context it is clear that Palestinians can no longer look to the Palestinian Authority to assume this role. It is not simply that it has acquiesced to the perpetuation of colonial relations; rather, it is, by virtue of the fact that it is itself a product of these same relations, inherently counter-intuitive to assume that it can challenge or alter them. Indeed, far from seeking to establish the basis for this challenge, the PA more often – in the guise of security 'cooperation' – seeks to frustrate or limit them.

As Edward Said argued, the Oslo Accords were not the point at which the Palestinian leadership agreed to enter, as co-equals, into negotiations with their Israeli counterparts. Rather this was an abject surrender, in which a weakened PLO was forced to compromise internationally recognized rights and entitlements. In return for the dubious benefits of limited self-rule and inflows of development aid, the newly established PA agreed to administer Israel's occupation on its behalf.

In contrast to the PA, which took Palestinian rights as the 'framework' for negotiations, both UNLU and BDS insist that these rights must be the foundation of any sustainable agreement. Furthermore, it is significant that these rights are demanded. In contrast, both the Accords and the P2PP all too frequently gave rise to the impression that Palestinians were beneficiaries of Israeli compromise. In celebrating Ehud Barak's historic compromise, for instance, observers generally failed to acknowledge that his 'concessions' still fell short of the international consensus on the issue.

BDS also has an essential contribution to make in shifting the terms of discussion from 'peace' to 'justice'. Palestinians previously spoke of the term as synonymous ('peace with justice'), but now the former has become discredited to the point where it seems best to dispose of it entirely. The peacebuilding agenda is now an external agenda which is almost entirely divorced from the everyday struggles of Palestinians. Even from the outset, the 'peace process' was essentially a performance that was conducted for the benefit of international audiences.

For these same audiences, BDS is discomforting because it forces them to recognize their complicity within the ongoing occupation and to actively consider how they can distance or detach themselves. The P2PP, in contrast, does not make a similar demand and also enables international actors to persist in the illusion that, far from sustaining the conflict, they are actually helping to overcome it. In operating at a symbolic level, the P2PP also does not place extensive demands upon time and resources.

For Israeli participants, the P2PP also enabled them to engage upon terms that were suited to their own interests and priorities. The activities of Israeli peace groups are linked into wider public opinion. This became clear during the *Al-Aqsa Intifada*, when many groups had no choice but to align themselves with the shifting currents of Israeli public opinion. By virtue of the efficiency of the Israeli ideological apparatus, Israeli participants did not have the same need to establish a clear agenda in advance of engaging with the P2PP: rather, there was instead a tacit understanding of the parameters within which engagement should operate, as the 'security first' attitude of many participants clearly demonstrated (Bar-On, 1996; Kaminer,1996). The belief that NGOs could proactively lead public opinion was therefore, at least on the Israeli side, open to question.

BDS could also be viewed as a response to the Israeli claim that Palestinians should take a greater degree of responsibility for their current circumstances. There was some justification to this criticism. The Oslo Accords in many respects highlighted the lack of accountability and transparency within Palestinian political life. While external political actors (most notably those who turned a blind eye to the PA's suppression of human and political rights) must shoulder part of the responsibility, it was ultimately Palestinians themselves who were responsible for holding their own political representatives to account. Furthermore, within the context of the P2PP, Palestinian NGOs repeatedly failed to engage with their Israeli counterparts in pushing for an alteration within the terms of engagement.

In conclusion, this book has sought to integrate a range of different themes, with a view to providing a more comprehensive and encompassing analysis of the theme of contact. In initially observing the ongoing international attachment to the principle of contact, it suggested that this commitment owes more to external priorities than the interests and priorities of the contemporary inhabitants of the OPT.

In then referring back to the historical example of the P2PP, it sought to situate this theme of contact within wider historical and political context, doing so in the belief that this was essential if the actual Palestinian position was to be 'retrieved' from some of the false accusations and insinuations that have been hurled in its direction. The contemporary Palestinian position on contact, which is embodied within an ongoing opposition to normalization, is, it argued, grounded within past experience.

But it is in a shared existence that Palestinians and Israelis can find hope of a better future. In my encounters with older Palestinians, I have frequently been reminded of the positive relationships that used to prevail between Palestinians and Jews. Elias Nasrallah had, for example, similarly recalled how he used to play with an Arab Jew boy from a transit camp (which were established for Jews from Arab countries in the early 1950s). The camp was then replaced by a settlement and he never saw the boy again (Nasrallah, 2016: 304). Nasrallah's encounters with the Israeli Left were also more positive than those of many contemporary Palestinians (ibid.).

These generally positive relations were later corrupted by colonialism (Taiaiake and Corntassel, 2005: 611) and it will most likely take several generations to change the negative views that Israelis have of Arabs (Bar-Tal and Teichman, 2005: 175; see also Peled, 2012). Hope can however be found in a one-state solution (Halper, 2018) that seeks to acknowledge past injustice (Dunbar-Ortiz, 2015). This is a significant divergence from the 'forward-looking' predisposition that was frequently evidenced by Israeli participants during the P2PP (Salamanca et al., 2012: 3). This is not simply a question of how Israelis engage with past history: rather, for Palestinians, the events of the Nakba are inscribed on the contemporary outlines of the occupation and continued Palestinian dispossession (ibid.: 2). One of the main 'contributions' of the peace process was to undermine this dimension of the conflict by misrepresenting and distorting Palestinian history and narrative (Hilal, 2015: 2). A settler-colonial analysis is, to this extent, a prelude to improved Palestinian–Israeli relations. In a recent example and during the Palestinian protest in Gaza, known as the Great Return March, Palestinians invited Israeli activists on the other side of the so-called 'fence' to have tea with them (Baum, 2018).

In engaging with the P2PP, this book has discussed its design, implementation and evaluation. It has observed that its main issues did not relate to implementation but were instead rooted within the conceptual framing of the P2PP and its unwillingness to engage with the wider context. This unwillingness, it was suggested, originated within a clear sense that this context was ultimately the object of reform: the key insight that it might be an active consideration in itself was insufficiently acknowledged or overlooked entirely by external observers. Meanwhile, the implementation of the P2PP was questioned on the grounds that deeply embedded inequalities were not sufficiently engaged.

This inattention to context led into a discussion of theories of settler colonialism, and it was observed that the ostensible neutrality of the P2PP served, in many respects, as the means through which these relations were circulated and more completely embodied. In addition, theories of settler colonialism were also advanced on the basis that they provided a clear insight into both the P2PP and a number of key dimensions of the wider conflict.

In broad perspective, this book has sought to highlight the limitations of conflict resolution theory when it is applied to the precise exigencies of the Palestinian–Israeli conflict. It has been argued that this application is, to all intents and purposes, an obfuscation which conceals the true dynamics of the ongoing conflict. The BDS movement, it was suggested, makes an essential contribution by shifting the debate from 'peace' to 'justice'.

The inadequacy of conflict resolution frameworks, and more specifically their precise application to the Palestinian–Israeli conflict, has been noted. This has in turn compelled a search for an alternative theoretical framework, which ultimately converged upon theories of settler colonialism. This framework, in enabling and sustaining a new interpretation and reading of the conflict, in turn established the basis for an assessment, and ultimate recommendation, of the BDS movement, which was conceived as the basis upon which alternative possibilities of political mobilization and engagement could be explored and developed.

Ultimately, and perhaps most importantly, this book is about hope and the limits of hegemony. It is in action-based activities, which have a concrete and clearly discernible impact, that the outlines of future resistance can be identified and traced.

In retrospect, the P2PP appears almost as an unfortunate interlude, which interjects itself into the space that separates the events of the First *Intifada* and the contemporary resistance of BDS. There is, to mind, a clear continuity which conjoins the two. This thread must be further unravelled, with the intention of lending renewed impetus to contemporary struggle. It is in decolonization that Palestinians and Israelis find a joint cause and the prospect of a better future.

Notes

Introduction

1. The *Al-Aqsa Intfiada* was anticipated in September 1996 when the Israeli government authorized the construction of a tunnel alongside the Al-Aqsa mosque/Al-Haram al-Sharif (which is sacred to Muslims). This sparked armed confrontations, resulting in the deaths of sixty Palestinians and fifteen Israeli soldiers.
2. Israeli proposals for the Haram Al-Sharif were particularly convoluted.
3. Issa Rabadi, co-director, IPCRI-Peace Education Department, interview, 15 December 2003.
4. Independent Institute for Applied Social Science, Centre for International Studies, Oslo, Norway.
5. Zochrot is a good example in this respect. It is an Israeli organization that was founded in 2002 with the intention of educating the Israeli public about the Nakba and the associated destruction of Palestinian villages.
6. Interview with Ziad Abu-Zayyad, Jerusalem, 24 August 2001. Ziad Abu-Zayya was a Palestinian leader and lawyer who was among the first Palestinians who sought to engage the Israeli public with the intention of explaining the Palestinian view.
7. The P2P Guidelines for Applicants, which established clear conditions and expectations for participant NGOs, remained in place until the outbreak of the *Al-Aqsa Intifada*.
8. The division between Fatah and Hamas began in 2006 when Hamas won the elections which led to internal fighting. In 2007 Hamas took over Gaza Strip, which resulted in two leaderships: one in the West Bank led by Fatah and second in the Gaza strip led by Hamas.
9. Former deputy mayor of Jerusalem.
10. The Jerusalem Media and Communication Centre (JMCC) is a Palestinian media centre that is based in Jerusalem. Its services include research and opinion polls. JMCC carries out fieldwork in Palestine and Israel. A number of the field staff have Jerusalemite identity cards, which gives them freedom of movement, enabling them to distribute questionnaires and surveys to areas under siege.

11 This is the Israeli NGO that implemented the 'From Both Sides' (FBS) project.
12 I paid for an Israeli assistant to contact the Israeli participants, to post the questionnaires and to collect them when completed.

1 The context of P2PP

1 Refer to Annex VI (Article VIII) of Oslo Agreement II.
2 Details of the funding allocation can be found at http://www.ipcri.org (17 February 2004).
3 Details of the funding allocation can be found at http://www.ipcri.org (17 February 2004).
4 Reported at http://www.usembassy.it (accessed 17 February 2004).
5 Annex VI in the interim agreement refers to cooperation in other sectors – it conceives of, inter alia, cultural, educational, scientific and technological cooperation.
6 Terje Rod Larsen, the then director of Fafo, was one of the key facilitators of the 'secret channel' negotiations that resulted in the Oslo Accords.
7 Article III, 2, (d) states, 'The SCC (Standing Co-operation Committee) may set up working groups of bodies for the implementation of this Annex.'
8 The Palestinian head of the SCC was Sufian Abu Zaideh (the general director of the Ministry of Planning, who later became the deputy minister of the Ministry of Civil Affairs); his Israeli counterpart was Itan Ben, the director of the Israeli Ministry of Foreign Affairs.
9 Lena Endresen was the People-to-People Programme coordinator between May 1996 and July 1997.
10 The Joint Planning Group provided administrative and logistical assistance to Israeli and Palestinian participants. It also retained records and information on people-to-people activities.
11 Andrea and Charles Bronfman Philanthropist Foundation (which I refer to as the CRB Foundation). CRB, in cooperation with the Israeli Ministry of Foreign Affairs, funded the educational programme in Israel.
12 The first Palestinian planning group was represented by Hassan Abu-Libedeh, the former head of the Palestinian Central Bureau of Statistics (PCBS) who is currently chief of staff in the Prime Minister's Office. Whereas the CRB had close links with the Israeli Foreign Ministry, the PA did not have a Foreign Ministry at the time and so the PCP was not in a position to liaise directly with official Palestinian representatives (this feature was mitigated by the fact that Abu Mazen was on the PCP board of directors).

13. Russian language projects brought together immigrants from Russia with Russian-speaking Palestinians (mainly those who had studied in the former Soviet Union). A number of the respondents to my questionnaire had a Russian background.
14. Based on an unpublished paper by Fafo; also see www.people-to-people.org.
15. Refer to Annex VI (Article VIII) of Oslo Agreement II.
16. Social categorization theory uses 'minimal group' models to demonstrate that individuals categorize themselves and discriminate against the out-group even in the absence of interpersonal attraction. Participants are divided into two groups and are asked to indicate their preferences by reacting to picture slides. When subjects are asked to distribute money, as a reward, they tend to give more money to their own group. This suggests that the process of group affiliation is entirely cognitive.
17. Dr Zakaria Al Qaq, co-director, IPCRI, interview, 15 December 2003, Jerusalem.
18. Yolla Haddadin, telephone interview, 21 October 2003.
19. Naseef Mu'allem, interview, 14 August 2001, Ramallah.
20. Lena Endresen was the P2P programme coordinator between May 1996 and July 1997.
21. For more information, see www.people-to-people.org.
22. To take one example, the Palestinian Ministry of Education refused to cooperate with twinning initiatives and expressly forbade any government schools from participating. The seventeen school twinning projects THEREFORE brought together Israeli government (state) schools and Palestinian private schools.
23. Ghassan Al-Khatib, in his capacity as the then minister of labour in the Palestinian Authority. Follow-up interview, 9 March 2004, Ramallah.

2 The colonial context of P2PP

1. This is a small village near Jerusalem that was, subsequent to a High Court of Justice ruling, relocated in order to enable settlement expansion.
2. 'As in North America, the settler in Israel is not interested in Palestinians as a source of labo[u]r; he or she wants their land' – Mamdani, 2015: 610.
3. BDS was formed one year after and International Court of Justice (ICJ) ruling which found that the construction of the so-called 'separation wall' was contrary to international law. In the aftermath of its establishment, 170 Palestinian civil society organizations called for the international community to support the BDS movement (Qumsiyeh, 2016).

3 Contact between 1967 and 1987

1. The Arab Summit Conference (which took place in Khartoum between 28 August–2 September 1967) was unequivocal on this point: no recognition, no negotiation and no peace with Israel.
2. Ziad Abu-Zayyad, interview, 24 August 2001, Jerusalem.
3. Interview, 26 August 2001, Ramallah.
4. Interview with Nuha Bargouti, 8 September 2001, Ramallah.
5. Interview with Taysir Aruri, 5 September 2001, Ramallah.
6. Felicia Langer was the first Israeli lawyer who defended Palestinian prisoners in Israeli courts. She fought against land confiscation, deportation, house demolitions and torture. Two of her books (*With My Own Eyes* (1975) and *These Are My Brothers* (1975)) documented Palestinian suffering in Israeli jails.
7. Taysir Aruri, interview, 5 September 2001, Ramallah.
8. Ibid.
9. Interview with Taysir Aruri, 5 September 2001, Ramallah.
10. Said Hammami was the PLO representative in England at that time.
11. Avnery, telephone conversation, 21 October 2003.
12. Ibid.
13. Ibid.
14. Interview with Taysir Aruri, 5 September 2001, Ramallah.
15. *Al-Fajr* was a weekly Palestinian English-language newspaper that was based and published in East Jerusalem. It was distributed in Jerusalem and Israel between 1980 and 1993. The Israeli authorities banned it from being distributed in the West Bank and Gaza Strip.

4 Contact during the First *Intifada* (1987–93)

1. Interview with Ghassan Khatib, Ramallah.
2. Interview, 5 September 2001, Ramallah.
3. As a direct consequence of the group's activism, around two thousand Israeli soldiers were either jailed or discharged.
4. Interview, 15 September 2001, Ramallah.
5. Ziad Abu-Zayyad, interview, 24 August 2001.
6. Ziad Abu-Zayyad, interview, 24 August 2001, Jerusalem.
7. IPCRI was initially co-directed by Gershon Baskin, an Israeli activist whose work is engaged with coexistence and peace education, and Adel Yahia, a Palestinian communist who lectures at Birzeit University. The Centre's research is focused

on the identification of solutions that can be applied to the Palestinian–Israeli conflict.
8 Gershon Baskin, interview, 15 December 2003, Jerusalem.
9 Taysir Aruri, interview, 5 September 2001, Ramallah.
10 Taysir Aruri, interview, 5 September 2001, Ramallah.
11 For more details, see www.nad-plo.org (12 March 2004).

5 The 'Oslo years' and 'facts on the ground'

1 Under the Oslo Accords Hebron had, in acknowledgement of the Israeli settlement in the centre of the city, been granted a special status. The rights of the 154,714 Palestinians who live in Hebron City (the total population of Hebron District is 505,694) were therefore subordinated to the 'security' needs of 479 settlers (PASSIA, 2003). Palestinian observers noted that the Hebron Protocol and Wye River Memorandum enshrined Israeli security and understated Palestinian rights (Andoni, 1997; Aruri, 1999; Said, 1997).
2 The Israeli government and the PA signed the Hebron Protocol on 15 January 1997. The implementation of this agreement was set out in the Wye River Memorandum, which was signed in Washington, DC, on 23 October 1998. The Hebron Protocol was based on the Guidelines for Hebron set out in Oslo II (JMCC, 1996: 41–3). Annex I (Article VII) establishes that Hebron will be divided into two areas (Area H-1 and H-2). H-1 would come under the authority of the PA. Area H-2, where Israeli settlers were resident, was placed under Israeli military control.
3 It could be argued that, under the political circumstances, any agreement constituted success. Aruri offered a more measured appraisal. He notes, 'The section on security consumes about 60 percent of the memorandum, while the rest take up with further redeployment (itself linked to security needs) and unresolved interim issues, including Israeli commitments to negotiate safe passage between the West Bank and Gaza as well as the opening of Gaza airport and eventually a seaport. Extremely brief sections deal with final status talks and "unilateral actions"' (1999: 18).
4 Moshe Ma'oz is an eminent Israeli historian. He is currently a director within Hebrew University's Truman Institute.
5 'Neither Party shall initiate or take any step that will change the status of the West Bank and the Gaza Strip pending the outcome of the permanent status negotiations' (JMCC, 1996: 24).

6. The Netanyahu government also authorized settlers to seize Jabal Abu, in East Jerusalem.
7. The motives underlying Israel's land confiscation were the same in both Jerusalem and West Bank (see Mustafa Walid (2000: 71–95) for more information on Israeli settlement activity in Jerusalem).
8. Khalil Tufakji is director of the Maps and Survey Centre, which is based in Jerusalem's Orient House.
9. This represented a *hardening* of the traditional Israeli stance. Settlements and settlers had originally been defined by their proximity to the Green Line (Baskin, Qaq and Israel/Palestine Center for Research and Information, 1997: 49–50). Although the Palestinian leadership has evidenced a willingness to negotiate upon this basis, it is willing to trade on up to around 3 per cent of land, whereas the Israeli preference is closer to 6 per cent (Mohamed Rachid, Interview, London, 2 February 2003). The Israeli position to land swaps however fails to acknowledge either the illegality of the settlements (see Chazan, 2000; Tufajki, 2000) or the fact that Palestinians view the very existence of the settlements as proof of Israeli bad faith (as joint meetings frequently demonstrated).
10. Jamil Hilal, interview, 25 August 2001, Ramallah.
11. Ifat Maoz, PhD, Department of Communication, the Hebrew University of Jerusalem.
12. Endresen also remarks upon the profound and far-reaching consequences of this 'geo-aspect' (2001: 20).
13. Interview, Marwan Al-Bargouti, 26 August 2001, Ramallah.
14. Dr Said Zeedani, a prominent Palestinian academic and activist, argues, 'Joint projects did not build a strong base to include human resources or a data base to guarantee continuity of relationships. Funding remained a major motivation for those projects' (interview with Dr Said Zeedani, 6 September 2001, Ramallah).
15. Samir Saif, interview, 18 January 2004, Ramallah.
16. Interview with Sarah Ozacky-Lazar, 28 August 2001, Jerusalem.
17. A letter from the Palestinian and the Israeli co-directors of IPCRI, which was sent on 8 June 2003, points out that the 'US Wye River People-to-People fund was taken from the $400 million that President Clinton promised to the Palestinians and not one cent from the more than $1 billion that was allocated to Israel was taken for the People-to-People fund'. See Letter to President Bush: 'Peace Education Now!' at www.ipcri.org.

6 'From Both Sides': A case study of the programme

1. Samir Saif, interview, 10 August 2001, Ramallah.
2. It is worth noting here that it is always the case that Palestinians are invited to lecture to Israeli audiences and not the other way around. However, in some academic interactions lecturers from both sides are invited to address Palestinian audiences.
3. Melitz is a Hebrew word that means 'interpreter' (Gen. 42.23). Melitz interpreted when Joseph and his brothers met with the governor of Egypt.
4. Participants did engage with 'final status' issues at different points.
5. The most popular way of recruiting Palestinians participants was through a 'snowball' method. Facilitators also played a substantial role in recruiting, usually by inviting friends to projects. These methods were used because a lack of Palestinian support meant that P2P projects could not be advertised publicly.
6. Lee Perlman, interview, 29 June 2001, Londonderry, Ireland.
7. Lee Perlman, interview, 29 June 2001, Londonderry, Ireland.
8. Lee Perliman, interview, 29 June 2001, Londonderry, Ireland.
9. Israeli visits to settlements were intended to demonstrate the advantages and privileges that Israeli occupants of the OPT possessed. They were consistent with the general Palestinian position on settlements, which presents them as a violation of UN Resolution 242.
10. Nisreen Abu-Zayyad, interview, August 2001, Jerusalem.
11. Interview with Haseeb Ali, teacher at Friends School, interview, 29 January 2004, Ramallah.
12. It was originally anticipated that the project would extend across two years. However, EU funding was ultimately only committed for a single year.
13. Palestinians were allowed to enter Israel only after obtaining a permit from the Israeli authorities. The usual arrangement was that the Israeli coordinator would be responsible for taking this list to the relevant authority. When the permits were issued, the Palestinian participants then had to collect them from the Palestinian–Israeli coordinating office.
14. Lee Perliman, interview, Londonderry, Northern Ireland, 29 June 2001.
15. Muhammad Shahin, director, Centre for Development in Primary Health Care, Al-Quds University interview, 30 October 2003, Ramallah.
16. Lee Perlman, interview, 29 June 2001, Londonderry, Northern Ireland.
17. One Palestinian participant observes, 'I always thought that Israelis think of peace in a different way from us, but I became sure about it when I spoke to Israelis in this project.'

18 It is worth noting here that it is always the case that Palestinians are invited to lecture to Israeli audiences and not the other way around. However, in some academic institutions lecturers from both sides have been invited to address Palestinian audiences.
19 Interview, 10 August 2001, Ramallah; and a follow-up interview, 18 January 2004.
20 Taysir Al-Aruri, a Palestinian who had been involved in contact initiatives with Israelis since the mid-1980s, agrees that the appearance of a peace process made it 'hard to convince the international community that we still suffered from Israeli occupation'.
21 Hassan Abu-Libedeh, who then represented the Palestinian Central Bureau of Statistics, is now the minister/chief of staff in the Prime Minister's Office.
22 The Palestinian plan is documented in the Palestinian National Authority archives but it is not currently available to the public.
23 A small number of Palestinians did nonetheless engage with Israeli settlers, and eight joint meetings took place between June 1995 and June 1996. A Palestinian official who participated in those meetings observes that they had a clear tactical rationale: both sides wanted to learn more about the opposing side and to communicate their position. He notes that, subsequent to these meetings, Palestinian participants identified subtle differences and nuances in the positions adopted by their opponents.
24 Interview, 26 August 2001, Ramallah.
25 Lee Perlman, interview, Londonderry, Northern Ireland, 29 June 2001.
26 The conference was initiated by 'Peace Research Institute in the Middle East' (PRIME). Palestinian and Israeli representatives who were engaged with joint projects were invited to exchange ideas, evaluate their respective experiences and identify the support that PRIME could lend to future initiatives.
27 The conference papers and conclusions were published in January 2000.
28 Dan Bar-On and Sami Adwan, the co-directors of PRIME, observe, 'While some are committed to a specific area (for example, environmental issues), others are more comprehensive in their approach, trying to cover many issues as they can' (2000: 68).
29 The Ministry of NGO Affairs was established in October 1999. Israeli–Palestinian joint projects and the P2PP were both major items on its agenda.
30 I was a member of the follow-up committee.
31 Orient House provides political, social and economic support to Palestinians who live in Jerusalem. Its political significance is attested to by the fact that it has become the official Palestinian address for many international diplomatic missions. It embodies the Palestinian aspiration that Jerusalem will one day be the capital of the Palestinian state.

32 The organizations that rejected contact with Israelis tended to be associated with political parties that had rejected the Oslo agreement (e.g. the Popular Front and Hamas). Those that participated tended to be associated with parties that supported this process (e.g. Fatah, the largest Palestinian political party).
33 Akram Atallah, interview, 19 February 2004, Jerusalem.
34 Akram Atallah, interview, 19 February 2004, Jerusalem.

7 The P2PP – a critical assessment

1 Mohamed Rachid, interview, 2 February 2003, London.
2 Amneh Badran, interview, 26 September 2002, Exeter.
3 Amneh Badran, interview, 26 September 2002, Exeter. The Jerusalem Centre for Women is the partner of the Palestinian–Israeli 'Jerusalem Link'.
4 Mahdi Abdul-Hadi, interview, 27 August 2001, Ramallah.
5 UN Resolution No. 194 (III) clearly states, 'Refugees wishing to return to their home and live at peace with their neighbours should be permitted to do so at the earliest practicable date, and that compensation should be paid for the property of those choosing not to return and for loss of or damage to property of those choosing not to return which, under principles of international law or in equity, should be made good by the Governments or authorities responsible' (Tomeh, 1975: 16).
6 Mohamed Rachid, interview, London, 2 February 2003.
7 Interview, 26 January 2004, Jerusalem.
8 Samir Saif, interview, 10 August 2001, Ramallah.
9 Janet Aviad, interview, 26 January 2004, Jerusalem.
10 Yolla Haddadin, telephone conversation, 21 February 2003.
11 Yolla Haddadin, telephone conversation, 21 February 2003.
12 http://www.enpi-info.eu/mainmed.php?id=478&id_type=10.
13 http://eeas.europa.eu/delegations/israel/documents/projects/20160216_eupi-eupfp_programme_at_a_glance_2016_en.pdf. https://www.devex.com/projects/grants/eu-peacebuilding-initiative-in-mediterranean-region/7465.
14 The Arab Peace Initiative was formally proposed by Saudi Arabia's Crown Prince Abdullah in 2005 and was later adopted by the Arab League. It pledged to recognize Israel (conditional upon its full withdrawal from occupied territory), endorsed a two-state solution and called for the full implementation of UN Security Council Resolution 194.
15 The Road Map to Peace was first proposed in 2002 and was sponsored by the International Quartet (the United States, European Union, Russia and the United

Nations). It called upon Israel to freeze settlement activity as a first step towards a final political settlement premised upon two independent states. It also endorsed increasing funding for P2P activities.

16 People-to-People Peace Building: A Program Guide, Produced by the USAID Office of Conflict Management and Mitigation USAID/DCHA/CMM, January 2011. https://www.usaid.gov/sites/default/files/documents/1866/CMMP2PGuidelines2010-01-19.pdf.
See also, https://www.usaid.gov/west-bank-and-gaza/fact-sheets/conflict-management-and-mitigation-program-november-2015.

17 Conflict Management and Mitigation Program Fact Sheet. https://www.usaid.gov/west-bank-and-gaza/fact-sheets/conflict-management-and-mitigation-program.

18 Ra'id Malki, Senior Development Program Officer, Deputy Head of Aid, CanaDain Representative Office, interview, 7 September 2001, a follow-up interview, 26 March 2004, Ramallah.

19 Palestinian and Israeli employees work in the same office of IPCRI in Jerusalem. Issa Rabadi, co-director, Peace Education Department-IPCRI, was interviewed on 15 December 2003.

20 The Peace Education Program was initiated by IPCRI. Palestinian and Israeli teachers worked on developing peace education curricula that were to be integrated in subjects taught to tenth-grade students in Palestinian and Israeli schools. The programme brought together students and teachers from both sides (for more details, see www.ipcri.org).

21 Uri Savir was the chief Israeli negotiator during the pre-Oslo negotiations. He founded Yala Young Leaders movement in May 2011. This was an online and Facebook initiative that brought together Palestinians, Israelis and participants from across the Middle East.

22 'Proceeding of the Assessing and Evaluating P2P Activities' was held in Jerusalem on 5 April 2005. Unpublished.

23 People to People (P2P) (2001), 'People to People Programme under crisis, Oslo Workshop Statement', unpublished paper, Oslo, 20–24 June 2001.

24 Ghassan Al-Khatib, interview, 9 March 2004, Ramallah.

25 Ghassan Al-Khatib, interview, 10 August 2001, Ramallah.

26 Dr Hanna Nasir was the president of Bir Zeit University.

27 www.infopal.org/plnews.

28 'Proceeding of the Assessing and Evaluating P2P Activities' was held in Jerusalem on 5 April 2005. Unpublished.

29 JMCC is a media centre that was established in 1988 by a group of Palestinian journalists and researchers. Its services, which include research and opinion poll analysis, are drawn upon by journalists, researchers and international agencies.

8 The P2PP during and after the *Al-Aqsa Intifada*

1. The Arab Peace Initiative was proposed by Prince Abdullah Bin Abdullaziz, the crown prince of the Kingdom of Saudi Arabia, in March 2002. The Roadmap for peace was proposed by the Quartet (the United States, EU, Russia and the UN) in November 2002. The Annapolis Conference, November 2007, was a US initiative that sought to implement the Road Map as a basis for the resolution of final status issues. The United States also brokered peace talks over a nine-month period (from July 2013 onwards), with John Kerry, the then US secretary of state assuming a leading role.
2. During this period, Palestinians required Israeli permits to move between Palestinian areas.
3. Interview, 18 January 2004, Ramallah.
4. Ghassan Al-Khatib, interview, 9 March 2004, Ramallah.
5. Akram Atallah, interview, 19 February 2004, Jerusalem.
6. Ghassan Al-Khatib, at the time of writing minister of Labour in the Palestinian Authority, interview, 9 March 2004, Ramallah.
7. Ra'id Malki, senior development programme officer, deputy head of aid, Canadian Representative Office, interview, 7 September 2001 (follow-up interview, 26 March 2004), Ramallah.
8. Ghassan Al-Khatib, interview, 9 March 2004, Ramallah.
9. http://www.geneva-accord.org/mainmenu/mission-statement (accessed 22 September 2017).
10. http://www.geneva-accord.org/mainmenu/mission-statement (accessed 22 September 2017).
11. Nabil Kassis, minister of Ministry of Planning, interview, 13 March 2004, Ramallah.
12. Interview, 6 October 2003, Ramallah.
13. Nabil Kassis, the present minister of Ministry of Planning, interview, 13 March 2004, Ramallah.
14. For public opinion polls on the Geneva Initiative, see www.ccmep.org (12 March 2004).
15. Interview, 6 October 2003, Ramallah.
16. Ibid.
17. Taysir Al-Aruri is a lecturer at Birzeit University and general coordinator of the Palestinian Democratic Coalition, interview, 5 September 2001 (follow-up interview, 13 March 2004), Ramallah.
18. Al-Bargouti was one of the leaders of the *Al-Aqsa Intifada* who was arrested in 2002. He is currently serving five life sentences in an Israeli jail.

19 Interview, Marwan Al-Bargouti, 26 August 2001, Ramallah.
20 For more details, see www.nad-plo.org (12 March 2004).
21 www.batshalom.org, accessed 25 February 2004.
22 After Hamas was elected in 2006, a division emerged and resulted in a 2007 coup, which left the Strip under the control of Hamas. Three successive wars then followed.
23 West Bank Palestinians have adopted this approach. The Gaza Strip, which has been blockaded since 2007 when Hamas seized power, has instead adopted a military approach. This resulted in three devastating wars in 2009, 2012 and 2014.
24 Women Wage Peace is an Israeli women's movement that was created in response to the 2014 war in Gaza. It was created with the intention of pressurizing the Israeli government to reach a peace agreement. See http://womenwagepeace.org.il/en/mission-statement/.
25 See the BDS leaflet (in Arabic): https://bdsmovement.net/ar/news/-اللجنة-الوطنية-الفلسطينية-للمقاطعة-تندين-الدعوة-لمسيرة-نسوية-تطبيعية-في-أريحا-وتدعو-لمقاطعتها.
26 Breaking the Silence: http://www.breakingthesilence.org.il/about/organization.
27 See http://zochrot.org/en/tour/all.
28 In Hebrew, *Ta'ayush* means 'life in common'.
29 Ta'ayush was formed in 2000 after the *Al-Aqsa Intifada* broke out. See http://www.taayush.org (accessed 6 March 2004).
30 In Hebrew, *Machsom* means 'checkpoint'.
31 Machsom Watch was formed in January 2001. See http://www.machsomwatch.org (accessed 6 March 2004).
32 Rabbis for Human Rights was formed during the First *Intifada* (in 1988). See their website: http://www.rhr.israel.net (6 March 2004).
33 See the website at www.icahd.org (10 January 2004).
34 http://www.awalls.org.
35 See http://www.theparentscircle.com.
36 The conference was held in the Seven Arches Hotel in Jerusalem on 23 January 2004. I attended as an observer for the purposes of this study.
37 Dr Adel Misk, co-chairperson, Parents' Circle-Families Forum, 23 January 2004, Jerusalem.
38 Yitzhak Frankenthal established the Parents' Circle in 1994 when his (nineteen-year old) son, who was serving as a solider, was kidnapped and killed by Hamas.
39 Yitzhak Frankenthal, co-chairperson, Parents' Circle-Families Forum, 23 January 2004, Jerusalem.
40 JVP, https://jewishvoiceforpeace.org/boycott-divestment-and-sanctions/jvp-supports-the-bds-movement/.

Bibliography

Abarbanel, Avigail (2012), *Beyond Tribal Loyalties Personal Stories of Jewish Peace Activists*. Newcastle: Cambridge Scholars.

Abbas, Mahmoud (Abu Mazen) (1994), *Tarīq Ūslū: Mūwaqqi' Al-'Itifāq Yarwī al-'asrār Al-haqīqīyah Lil-mufāwadāt*. Bayrūt: Sharikat al-matbū'āt lil-tawzī' wa al-nashr.

Abu-Lughod, Ibrahim (1990), 'Introduction: On Achieving Independence in Nassar and Heacock'. In Jamal Nassar and Roger Heacock (eds.), *Intifada: Palestine at the Crossroads*. New York: Praeger.

Abu-Nimer, Mohammed (1999), *Dialogue, Conflict Resolution, and Change: Arab-Jewish Encounters in Israel*. Albany: State University of New York Press.

Abu-Saad, I. (2008), 'Where Inquiry Ends: The Peer Review Process and Indigenous Standpoints', *American Behavioral Scientist*, 51, 1902–18.

Adala, The Legal Center for Arab Minority Rights in Israel (2018), Adalah's Position Paper: Proposed Basic Law: Israel – The Nation State of the Jewish People UPDATE – 16 July 2018, https://www.adalah.org/en/content/view/9569 (accessed 13 August 2018).

Adwan, Sami, and Dan Bar-On (eds.) (2000), *The Role of Non-Governmental Organizations in Peace-Building between Palestinians and Israelis*. Beit Jala: PRIME.

Adwan, Sami, and Philip Veerman (2000), 'Reflections on Joint Israeli-Palestinian Cooperation Projects', *Palestine-Israel Journal of Politics, Economics and Culture*, 7 (1, 2), 110–25.

Ahern, M. (2012), 'The West Bank and Gaza Mark'. In R. P. Beschel and M. Ahern, Jr. (eds.), *Public Financial Management Reform in the Middle East and North Africa: An Overview of Regional Experience*, pp. 165–76. Washington, DC: World Bank.

Alazzeh, Ala (2015), 'Seeking Popular Participation: Nostalgia for the First Intifada in the West Bank', *Settler Colonial Studies*, 5 (3), 251–67.

Alfred, T. (2005), *Wasáse: Indigenous Pathways of Action and Freedom*. Toronto: University of Toronto Press.

Al-Hardan, A. (2014), 'Decolonizing Research on Palestinians: Towards Critical Epistemologies and Research Practices', *Qualitative Inquiry*, 20 (1), 61–71.

Al-Khatib, Ghassan (1995, Winter), 'The Inadequacy of an Interim Agreement', *Palestine-Israel Journal of Politics, Economics and Culture*, 2 (I), 13–17.

Al-Shu'aibi, A. (2012), 'Security Sector Reform in the Arab Countries: The Case of Palestine', *ARI Thematic Studies: Arab Securitocracies and Security Sector Reform*, https://www.arab-reform.net/en/node/580 (accessed 13 May 2019).

Allport, G. W. (1954), *The Nature of Prejudice*. Reading, MA: Addison-Wesley.

Amir, Yehuda (1969), 'The Contact Hypothesis in Ethnic Relations', *Psychological Bulletin*, 71 (5), 319–42.

Andoni, Lamis (1997), 'Redefining Oslo: Negotiating the Hebron Protocol', *Journal of Palestine Studies*, 25 (3), 17–30.

Aruri, Nasser H. (1999), 'The Wye Memorandum: Netanyahu's Oslo and Unreciprocal Reciprocity', *Journal of Palestine Studies*, 25 (2), 17–28.

Ashrawi, Hanan (1992), 'The Intifada: Political Analysis'. In Naim S. Ateek, Marc H. Ellis and Rosemary Randford Ruther (eds.), *Faith and the Intifada: Palestinian Christian Voices*. Maryknoll, NY: Orbis Books.

Avnery, Uri (1986), *My Friend, the Enemy*. London: Zed Books.

Badarin, E. (2015), 'Settler-Colonialist Management of Entrances to the Native Urban Space in Palestine', *Settler Colonial Studies*, 5 (3), 226–35.

Badarin, E. (2016), *Palestinian Political Discourse: Between Exile and Occupation*. New York: Routledge.

Barkar, Adam (2015), '"A Direct Act of Resurgence, a Direct Act of Sovereignty": Reflections on Idle No More, Indigenous Activism, and Canadian Settler Colonialism', *Globalizations*, 12 (1), 43–65.

Barnea, Nahum (2014), 'Inside the Talks' Failure: US Officials Open Up'. *Ynet News*, 5 February 2014, https://www.ynetnews.com/articles/0,7340,L-4515821,00.html.

Barnea, Tamara, and Ziad Abdeen (2002), 'Cooperate and Cooperate: The Role of Health Professionals in Promoting Israeli-Palestinian Coexistence'. In Tamara Barnea and Rafiq Husseini (eds.), *Separate and Cooperate, Cooperate and Separate: The Disengagement of the Palestine Health Care System from Israel and Its Emergence as an Independent System*. London: Praeger.

Bar-On, Mordechai (1996), *In Pursuit of Peace: A History of the Israeli Peace Movement*. Washington, DC: US Institute of Peace Press.

Bar-Tal, D., and Y. Teichman (2005), *Stereotypes and Prejudice in Conflict: Representations of Arabs in Israeli Jewish Society*. Cambridge, MA: Cambridge University Press.

Baskin, G., Z. Qaq and Israel/Palestine Center for Research and Information (1997), *The Future of the Israeli Settlements in Final Status Negotiations: A Policy Paper Featuring Recommendations for Negotiations in the Final Status Talks between Israel and the Palestinians*. Jerusalem: IPCRI.

Baum, Dalit (2018), 'Gazans Invite Israeli Activists over for Tea', +972 Magazine, 12 September 2018, https://972mag.com/gaza-blockade-israeli-activists-solidarity-tea/137698/ (accessed 22 September 2018).

BDS (2005), 'Open Letter: Palestinian Civil Society Call for BDS', 9 July 2005, https://bdsmovement.net/call (accessed 14 August 2018).

BDS (2016), *The Call for Boycott, Divestment and Sanctions* [online]. BDS Movement. https://bdsmovement.net/what-is-bds (accessed 22 January 2018).

Ben-Ozer, Ramar (2018), 'EU Passes Bill to Promote Anti-Hate Education in Palestinian Schools', *Jerusalem Post*. Available online. 18 April 2018. www.jpost.com/Middle-East/EU-passes-bill-to-promote-anti-hate-education-in-Palestinian-schools-551175 (accessed 6 May 2018).

Benvenisti, Meron (2003), 'Which Kind of Binational State?' *Ha'Aretz*, 20 November 2003. http://www.haaretz.com/print-edition/opinion/which-kind-of-binational-state-1.106273.

Benvenisti, Meron (2010), 'United We Stand: Do Israelis and Palestinians Belong to One Divided Society, or to Two Separate Societies in a Situation of Forced Proximity as a Result of a Temporary Occupation?' *Ha'Aretz*, 28 January 2010, https://www.haaretz.com/1.5091478 (accessed 12 May 2017).

Bishara, Marwan (2001), *Palestine/Israel: Peace or Apartheid: Prospects for Resolving the Conflict*. London: Zed Books.

Bouillon, Markus E. (2004), 'Gramsci, Political Economy, and the Decline of the Peace Process', *Critique: Critical Journal of Middle East Studies*, 13 (3), 239–64.

Bouris, Dimitris (2010), 'The European Union's Role in the Palestinian Territory after the Oslo Accords: Stillborn State-Building', *Journal of Contemporary European Research*, 6 (3), 376–94. http://www.jcer.net/ojs/index.php/jcer/article/view/205/232 (accessed 26 February 2017).

Brewer, Marilynn B., and N. Miller (1984), 'Beyond the Contact Hypothesis: Theoretical Perspectives on Desegregation'. In N. Miller and M. B. Brewer (eds.), *Groups in Contact: The Psychology of Desegregation*, pp. 281–302. San Diego, CA: Academic Press.

Brewer, Marilynn B. (1997), 'On the Social Origins of Human Nature'. In C. McGarty and S. A. Haslam (eds.), *The Massage of Social Psychology*. Oxford: Blackwell.

Brewer, Marilynn B., and Norma Miller (1996), *Intergroup Relations*. New York: Brooks/Cole.

Brown, R. (1988), *Group Processes: Dynamics within and between Groups*. Oxford: Basil Blackwell.

Brown, R. (1995), *Prejudice: Its Social Psychology*. Oxford: Blackwell.

B'Tselem (2010), 'By Hook and by Crook: Israel's Settlement Policy in the West Bank', Summary, Jerusalem, 5 July 2010.

B'Tselem – The Israeli Information Center for Human Rights in the Occupied Territories (2018), 'Three Israeli Supreme Court Justices Greenlight State to Commit War Crime', 27 May 2018, https://www.btselem.org/communities_facing_expulsion/20180527_supreme_court_greenlights_war_crime_in_khan_al_ahmar.

Buchanan, Paul G. (2000), 'Note sulla "Escuola Italiana": Using Gramsci in the Current International Moment', *Contemporary Politics*, 6 (2), 103–22.

Bush, G. W. (2002), 'Full Text of George Bush's Speech', *Guardian*, 25 June 2002, http://www.guardian.co.uk/ world/ 2002/ jun/ 25/ israel.usa.

Carey, Roane, and Jonathan Shainin (eds.) (2002), *The Other Israel: Voices of Refusal and Dissent*. New York: New Press.

Cavanaugh, Kathleen (1999), 'The Cost of Peace: Assessing Oslo', *Middle East Report*, 211, 10–12.

CBC News (2013), '9 Questions about Idle No More', *CBC News*, 5 January 2013, https://www.cbc.ca/news/canada/9-questions-about-idle-no-more-1.1301843 (accessed 13 August 2018).

Chacham, Ronit (2003), *Breaking Ranks: Refusing to Serve in the West Bank and Gaza Strip*. New York: Other Press.

Chaitin, Julia (2011), *Peace-Building in Israel and Palestine: Social Psychology and Grassroots Initiatives*. New York: Palgrave Macmillan.

Chazan, Naomi (2000), 'Toward a Settlement without Settlement', *Palestine-Israel Journal of Political, Economics and Culture*, 7 (3, 4), 46–51.

Chomsky, Noam (1999), *Fateful Triangle: The United States, Israel and the Palestinians*. London: Pluto Press.

Chomsky, Noam, Ilan Pappé and Frank Barat (2015), *On Palestine*. New York: Haymarket Books/London: Penguin.

Cohen, Stephen P., Herbert Kelman, D. Miller Frederick and Bruce L. Smith (1977), 'Involving Intergroup Techniques for Conflict Resolution: An Israeli-Palestinian Pilot Workshop', *Journal of Social Issues*, 33 (1), 165–89.

Cook, Jonathan (2017), 'How Israel Robs Palestinians of Citizenship', *Electronic Intifada*, 19 September 2017, https://electronicintifada.net/content/how-israel-robs-palestinians-citizenship/21751 (accessed 13 August 2018).

Cook, S. W. (1962), 'The Systematic Analysis of Socially Significant Events: A Strategy of Social Research', *Journal of Social Issues*, 18, 66–84.

Coulthard, Glen C. (2014), *Red Skin, White Masks: Rejecting the Colonial Politics of Recognition* (Minneapolis: University of Minnesota Press).

Cox, R. W. (1996a), 'Gramsci, Hegemony, and International Relations: An Essay in Method'. In Robert Cox (ed.), *Approaches to World Order* (Cambridge: Cambridge University Press).

Cox, R. W. (1996b), 'Social Forces, States, and World Orders: Beyond International Relations Theory (1981)'. In Robert Cox (ed.), *Approaches to World Order*, pp. 85–123 (Cambridge: Cambridge University Press).

Cox, R. W. (1996c), 'Realism, Positivism, and Historicism (1985)'. In *Approaches to World Order*, pp. 49–59. Cambridge: Cambridge University Press.

Dajani, Omar (2007), 'Forty Years without Resolve: Tracing the Influence of Security council Resolution 242 on the Middle East Peace process', *Journal of Palestine Studies*, 37 (1), 24–38.

Dalsheim, Joyce (2005), 'Ant/agonizing Settlers in the Colonial Present of Israel-Palestine', *Social Analysis: The International Journal of Social and Cultural Practice*, 49, 122–43.

Dana, Tariq (2015), 'The Symbiosis between Palestinian "Fayyadism" and Israeli "Economic Peace": The Political Economy of Capitalist Peace in the Context of Colonisation', *Conflict, Security & Development*, 15 (5), 455–77. doi: 10.1080/14678802.2015.1100013.

Darweish, Marwan (2016), 'Israeli Peace and Solidarity Organizations'. In Alpaslan Ozerdem, Chuck Thiessen and Mufid Qassoum (eds.), *Conflict Transformation and the Palestinians*, Chapter 13, pp. 229–45. Florence: Taylor and Francis.

Darweish, Marwan, and Andrew Rigby (2015), *Popular Protest in Palestine: The Uncertain Future of Unarmed Resistance*. London: Pluto Press.

Davis, Angela Y. (2016), *Freedom Is a Constant Struggle: Ferguson, Palestine, and the Foundations of a Movement*. Chicago, IL: Haymarket Books.

Dixon, John, and Steve Reicher (1997), 'Intergroup Contact and Desegregation in the New South Africa', *British Journal of Social Psychology*, 36, 361–81.

Dixon, John, and Kevin Durrheim (2003), 'Contact and the Ecology of Racial Division: Some Varieties of Informal Segregation', *British Journal of Social Psychology*, 42, 1–23.

Dunbar-Ortiz, Roxanne (2015), *An Indigenous Peoples' History of the United States (ReVisioning American History)*. Boston, MA: Beacon Press, p. 5.

Endresen, Lena (2001), *Contact and Cooperation: The Israeli-Palestinian People-to-People Program*. Oslo: Institute for Applied Social Science.

Endresen, Lena C., and Signe Gilen (2000), 'Consultations and Consensus: Implementing the Israeli-Palestinian People-to-People Programme for Development', *Development*, 43 (3), 29–33.

FACTS Information Committee, 'Towards a State of Independence: The Palestinian Uprising', December 1987–August 1988.

Fanon, Frantz (1963), *The Wretched of the Earth*. New York: Grove Press.

Fanon, Frantz (2008), *Black Skin, White Masks*. London, Pluto Press.

Farsakh, Leila (Spring 2008), 'Independence, Cantons or Bantustans: Whither the Palestinian State?', *Middle East Journal* 59 (2), 230–45.

Farsoun, Samih K., and Jean M. Landis (1990), 'The Sociology of an Uprising: The Roots of the Intifada', In Jamal Nassar and Roger Heacock (eds.), *Intifada: Palestine at the Crossroads*, pp. 53–71. New York: Praeger.

FCO (2016), 'Middle East: Overseas Aid'. Foreign and Commonwealth Office written question – answered on 25 May 2016. http://www.theyworkforyou.com/wrans/?id=2016-05-20.37735.h&s=israel#g37735.r0.

Fitzduff, Mari (1999), 'Changing History – Peace Building in Northern Ireland'. In *People Building Peace: 35 Inspiring Stories from Around the World*. Utrecht: European Centre for Conflict Prevention in cooperation with IFOR and the Coexistence Initiative of the State of the World Forum.

Foster, D., and G. Finchilescu (1986), 'Contact in a Non-Contact Society: The Case of South Africa'. In M. Hewstone and R. Brown (eds.), *Contact and Conflict in Intergroup Encounters*. Oxford: Basil Blackwell.

Foucault, M. (1980), *Power/Knowledge*, ed. Colin Gordon. New York: Pantheon Books.

Foucault, M. (1984), 'The Order of Discourse', In M. Shapiro (ed.), *Language and Politics*, trans. I. McLeod, pp. 108–38. New York: New York University Press.

Foucault, M. (1990), *History of Sexuality Vol. 1: An Introduction*. New York: Vintage.

Foucault, M. (1991), *Discipline and Punish: The Birth of a Prison*. London: Penguin.

Foucault, M. (May 1993), 'About the Beginning of the Hermeneutics of the Self' (Transcription of two lectures in Dartmouth on 17 and 24 November 1980), ed. Mark Blasius, *Political Theory*, 21 (2), 198–227.

Foucault, Michel (2002), *The Archaeology of Knowledge*. London: Routledge.

Gawerc, Michelle (2012), *Prefiguring Peace: Israeli-Palestinian Peacebuilding Partnerships*. Lanham, MD: Lexington Books.

Ghanem, As'ad (2010), *Palestinian Politics after Arafat: A Failed National Movement*. Bloomington: Indiana University Press.

Gordon, N. (2002), 'The Enemy Within'. In Roane Carey and Jonathan Shanin (eds.), *The Other Israel: Voices of Refusal and Dissent*. New York: New Press.

Gordon, N. (2009), 'An Israeli Comes to the Painful Conclusion That It's the Only Way to Save His Country [online]', *Los Angeles Times*, 20 August 2009. http://articles.latimes.com/2009/aug/20/opinion/oe-gordon20.

Gordon, Uri, and Ohal Grietzer (eds.) (2013), *Anarchists against the Wall: Direct Action and Solidarity with the Palestinian Popular Struggle*. Oakland, CA: AK Press.

Grande, Sandy (2004), *Red Pedagogy: Native American Social and Political Thought*. Lanham, MD: Rowman & Littlefield.

Gregory, Derek (2004), *The Colonial Present: Afghanistan, Palestine, Iraq*. Oxford: Blackwell.

Guardian (2015a), 'Letter: Over 100 Artists Announce a Cultural Boycott of Israel', *Guardian*, 13 February 2015.

Guardian (2015b), 'Star Authors Call for Israeli-Palestinian Dialogue Rather Than Boycotts', *Guardian*, 22 October 2015.

Haaretz (2003), 'Israel's Road Map Reservations', 27 May. Available online: http://www.haaretz.com/print-edition/news/israel-s-road-map-reservations-1.8935 (accessed 2 March 2015).

Haddad, Toufic (2016), *Palestine Ltd: Neoliberalism and Nationalism in the Occupied Territories*. London: I. B. Taurus.

Hadi, Mahdi Abdul F. (1987), *Notes on Palestinian-Israeli Meetings in the Occupied Territories (1967–1987)*. East Jerusalem: PASSIA.

Hall-Cathala, David (1990), *The Peace Movement in Israel, 1967–87*. London: Macmillan.

Halper, Jeff (2012), 'Our Vision of a Just One-State Solution – Jeff Halper of ICAHD'. MONDOWEISS, 24 September 2012, http://mondoweiss.net/2012/09/our-vision-of-a-just-one-state-solution-jeff-halper-of-icahd/ (accessed 21 June 2018).

Halper, Jeff (2015), *War against the People: Israel, the Palestinians and Global Pacification*. London: Pluto Press.

Halper, Jeff (2017), 'Ending the Occupation Isn't Enough', *+972 Magazine*, 10 June 2017, https://972mag.com/fifty-years-on-its-time-for-a-conflict-resolution-in-palestine-israel/128024/ (accessed 7 October 2017).

Halper, Jeff (2018), 'The "One Democratic State Campaign" Program for a Multicultural Democratic State in Palestine/Israel'. MONDOWEISS, 3 May 2018, https://mondoweiss.net/2018/05/democratic-multicultural-palestine/ (accessed 22 July 2018).

Hammami, Rema (1995), 'NGOs: The Professionalization of Politics', *Race & Class*, 37 (2), 51–63.

Hammami, Rema, and Salim Tamari (2001), 'The Second Uprising: End or New Beginning?' *Journal of Palestine Studies*, 30 (2), 5–25.

Hanafi, Sari (2007), 'Dancing Tango during Peacebuilding: Palestinian-Israeli People-to-People Programs for Conflict Resolution'. In Judy Kuriansky (ed.), *Beyond Bullets & Bombs: Grassroots Peacebuilding between Israelis and Palestinians*, pp. 69–80. Westport, CT: Praeger.

Hanafi, Sari (2013), 'Explaining Spacio-Cide in the Palestinian Territory: Colonization, Separation and State of Exception', *Current Sociology*, 61 (2), 190–205.

Hanafi, Sari, and Linda Tabar (2005), *The Emergence of a Palestinian Globalised Elite: Donors, International NGOs and Local NGOs*. Ramallah: Muwatin and the Institute for Jerusalem Studies.

Hanieh, Akram (2000), 'Special Document: The Camp David Papers', *Journal of Palestine Studies*, 30 (2), 75–97.

Hanieh Badarin, Adam (2008), 'Palestine in the Middle East: Opposing Neoliberalism and US Power', *MRzine*, 19 July 2008, http://www.monthlyreview.org/mrzine.

Hanieh, Adam (2013), *Lineages of Revolt: Issues of Contemporary Capitalism in the Middle East*. Chicago, IL: Haymarket Books.

Hanieh, Adam (2016), 'Development as Struggle: Confronting the Reality of Power in Palestine', *Journal of Palestine Studies*, 45 (4), 32–47.

Hanssen-Bauer, Jon (2000), 'The Israeli-Palestinian People-to-People Program: The Fafo Model of People-to-People', paper presented to the *Helsinki Workshop on Evaluating Israeli-Palestinian Civil Society Cooperative Activities*, 27–28 November 1999, KATU, 2000, pp. 35–40.

Hanssen-Bauer, Jon (2005), 'Bustling Backwards: Lessons from the Norwegian Sponsored Israeli-Palestinian People-to-People Program', *Palestine-Israel Journal*, 12–13 (4), 39–52.

Hassassian, Manuel (2000), 'The Role of Palestinian NGOs in Peace Building and Conflict Resolution'. In Sami Adwan and Dan Bar-On (eds.), *The Role of Non-Governmental Organizations in Peace-Building between Palestinians and Israelis*. Beit Jala: PRIME.

Hasson, Nir (2017), '30,000 Israelis, Palestinians Take Part in Women Wage Peace Rally in Jerusalem', *Haaretz*, 8 October 2017, https://www.haaretz.com/israel-news/1.816255 (accessed 8 October 2017).

Henry, M. (2000), 'Hillary Clinton: Link PA to End to Antisemitism', *Jerusalem Post*, 26 September.

Hermann, T. (2009), *The Israeli Peace Movement: A Shattered Dream*. Cambridge: Cambridge University Press.

Hever, Shir (2010), *The Political Economy of Israel's Occupation: Repression beyond Exploitation*. London: Pluto Press.

Hewstone, Miller, and R. Brown (1986), 'Contact Is Not Enough: An Intergroup Perspective on the "Contact Hypothesis"'. In M. Hewstone and R. Brown (eds.), *Contact and Conflict in Intergroup Encounters*. New York: Basil Blackwell.

Hilal J. (1976), 'Imperialism and Settler Colonialism in West Asia: Israel and the Arab Palestinian Struggle', *Utafi* 1 (1), 51–70.

Hilal, J. (ed.) (2007), *Where Now for Palestine? The Demise of the Two-State Solution*. London: Zed.

Hilal, J. (2010a), 'The Polarization of the Palestinian Political Field', *Journal of Palestine Studies*, 39 (3), 24–39.

Hilal, J. (2010b), *The Pauperization of Women, Men and Children in the West Bank and Gaza Strip*. Birzeit: Institute for Women's Studies, Birzeit University.

Hilal, J. (2015), 'Rethinking Palestine: Settler-Colonialism, Neoliberalism and Individualism in the West Bank and Gaza Strip', *Contemporary Arab Affairs*, 8 (3), 351–62. doi: 10.1080/17550912.2015.1052226.

Hilal, J., and Mushtaq Husain Khan (2004), 'State Formation under the PNA'. In Mushtaq Husain Khan, George Giacaman and Inge Amundsen (eds.), *State Formation in Palestine: Viability and Governance during a Social Transformation*. London: Routledge.

Hiltermann, Joost R. (1991), *Behind the Intifada: Labor and Women's Movements in the Occupied Territories* (Princeton, NJ: Princeton University Press).

Hirschfield, Yair (2000), 'The Oslo Process and the People-to-People Strategy', Society for International Development, *Peoples' Peace Movements*, 43 (3), 13–28.

Hirschfield, Yair, and Sharon Roling (2000), 'The Oslo Process and the People-to-People Strategy', *Development: Journal of the Society for International Development*, 43 (3), 13–28.

Gramsci, Antonio, Quintin Hoare and Geoffrey Nowell-Smith (eds.) (1971), *Selections from the Prison Notebooks of Antonio Gramsci*. New York: International.

Hogg, M. A., and Barbara A. Mullin (1999), 'Joining Groups to Reduce Uncertainty: Subjective Uncertainty Reduction and Group and Identification'. In D. Abraham and M. Hogg (eds.), *Social Identity and Social Cognition*. Oxford: Blackwell.

Husseini, Faisal (1991), 'Palestinian Politics after the Gulf War: An Interview with Faisal Husseini', *Journal of Palestine Studies*, 20 (4), 99–108.

Jabotinsky, V. (1923), *The Iron Wall (We and the Arabs)*. Essay, http://en.jabotinsky.org/media/9747/the-iron-wall.pdf (accessed 14 March 2016).

Jabri, V. (2006), 'Revisiting Change and Conflict: On Underlying Assumptions and the De-Politicisation of Conflict Resolution'. In D. Bloomfield, M. Fischer and B. Schmelzle (eds). *Berghof Handbook Dialogue Series No. 5: Social Change and Conflict Transformation*, pp. 69–76. Berlin: Berghof Research Center for Constructive Conflict Management.

Jad, Islah (1990), 'From Salons to the Popular Committees: Palestinian Women, 1919–1989'. In Jamal R. Nassar and Roger Heacock (eds.), *Intifada: Palestine at the Crossroads*, pp. 125–42. New York: Praeger.

Jerusalem Media and Communications Centre (JMCC) (1993), *Israeli Military Orders in the Occupied Palestinian West Bank (1967–1992)*. JMCC: Jerusalem.

Jerusalem Media and Communication Centre (JMCC) (1996), 'Israeli–Palestinian Interim Agreement on the West Bank and the Gaza Strip', Washington DC, 28 September 1995, JMCC Occasional Document Series No. 7, August 1996.

Jerusalem Media and Communication Centre (JMCC) (1999), *On Palestinian Attitudes towards Politics and Media*, JMCC Public Opinion Polls, No. 33, October 1999.

Jerusalem Media and Communication Centre (JMCC) (2006), 'Palestinian-Israeli Public Debate on People-to-People Program: An Evaluation', Jerusalem Media and Communication Center.

Kaminer, Reuven (1996), *Politics of Protest: The Israeli Peace Movement and the Palestinian Intifada*. Brighton: Sussex Academic Press.

Karmi, Ghada (2011), 'The One-State Solution: An Alternative Vision for Israeli-Palestinian Peace', *Journal of Palestine Studies*, 40 (2), 62–76.

KATU (2000), 'Declaration of Recommendations to Donors Supporting Israeli-Palestinian Civil Society Cooperative Activities', Report of the Workshop on the Israeli-Palestinian Civil Society Cooperative Activities, 27–28 November 1999, Helsinki, Finland, p. 71.

Katz, Sheila (2016), *Connecting with the Enemy: A Century of Palestinian-Israeli Joint Nonviolence*, 1st ed. Austin: University of Texas Press.

Kaufman, Edy (1988), 'The Intifadah and the Peace Camp in Israel: A Critical Introspective', *Journal of Palestine Studies*, 17 (2), 66–80.

Kaufman, Edy, and W. Salem (eds.) (2006), *Bridging the Divide: Peace-Building in the Israeli–Palestinian Conflict*. pp. 87–109. London: Lynne Rienner.

Keinon, H. (2014), 'Netanyahu: Palestinian Incitement Spurs Mideast Conflict', *Jerusalem Post*, 1 January. Available online: http://www.jpost.com/Diplomacy-and-Politics/Netanyahu-Palestinian-incitement-spurs-Mideast-conflict-337133 (accessed 2 April 2017).

Keller, Adam (1987), *Terrible Days: Social Divisions and Political Paradoxes in Israel*. Cyprus: Amstelveen.

Kelman, Herbert C. (1996), 'Negotiation as Interactive Problem Solving', *International Negotiation*, 1, 99–123.

Kelman, Herbert C. (1998), 'Informal Mediation by the Scholar/Practitioner'. In E. Weiner (ed.), *The Handbook of Interethnic Coexistence* (foreword A. B. Slifka). New York: Continuum/The Abraham Fund.

Kelman, Herbert C. (2005), 'Interactive Problem Solving in the Israeli-Palestinian Case: Past Contributions and Present Challenges'. In R. Fisher (ed.), *Paving the Way: Contributions of Interactive Conflict Resolution to Peacemaking*, pp. 41–63. Lanham, MD: Lexington Books.

Khalidi, Rashid (2006), *The Iron Cage: The Story of the Palestinian Struggle for Statehood*. Boston, MA: Beacon Press.

Khalidi, Rashid (2013), *Brokers of Deceit: How the US Has Undermined Peace in the Middle East*. Boston, MA: Beacon Press.

Khalidi, Raja, and Sobhi Samour (2011), 'Neoliberalism as Liberation: The Statehood Programme and the Remaking of the Palestinian National Movement', *Journal of Palestine Studies*, XL (2), 6–25.

Khalidi Raja, and Sobhi Samour (2014), 'Neoliberalism and the Contradictions of the Palestinian Authority's State-Building Programme'. In M. Turner and O. Shweiki (eds.), *Decolonizing Palestinian Political Economy: Rethinking Peace and Conflict Studies*. London: Palgrave Macmillan.

Kimmerling, Barach (1983), *Zionism and Territory: The Socio-Territorial Dimensions of Zionist Politics*. Berkeley: Institute of International Studies, University of California.

Kimmerling, Baruch (1995), 'Academic History Caught in the Cross-Fire: The Case of the Israeli-Jewish Historiography', *History and Memory*, 7 (1), 41–65.

King, Mary Elizabeth (2007), *A Quiet Revolution: The First Palestinian Intifada and Nonviolent Resistance*. New York: Nation Books.

Levy, Gideon (2002), 'The People's War'. In Roane Carey and Jonathan Shanin (eds.), *The Other Israel: Voices of Refusal and Dissent*. New York: New Press.

Levy, Gideon (2014), 'The Dayan's Dynasty: Israel's Story', *Haaretz*, 4 May 2014, http://www.haaretz.com/opinion/.premium-1.588812.

Li, T. M. (2000), 'Articulating Indigenous Identity in Indonesia: Resource Politics and the Tribal Slot', *Comparative Studies in Society and History*, 42 (1), 149–79.

Li, T. M. (2014), *Land's End: Capitalist Relations on an Indigenous Frontier*. Durham, NC: Duke University Press.

Li, T. M. (2017), 'After Development: Surplus Population and the Politics of Entitlement', *Development and Change*, 48, 1247–61.

Lloyd, David (2012), 'Settler Colonialism and the State of Exception: The Example of Palestine/Israel', *Settler Colonial Studies*, 2 (1), 59–80.

Lloyd, David, and Patrick Wolfe (2016), 'Settler Colonial Logics and the Neoliberal Regime', *Settler Colonial Studies*, 6 (2), 109–18.

Lockman, Zachary (July 1976), 'Zionism versus Socialism', *MERIP Reports*, 49, 3–18.

Lonning, D. J. (1995), *Bridge over Troubled Water, Inter-Ethnic Dialogue in Israel-Palestine*. Bergen: Norse.

Ma'an News Agency (2010), 'Israel to Adjust Wall's Route in Bil'in', 6 February 2010, http://www.maannews.com/Content.aspx?id=259487 (accessed 5 August 2018).

Makdisi, S. (2010), *Palestine Inside Out: An Everyday Occupation*. New York: Norton.

Mamdani, Mahmood (2015), 'Settler Colonialism: Then and Now', *Critical Inquiry*, 41 (3), 596–614.

Ma'oz, Moshe (1999), 'The Oslo Agreement: Toward Arab-Jewish Reconciliation'. In Robert L. Rothstein (ed.), *After the Peace: Resistance and Reconciliation*. London: Lynne Rienner.

Maoz, Ifat (2000), 'Issues in Grassroot Israeli-Palestinian Cooperation: A Report on the NGO Discussion Panels.' In Sami Adwan and Dan Bar-On (eds.), *The Role of Non-Governmental Organizations in Peace-Building between Palestinians and Israelis*. Beit Jala: PRIME.

Maoz, Ifat (2004), 'Peace Building in Violent Conflict: Israeli-Palestinian Post-Oslo People-to-People Activities', *International Journal of Politics, Culture, and Society*, 17 (3), 563–74.

Marilynn B., and Norman Miller (1996), *Intergroup Relations*. New York: Brooks/Cole.

Masalha, Nur (1992), *Expulsion of the Palestinians: The Concept of 'Transfer' in Zionist Political Thought, 1882–1948*. Washington, DC: Institute for Palestine Studies.

Massad, Joseph (Summer 1996), 'Zionism's Internal Others: Israel and the Oriental Jews', *Journal of Palestine Studies*, 25 (4), 53–68.

Melhem, Ahmad (2016), 'Will Palestinian Interaction with Israel Be Stopped?' *Al Monitor*, 6 April 2016. https://www.al-monitor.com/pulse/originals/2016/04/committee-israeli-interaction-dissolved-possibility-bds.html (accessed 6 October 2017).

Memmi, A. (1974), *The Colonizer and the Colonized*. London: Souvenir Press.

Middle East Monitor (MEMO) (2018), 'One Democratic State in Palestine', campaign launched within the Green Line, 24 April 2018. https://www.middleeastmonitor.com/20180424-one-democratic-state-in-palestine-campaign-launched-within-the-green-line/ (accessed 22 June 2018).

Miller, Norman, Lynn M. Urban and Eric Vanman (1998), 'A Theoretical Analysis of Crossed Social Categorization Effects'. In Constantine Sedikides, John Schopler and Chester A. Insko (eds.), *Intergroup Cognition and Intergroup Behavior*. Mahwah, NJ: Lawrence Erlbaum.

Morgensen, S. L. (2011), 'The Biopolitics of Settler Colonialism: Right Here, Right Now', *Settler Colonial Studies* 1 (1), 53.

Morris, Kim T., and James M. Jones (1993), "Individual versus Group Identification as a Factor in Intergroup Racial Conflict'. In Stephan Worchel and Jeffery A. Simpson (eds.), *Conflict between People and Groups: Causes, Processes, and Resolutions*. Chicago, IL: Nelson-Hall.

Mualem, M., and A. Benn (2004), 'Sharon: PA's Real Test Is Ending Incitement', *Haaretz*, 19 November.

Mu'allem, N. (27–28 November 1999). 'Palestinian Israeli Civil Society Co-Operative Activities', paper presented to Workshop 'Peace Building between Israelis and Palestinians', Helsinki, Finland.

Mu'allem, N. (2000), 'Palestinian-Israel Civil Society Co-Operative Activities', paper presented to the Helsinki Workshop on Evaluating Israeli-Palestinian Civil Society Cooperative Activities, 27–28 November 1999, in *Report of the Workshop on the Israeli-Palestinian Civil Society Cooperation Activity*, KATU, 2000, pp. 8–18.

Muslih, Muhammad (1990), 'Towards Coexistence: An Analysis of the Resolutions of the Palestine National Council', *Journal of Palestine Studies* 16 (4): 3–29.

Muslih, Muhammad (1995), 'Palestinian Civil Society'. In Augustus Richard Norton (ed.), *Civil Society in the Middle East*, vol. 1. Leiden: Brill.

Nakhleh, K. (2012), *Globalized Palestine: The National Sellout of a Homeland*. New Jersey: Red Sea Press.

Nasasra, Mansour, et al. (2015), *The Naqab Bedouin and Colonialism: New Perspectives*. London: Routledge.

Naser-Najjab, N. (2014), 'Between Myth and Reality: The Palestinian Political Elite and the Two-State Solution', *Holy Land Studies*, 13 (2), 139–58.

Naser-Najjab, N. (2017), '*Connecting with the Enemy: A Century of Palestinian-Israeli Joint Nonviolence* by Sheila H. Katz (review)', *Middle East Journal*, 71 (2), 312–14. Middle East Institute. Retrieved 29 June 2018, from Project MUSE database.

Naser-Najjab, N., and I. Pappé (2016), 'Palestine: Reframing Palestine in the Post-Oslo Period'. In R. Guyver (ed.), *Teaching History and the Changing Nation States: Transnational and International Perspectives*. London: Bloomsbury.

Nasir, Hanna (2001), 'The Intifada is Not a Palestinian picnic', Open letter to members of a Jerusalem synagogue, 15 February 2001, https://al-bushra.org/hedchrch/feb15.htm (accessed 1 August 2019).

Nasrallah, Elias (2016), *Testimonies on the First Century of Palestine*. Dar Al-Farabi: Beirut.

NGO Monitor (2016), 'Israeli Committee against House Demolitions (ICAHD)', 27 December 2016, http://www.ngo-monitor.org/ngos/israel_committee_against_house_demolitions_icahd_/ (accessed 27 January 2017).

OCHA (2008), 'Closure Update: Main Findings and Analysis', 30 April–11 September 2008, Jerusalem, pp. 4–5.

OCHA (2011a), 'East Jerusalem: Key Humanitarian Concerns Special Focus', March 2011, United Nations, OCHA. http://www.ochaopt.org/documents/ocha_opt_jerusalem_report_2011_03_23_web_english.pdf.

OCHA (2011b), 'Displacement and Insecurity in Area C of the West Bank', Executive Summary, East Jerusalem, August 2011.

Omer-Man, Michael Schaeffer (2018), 'A State That Belongs to Only Some of Its Citizens', 13 July 2018, https://972mag.com/a-state-that-belongs-to-only-some-of-its-citizens/136710/ (accessed 13 August 2018).

Ophir, A. (2002), 'A Time of Occupation.' In Roane Carey and Jonathan Shanin (eds.), *The Other Israel: Voices of Refusal and Dissent*. New York: New Press.

Ophir, A., M. Givoni, and S. Hanafl (eds.) (2009), *The Power of Inclusive Exclusion: Anatomy of Israeli Rule in the Occupied Palestinian Territories*. New York: Zone Books.

PACBI Statement (2011), 'Israel's Exceptionalism: Normalizing the Abnormal', 31 October 2011, https://bdsmovement.net/news/israel%E2%80%99s-exceptionalism-normalizing-abnormal (accessed 21 January 2017).

Palestinian Health Sector Signatories, Occupied Palestine | Palestinian Committee for the Academic and Cultural Boycott of Israel (2005), 'An Open Letter to the Palestinian and International Community Regarding Palestinian-Israeli Cooperation in Health', http://www.monabaker.com/pMachine/more.php?id=2903_0_1_84_M5 (accessed 22 May 2016).

Palestinian Ministry of NGOs (2000), 'The Basic Concept in Dealing with Israeli NGOs', 24 January 2000, unpublished paper.

'Palestinians Ready to Push for One State', *Associated Press*, 9 January 2004.

Palestine Papers (2008), Document 2352. Minutes of First Meeting on Culture of Peace, http://transparency.aljazeera.net/files/2352.PDF (accessed 1 August 2017).

Palestinian Academic Society for the Study of International Affairs (PASSIA) (2001), 'Settlements and the Final Status Talks', Special Bulletin, March 2001, Jerusalem/Al-Quds.

Palestinian Peace Information Centre (PPIC)-Al-Jiser and Melitz (1999a), 'Building the Moct: Final Report', unpublished paper, Jerusalem.

Palestinian Peace Information Centre (PPIC)-Al-Jiser and Givat Haviva (1999b), 'PeEducation Forum for Israeli and Palestinian Educators: Proposal', unpublished paper, Jerusalem.

Pappé, Ilan (1997), 'Post-Zionist Critique on Israel and the Palestinians: Part I: The Academic Debate', *Journal of Palestine Studies*, 26 (2), 29–41.

Pappé, Ilan (2002), 'Break the Mirror Now'. In Roane Carey and Jonathan Shanin (eds.), *The Other Israel: Voices of Refusal and Dissent*. New York: New Press.

Pappé, Ilan (2006), *A History of Modern Palestine: One Land, Two Peoples*. Cambridge: Cambridge University Press.

Pappé, Ilan (2009), 'The Vicissitude of 1984 Historiography of Israel', *Journal of Palestine Studies*, 39 (1), 6–23.

Pappé, Ilan (2011), *The Forgotten Palestinians: A History of the Palestinians in Israel*. New Haven, CT: Yale University Press.

Pappé, Ilan (2013), 'Revisiting 1967: The False Paradigm of Peace, Partition and Parity', *Settler Colonial Studies* 3 (3–4), 341–51.

Pappé, Ilan (2017a), *The Biggest Prison on Earth: A History of the Occupied Territories*. London: Oneworld.

Pappé, Ilan (2017b). *Ten Myths about Israel*. London: Verso.

Partnership for Peace (2012), *The EU Partnership for Peace Programme: Guidelines for Grant Applicants: Open Call for Proposals 2012*. http://www.europafacile.net/Formulari/ENPI/PartnershipforPeace/2012/Guidelines.pdf (accessed 12 December 2016).

Partnership for Peace (2014), *EU Partnership for Peace: Call for Proposals 2013*. http://www.eeas.europa.eu/archives/delegations/westbank/documents/news/2013/20140130_pfptable_en.pdf (accessed 12 December 2016).

Peace Now (2000), *Summary Data*, 4 December 2000.

Peled, Yoav (2006), 'Zionist realities', *New Left Review* (38), March–April, at: http://newleftreview.org/II/38/yoav-peled-zionist-realities-debating-israelpalestine (accessed 15 December 2016).

Peled-Elhanan, N. (2012), *Palestine in Israeli School Books: Ideology and Propaganda in Education*. London: I.B. Tauris.

Perlman, Lee, and Raviv Schwartz (2000), 'A Preliminary Stocktaking of Israeli Organizations Engaged in Palestinian-Israeli People-to-People Activity', paper presented to the Helsinki Workshop on Evaluating Israeli-Palestinian Civil Society Cooperative Activities, 27–28 November 1999, in *Report of the Workshop on the Israeli-Palestinian Civil Society Cooperative Activities*, KATU, 2000, 8–18.

Pettigrew, T. F. (1971), *Racially Separate or Together?* New York: McGraw-Hill.

Pettigrew, T. F. (1986), 'The Intergroup Contact Hypothesis Reconsidered'. In M. Hewstone and R. Brown (eds.), *Contact and Conflict in Intergroup Encounters*. New York: Basil Blackwell.

Piterberg, G. (2008), *The Returns of Zionism: Myths, Politics and Scholarship in Israel*. London: Verso.

Pogodda, Sandra, and Oliver P. Richmond (2015), 'Palestinian Unity and Everyday State Formation: Subaltern "Ungovernmentality" versus Elite Interests', *Third World Quarterly*, 36 (5): 890–907. doi: 10.1080/01436597.2015.1029909.

Pundak, Ron (2005/06), 'Looking Back: An Evaluation of People-to-People', *Palestine-Israel Journal of Politics, Economics and Culture*, 12–13 (4), 34–8.

Qumsiyeh, Mazin (2011), *Popular Resistance in Palestine: A History of Hope and Empowerment*. London: Pluto Press.

Qumsiyeh, Mazin (2012), *Popular Resistance in Palestine: A History of Hope and Empowerment*. London: Pluto Press.

Qumsiyeh, Mazin B. (2016), 'A Critical and Historical Assessment of Boycott, Divestment, and Sanctions (BDS) in Palestine'. In Alpaslan Ozerdem, Chuck Thiessen and Mufid Qassoum (eds.), *Conflict Transformation and the Palestinians*, chapter 5, pp. 89–113. Florence: Taylor and Francis.

Quray, Aḥmad (2005), *al-Riwāyah al-Filusṭīnīyah al-kāmilah lil-mufāwaḍāt: min Ūslū ilá Kharīṭat al-ṭarīq*, vol. 1. Bayrūt: Mu'assasat al-Dirāsāt al-Filasṭánīyah.

Qutaineh, Hazem (2000), 'Donors' Interests and Priorities within the People-to-People program', paper presented to the Helsinki Workshop on Evaluating Israeli-Palestinian Civil Society Cooperative Activities, 27–28 November 1999, KATU, 2000, pp. 41–6.

Ravid, Barak (2014), 'Kerry: Trust between Israel, Palestinians at All-Time Low', *Haaretz*, 13 March 2014, http://www.haaretz.com/israel-news/.premium-1.579516.

Raz, Avi (2012), *The Bride and the Dowry: Israel, Jordan and the Palestinians in the Aftermath of the June 1967 War*. New Haven, CT: Yale University Press.

Richmond, Oliver P. (2007), 'Critical Research Agendas for Peace: The Missing Link in the Study of International Relations', *Alternatives*, 32 (2), 247–74.

Richmond, Oliver P. (2013), 'Jekyll or Hyde: What Is Statebuilding Creating? Evidence from the "field"', *Cambridge Review of International Affairs*, 27 (1), 1–20. doi: 10.1080/09557571.2013.810590.

Rishmawi, Mona (1986), *Planning in Whose Interest? Land Use Planning as a Strategy for Judaization*. Ramallah: Al-Haq.

Robinson, Jerry W., and James D. Preston (1976), 'Equal-Status Contact and Modification of Racial Prejudice: A Reexamination of Contact Hypothesis', *Social Forces*, 54 (4), 911–24.

Rodinson, Maxime (1973), *Israel: A Colonial-Settler State?* Atlanta, GA: Pathfinder Press.

Rogin, Josh (2014), 'Exclusive: Kerry Warns Israel Could Become "An Apartheid State"', *Daily Beast*, 27 April 2014, https://www.thedailybeast.com/exclusive-kerry-warns-israel-could-become-an-apartheid-state.

Rosetti, Dominique (2005/06), 'Peacebuilding Programs: A Canadian View. A New Canadian Project for the Advancement of Peace', *Palestine-Israel Journal of Politics, Economics and Culture*, 12–13 (4), 64–6.

Rothstein, R. (1999) (ed.), *After the Peace: Resistance and Reconciliation*. London: Lynne Rienner.

Rouhana, Nadim (1990), 'The Intifada and the Palestinians of Israel: Resurrecting the Green Line', *Journal of Palestine Studies*, 19 (3), 58–75.

Rouhana, Nadim N. (2004), 'Group Identity and Power Asymmetry in Reconciliation Processes: The Israeli-Palestinian Case', *Peace and Conflict: Journal of Peace Psychology*, 10 (1), 33–52.

Rouhana, Nadim, and Areej Sabbagh-Khoury (2015), 'Settler-Colonial Citizenship: Conceptualizing the Relationship between Israel and Its Palestinian Citizens', *Settler Colonial Studies*, 5 (3), 41.

Roy, S. (1995), *The Gaza Strip: The Political Economy of De-Development*. Washington, DC: Institute for Palestinian Studies.

Roy, Sara (December 2002), 'Ending the Palestinian Economy', *Middle East Policy*, 9 (4).

Roy, Sara (2004), 'The Palestinian-Israeli Conflict and Palestinian Socioeconomic Decline: A Place Denied', *International Journal of Politics, Culture and Society*, 17 (3), 365–403.

Roy, Sara (2012), 'Reconceptualizing the Israeli-Palestinian Conflict: Key Paradigm Shifts', *Journal of Palestine Studies*, 41 (3), 71–91.

Said, Edward (1979), 'Zionism from the Standpoint of Its Victims, *Social Text*, 1, 7–58.

Said, Edward (1989), 'Intifada and Independence', *Social Text*, 22, 23–39.

Said, Edward (1993a). 'The Limits to Cooperation'. In Edward Said (ed.), *Peace and Its Discontents: Essays on Palestine in the Middle East Process*, pp. 32–9. New York: Vintage.

Said, Edward (1993b, reprinted 1995), 'The Morning After'. In Edward Said (ed.), *Peace and Its Discontents: Essays on Palestine in the Middle East Peace Process*. New York: Vintage/Random House.

Said, Edward, (1997), 'The Real Meaning of the Hebron Agreement', *Journal of Palestine Studies*, 26 (3), 31–6.

Said, E. W. (2003), *Orientalism*. London, Penguin.

Salamanca, O. J., M. Qato, K. Rabie and S. Samour (2012), 'Past Is present: Settler Colonialism in Palestine', *Settler Colonial Studies*, 2 (1), 1–8.

Save the Children, Fact Sheet (October 2011), 'Children's Right to Education in Armed Conflict', Save the Children. http://www.protectingeducation.org/sites/default/files/documents/save_the_children_fact_sheet_childrens_right_to_education_in_armed_conflict.pdf.

Savir, Uri (1998), *The Process: 1,100 Days That Changed the Middle East.* New York: Random House.

Sayegh, Fayez (2012), *Zionist Colonialism in Palestine, 1965.* Beirut: Research Center, Palestine Liberation Organization.

Sayigh, Y. (1997), *Armed Struggle and the Search for State: The Palestinian National Movement, 1949–1993.* Oxford: Oxford University Press.

Sayigh, Y. (2009), 'Fixing Broken Windows', Security Sector Reform in Palestine, Lebanon and Yemen, *Carnegie Papers.* Washington, DC: Carnegie Endowment for International Peace.

Scham, P. (2000, September), 'Arab-Israeli Research Cooperation, 1995–1999', *Middle East Review of International Affairs*, 4 (3).

Segev, Tom (2007), *1967: Israel, the War and the Year That Transformed the Middle East.* London: Little, Brown.

Selby, Jan (2003), 'Dressing Up Domination as "Cooperation": The Case of Israeli-Palestinian Water Relations', *Review of International Studies* 29 (1), 121–38.

Shadid, Mohammed, and Caroline Qutteneh (eds.) (2000), 'Palestinian Governmental/NGO Relations: Cooperation and Partnership', *Proceedings of the International Conference, Welfare Association Consortium*, 14–16 February, Ramalla: Masar.

Shafir, Gershon (1984), 'Changing Nationalism and Israel's "Open Frontier" on the West Bank', *Theory and Society*, 12 (6), 803–27.

Shafir, Gershon (1989), 'Zionism and Colonialism: A Comparative Approach' in I, Pappé, *The Israel/Palestine Question: A Reader*, 2nd ed., pp. 81–96. London: Routledge.

Shalhoub-Kevorkian, N. (2015), *Security Theology, Surveillance and the Politics of Fear.* Cambridge: Cambridge University Press.

Shehadeh, Raja (1997), *From Occupation to Interim Accords: Israeli and the Palestinian Territories.* London: Kluwer Law International.

Shehadeh, Raja (2015), *Language of War, Language of Peace.* London: Profile Books.

Sherwood, Harriet, Kim Willsher and Andrew Sparrow (2012), 'Israel Stands by Settlements Plan despite Growing Diplomatic Crisis', *Guardian*, 3 December, at http://www.guardian.co.uk/politics/2012/dec/03/uk-mayrecall-israel-ambassador-settlement.

Shikaki, Khalil (1999), 'The Internal Consequences of Unstable Peace: Psychological and Political Responses of the Palestinians'. In Robert L. Rothstein (ed.), *After the Peace: Resistance and Reconciliation.* London: Lynne Rienner.

Shlaim, Avi (1995), 'The Debate about 1948', *International Journal of Middle East Studies*, 27 (3), 287–304.

Shlaim, Avi (2000), *The Iron Wall: Israel and the Arab World*. London: Penguin.

Silver, Charlotte (2016), 'Israel Has Destroyed $74 Million Worth of EU Projects', *The Electronic Intifada*, 5 June 2016, https://electronicintifada.net/blogs/charlotte-silver/israel-has-destroyed-74-million-worth-eu-projects (accessed 30 July 2018).

Simpson, L. (2011), *Dancing on Our Turtle's Back: Stories of Nishnaabeg Re-Creation, Resurgence and a New Emergence* (Winnipeg: Arbeiter Ring Press).

Simpson, L. (2013, March 5), 'Dancing the World into Being: A Conversation with Idle No More's Leanne Simpson', Yes! *Magazine*, interviewed by Naomi Klein, https://www.yesmagazine.org/peace-justice/dancing-theworld-%20into-being-a-conversation-with-idle-no-more-leanne-simpson (accessed 14 August 2018).

Smith, Linda Tuhiwai (2012), *Decolonizing Methodologies*. London: Zed.

Staff, Toi (2016), 'Liberman Bars PA Liaison from Israel for "subversive" behavior', *Times of Israel*, 15 June 2016, https://www.timesofisrael.com/liberman-bars-pa-liaison-from-israel-for-subversive-behavior/ (accessed 7 October 2017).

Sussman, Gary (2004), 'The Challenge to the Two-State Solution', *Middle East Report*, at http://www.globalpolicy.org/nations-a-states/emerging-states–claimsto-autonomy-and-independence/palestine/29825.html (accessed 2 December 2016).

Sussman, Gary, A.-R. Abu-Saleh, H. Ajjuri and Pundik (2002), 'Building Bridges through Health: The Experience of the Palestine Council of Health and the Economic Cooperation Foundation, 1995–1999'. In Tamara Barnea and Rafiq Husseini (eds.), *Separate and Cooperate, Cooperate and Separate: The Disengagement of the Palestine Health Care System from Israel and Its Emergence as an Independent System*. London: Praeger.

Svirsky, Gila (2001), 'The Israeli Peace Movement since the Al-Aqsa Intifada'. In Roane Carey (ed.). *The New Intifada: Resisting Israel's Apartheid*, pp. 324–30. London: Verso.

Svirsky, Gila (2002), 'Nonviolent: Direct Action for Peace', *Common Ground News Service*, 7 June 2002, http://www.commongroundnews.org/print_article.php?artId=21085&dir=left&lan=en&sid=0.

Swisher, Clayton E. (2011), *The Palestine Papers: The End of the Road*. London: Hesperus.

Tabar, Linda, and Omar Jabary Salamanca (2015), 'After Oslo: Settler Colonialism, Neoliberal Development and Liberation in Critical Readings of Development under Colonialism: Towards a Political Economy for Liberation in the Occupied Palestinian Territories', Birzeit University, Center for Development Studies.

Taiaiake, Alfred (1999), *Peace, Power, Righteousness: An Indigenous Manifesto*. New York: Oxford University Press.

Taiaiake Alfred (2005), *Wasáse: Indigenous Pathways of Action and Freedom*. Peterborough: Broadview Press.

Taiaiake, Alfred, and Jeff Corntassel (2005), 'Being Indigenous: Resurgences against Contemporary Colonialism', *Government and Opposition* 40 (4), 597–614.

Tajfel, H. (1974), 'Social Identity and Intergroup Behavior', *Social Science Information*, 13, 65–93.

Tajfel, H. (1981), *Human Groups and Social Categories: Studies in Social Psychology*. London: Cambridge University Press.

Tajfel, H., et al. (1971), 'Social Categorization and Intergroup Behavior', *European Journal of Social Psychology*, I, 149–78.

Tajfel, H., and J. C. Turner (1979), 'An Integrative Theory of Intergroup Conflict', In William G. Austin and Stephen Worchel (eds.), *Social Psychology of Intergroup Relations*, pp. 33–7. Monterey, CA: Brook/Cole.

Tajfel, H, and J. C. Turner (1985), 'The Social Identity Theory of Intergroup Behaviour'. In S. Worschel and W. G. Austin (eds.), *Psychology of Intergroup Relations*, pp. 7–24. Chicago, IL: Nelson-Hall.

Tamari, Salim (1988), 'What the Uprising Means', Middle East Report, No. 152. *The Uprising*, pp. 24–30.

Tamari, Salim (1995), 'Tourists with Agendas', *Middle East Report*, 196.

Tamari, Salim (2004), 'The Case of Geneva', *Guardian*, 6 January 2004.

Taraki, Lisa (1990), 'The Development of Political Consciousness among Palestinians in the Occupied Territories, 1967–1987'. In Nassar and Heacock (eds.), *Intifada: Palestine at the Crossroads*. London: Praeger.

Tartir, Alaa (2015), 'The Evolution and Reform of Palestinian Security Forces 1993–2013', *Stability: International Journal of Security and Development*, 4 (1), 1–20.

Tartir, Alaa (2017), 'The Palestinian Authority Security Forces: Whose Security?', al-shabaka the Palestinian policy network, 16 May 2017, https://al-shabaka.org/briefs/palestinian-authority-security-forces-whose-security/ (accessed 25 July 2017).

Thiessen, Chuck (2016), 'The Evolution of Conflict Transformation Theory and Practice in Israel and the Occupied Palestinian Territory'. In Alpaslan Ozerdem, Chuck Thiessen and Mufid Qassoum (eds.), *Conflict Transformation and the Palestinians*, pp. 3–19. Florence: Taylor and Francis.

Tilley, Virginia (2005), *The One-State Solution: A Breakthrough for Peace in the Israeli-Palestinian Deadlock*. Manchester: Manchester University Press.

Tilley, Virginia (2006), 'The Secular Solution: Debating Israel-Palestine', *New Left Review*, 38, 37–57.

Tomeh, George J. (ed.) (1975), *United Nations Resolutions on Palestine and the Arab-Israeli Conflict 1947–1974*. Beirut: Institute for Palestine Studies.

Touma Khalil (1986), *Al-Fajr* (English edition), 5 December 1986 and 25 December 1986, 'Is Palestinian Israeli Dialogue Beneficial?', Jerusalem.

Trew, Karen (1986), 'Catholic-Protestant Contact in Northern Ireland'. In M. Hewstone and R. Brown (eds.), *Contact and Conflict in Intergroup Encounters*. New York: Basil Blackwell.

Trouillot, Michel-Rolph (2015), *Silencing the Past: Power and the Production of History*, 2nd rev. ed. Boston, MA: Beacon Press.

Tufakji, Khalil (2000), 'Settlements: A Geographic and Demographic Barrier to Peace', *Palestine-Israel Journal of Political, Economics and Culture*, 7 (3, 4), 52–8.

Turner, John C. (1999), 'Some Current Issues in Research on Social Identity and Self-Categorization Theories'. In N. Ellemers, R. Spears and B. Doosje (eds.), *Social Identity: Context, Commitment, Content*, pp. 6–34. Oxford: Basil Blackwell.

Turner, M. (2012). 'Completing the Circle: Peacebuilding as Colonial Practice in the Occupied Palestinian Territory', *International Peacekeeping*, 19 (4), 492–507. doi: 10.1080/13533312.2012.709774.

Turner, M. (2015), 'Peacebuilding as Counterinsurgency in the Occupied Palestinian Territories', *Review of International Studies*, 41, 73–98.

Turner M., and O. Shweiki (2014), 'Introduction: Decolonizing the Study of the Political Economy of the Palestinian People'. In M. Turner and O. Shweiki (eds.), *Decolonizing Palestinian Political Economy: Rethinking Peace and Conflict Studies*. London: Palgrave Macmillan.

United Nations (2006), *Report of the Special Rapporteur of the Commission on Human Rights, John Dugard, on the Situation of Human Rights in the Palestinian Territories Occupied by Israel Since 1967*, United Nations Commission on Human Rights, UN Doc. E/CN.4/2006/29, 17 January 2006.

UN Human Rights Council – UNHRC (2015), *Report of the Detailed Findings of the Independent Commission of Inquiry Established Pursuant to Human Rights Council resolution S-21/1*, http://www.ohchr.org/EN/HRBodies/HRC/CoIGazaConflict/Pages/ReportCoIGaza.aspx (accessed 2 July 2018).

United Nations Office for the Coordination of Humanitarian Affairs (UN-OCHA, occupied Palestinian territory) (February, 2018), 'West Bank Demolitions and Displacement'. (Online). www.ochaopt.org/content/west-bank-demolitions-and-displacement-february-2018 (accessed 20 April 2018).

USAID (2013), 'Conflict Management and Mitigation Program Fact Sheet'. https://www.usaid.gov/documents/1883/conflict-management-and-mitigation-program-fact-sheet-0.

USAID, People-to-People Peace Building: A Program Guide (2011), USAID Office of Conflict Management and Mitigation USAID/DCHA/CMM. https://www.usaid.gov/sites/default/files/documents/1866/CMMP2PGuidelines2010-01-19.pdf (accessed 7 June 2015).

Usher, Graham (1999), *Dispatches from Palestine: The Rise and the Fall of the Oslo Peace Process.* London: Pluto Press.

Veracini, Lorenzo (2006), *Israel and Settler Society.* London: Pluto Press.

Veracini, Lorenzo (2010), *Settler Colonialism: A Theoretical Overview.* Basingstoke: Palgrave Macmillan.

Veracini, Lorenzo (2011), 'Introducing', Settler Colonial Studies, 1 (1), 1–12.

Veracini, Lorenzo (Winter 2013), 'The Other Shift: Settler Colonialism, Israel, and the Occupation', *Journal of Palestine Studies*, 42 (2), 26–42.

Walid, Mustafa (2000), *Jerusalem: Population and Urbanization, from 1850–2000,* Jerusalem: Jerusalem and Communications Centre (JMCC), pp. 71–95.

Warschawski, Michel (Mikado) (1992), 'The Long March towards Israeli-Palestinian Cooperation'. In Deena Hurwitz (ed.), *Walking The Red Line: Israelis in Search of Justice for Palestine.* Philadelphia, PA: New Society.

Waziyatawin (2012), 'Malice Enough in Their Hearts and Courage Enough in Ours: Reflections on US Indigenous and Palestinian Experiences under Occupation', *Settler Colonial Studies*, 2 (1), 172–89.

Weizman, Eyal (2007), *Hollow Land: Israel's Architecture of Occupation.* London: Verso.

Wolfe, Patrick (1999), *Settler Colonialism and the Transformation of Anthropology: The Politics and Poetics of an Ethnographic Event.* London: Cassell.

Wolfe, Patrick (2006), 'Settler-Colonialism and the Elimination of the Native', *Journal of Genocide Research*, 8 (4), 387–409.

World Bank (2007), 'Movement and Access Restrictions in the West Bank: Uncertainty and Inefficiency in the Palestinian Economy', West Bank and Gaza, 9 May 2007.

World Bank (2011), *Coping with Conflict: Poverty and Inclusion in the West Bank and Gaza.* Gaza: World Bank Group.

Yiftachel, Oren (2005), 'Neither Two States Nor One: The Disengagement and "Creeping Apartheid" in Israel/Palestine', *Arab World Geographer* 8 (3), 125–9.

Yiftachel, Oren (2009), '"Creeping Apartheid" in Israel-Palestine', *Middle East Report*, 253, 7–15.

Zagha, Adel, and Husam Zumlot (2004), 'Israel and the Palestinian Economy: Integration or Containment?' In Mushtaq Husain Khan, George George Giacaman and Inge Amundsen (eds.), *State Formation in Palestine: Viability and Governance during a Social Transformation*, pp. 120–40. London: Routledge.

Zartman I. W. (2007). *Peacemaking and International Conflict: Methods and Techniques*. Washington, DC: United States Institution of Peace.

Zieve, Tamara (2018), 'In Response to Nation-State Law: Mass Arabic Class Held in Tel Aviv', *Jerusalem Post*, 30 July 2018, https://www.jpost.com/Israel-News/In-response-to-Nation-State-Law-Mass-Arabic-class-held-in-Tel-Aviv-563802 (accessed 14 August 2018).

Zureik, Elia (1994), 'Palestinian Refugees and Peace', *Journal of Palestine Studies*, 24 (1), 5–17.

Links

http://www.pngo.net (accessed 5 June 2002).

http://www.infopal.org/plnews (accessed 2 July 2003).

http://www.geneva-accord.org/mainmenu/mission-statement (3 April 2014).

http://www.batshalom.org (accessed 25 February 2004).

Palestinian Campaign for the Academic & Cultural Boycott of Israel (Arabic): http://www.pacbi.org/atemplate.php?id=100 (accessed 21 October 2017).

BDS leaflet (in Arabic): https://bdsmovement.net/ar/news/-اللجنة-الوطنية-الفلسطينية-للمقاطعة-ندين-الدعوة-لمسيرة-نسوية-تطبيعية-في-أريحا-وندعو-لمقاطعتها (accessed 19 October 2017).

UPWC: Palestinian women confront normalization and the so-called 'peace' deception, 7 October 2017: http://pflp.ps/english/2017/10/07/upwc-palestinian-women-confront-normalization-and-the-so-called-peace-deception/ (accessed 8 October 2017).

Breaking the Silence: http://www.breakingthesilence.org.il/about/organization

http://zochrot.org/en/tour/all (accessed 6 September 2017).

https://culturesofresistance.org/groups-we-support-AATW (accessed 1 August 2019).

JVP: https://jewishvoiceforpeace.org/boycott-divestment-and-sanctions/jvp-supports-the-bds-movement/ (accessed 3 May 2017).

Stand with Standing Rock, 'Standing Rock Sioux Applauds BNP Paribas' Decision to Divest from DAPL', 5 April 2017: http://standwithstandingrock.net/standing-rock-sioux-applauds-bnp-paribas-decision-divest-dapl/ (accessed 3 August 2018).

Stand with Standing Rock, 'In Victory for Standing Rock Sioux Tribe, Court Finds That Approval of Dakota Access Pipeline Violated the Law', 14 June 2017, http://standwithstandingrock.net/victory-standing-rock-sioux-tribe-court-finds-approval-dakota-access-pipeline-violated-law/ (accessed 2 August 2018).

Idle No More, 'The Story', http://www.idlenomore.ca/story (accessed 13 August 2018).

Index

Abarbanel, Avigail 54
Abbas, Mahmoud 42, 60, 90, 124, 152
Abdel-Shafi, Haidar 91
Abdul-Hadi, Mahdi 133
Abu-Libedeh, Hassan 188 n.12
Abu-Nimer, Mohammed 112, 119, 120
Abu-Saad, I. 7–8
Abu-Zayyad, Nisreen 118
Abu-Zayyad, Ziad 69, 81
Adwan, Sami 113, 135
agglomerations 101
Al-Ahmar, Khan 50
Al-Aqsa Intifada 2, 3, 4, 14, 20, 28, 42, 102, 107, 109, 126, 142, 143, 144, 148, 162, 183, 187 n.1
Alazzeh, Ala 167
Al-Barghouti, Marwan 106, 156–157
Albright, Madeline 31
Alfred, Taiaiake 51, 54
al-Hardan, A. 27
Al-Husseini, Faisal 115
Ali, Haseeb 119
Al-Jiser 112, 114, 134
Al-Khatib, Ghassan 80, 92, 143, 151, 152
Allon, Yigal 50, 68
Allon Plan 50
Allport, G. W. 139, 146
al-Madani, Muhammad 161
Al-Qaq, Zakaria 40
American Nightline (TV Programme) 91
Amir, Yehuda 139, 146
Amirav, Moshe 90
Anarchists against the Wall (AATW) 164
Annapolis Conference (2007) 3
anti-colonial struggle 64
Arab–Israeli conflict 69
Arab Peace Initiative (2002) 3, 141
Arab Studies Society (ASS) 115
Arab Summit Conference 190 n.1
Arafat, Yasser 2, 18, 59, 67, 91, 100
Aruri, Taysir 77, 86
Ashrawi, Hanan 77, 80, 91

Attalla, Akram 128
Aviad, Janet 134, 138
Avnery, Uri 74, 76, 107

Balfour Declaration of 1917 167
Bantustanization 101
Barak, Ehud 101
Barker 170
Bar-On, Dan 135
Baskin, Gershon 91
BDS movement *see* Boycott, Divestment and Sanctions (BDS) movement
BDS National Committee (BNC) 160
Begin, Menachem 76, 174
Beilen, Yossi 153
Beit Jala conference 1999 126
Benvenisti, Meron 17
Bethlehem 1
Bi'lin Popular Committee Against the Wall 167
Bishara 2
Black September 69
Boycott, Divestment and Sanctions (BDS) movement 5, 60, 158–159, 168, 169, 177, 183, 189 n.3
Brewer, Marilynn B. 36
British Foreign Office (FCO) 142
Brown, R. 37
B'tselem 88
Buchanan, Paul G. 159

Cairo Agreement 56, 97
Camp David agreement (1978) 3, 174
Canada Fund 15
Canadian International Development Agency (CIDA) 142, 152
cantonization of Palestinian land 100
capitalism 59
cautious optimism 1
Centre for Palestinian Research and Studies (CPRS) 1
civil disobedience 10

civil society 50, 179
Clinton, Hilary 137
Coalition of Women for Peace 24, 162
Cohen, Stephen P. 39
colonialism 11, 48, 49, 50, 51, 53, 62
   cultural horizon of 61
   normalizing 62–63
colonial peace 57
colonization 47, 49, 52, 54, 168, 169
   of Jerusalem 71
   of Palestine 51
Committee Against War in Lebanon (CAWL) 79
Communist Party 84
compartmentalization 157
Conflict Management 196 n.17
Conflict Management and Mitigation (CMM) 141
conflict resolution frameworks 19
Connecting with the Enemy (Katz) 7
constructive ambiguity 100
constructive dialogue 141
contact 5, 10
   1967–72 67–73
   1973–81 73–77
   1982–6 77–81
   different forms 10
   during First *Intifada* 1987–93 83–95
   hypothesis 146
   initiatives 123
   opposing 12
   post-Oslo period 12, 19
   from South Africa 140
   theory 36
contact-based initiatives 86, 91, 174
Core-Periphery and Dependency theory 65
Corntassel, Jeff 65
Coulthard, Glen C. 51
counterterrorism 59
Courage to Refuse 162
Cox, Robert 49, 137
CRB Foundation 188 n.11
cross-cultural contact 116
culture of coexistence 3
Culture of Peace committee (COP) 163
curriculum design 115

Dakota Access Pipeline (DAPL) 168
David, Camp 2, 53, 134, 136, 149
Davis, Angela 171
Dayan, Moshe 70, 121
decategorization 38
Declaration of Principles (DOP) (1993) 1
decolonization 27, 28, 45, 53, 170
Democratic Front for the Liberation of Palestine (DFLP) 77, 84
Dia Lakibush, diplomacy 88
dispossession 47, 54
distribution of power 53
divergences 128
donor-speak 105
Dori, Latif 80
Dunbar-Ortiz, Roxanne 54

Economic Co-operation Foundation (ECF) 15, 114
Edei Kibush 88
Education for Peace 134
Ellwood, Tobias 142
elimination 50, 51
empowerment 93, 176
Emunim, Gush 51
Endresen, Lena 33, 41, 188 n.9
Endresen, Lina 131
equal-status contact 147
Erekat, Sa'eb 80, 91
Eshkol, Levi 70
EU Peacebuilding Initiative (EU PI) 140
European colonization 52
European Union 15

facilitation 117
FACTS Information Committee 84–85
Fafo 42
   funding 103
family reunification 132
Fankenthal, Yitzhak 165
Fanon, Frantz 45, 53
Fatah 84
Fatah-Hamas reconciliation agreement 16
'Final Status' issues 97
Finchilescu, G. 37
Finnish Citizens' Security Council (KATU) 126
First *Intifada* 1987–93 43, 87, 88, 90, 124, 179
   contact during 83–95
Fitzduff, Mari 37

formal peace process 101
Foster, D. 37
Foucault, Michel 49, 62, 169, 180
Fragmentation of land 167
'From Both Sides' (FBS) 111–122
    divergences during 122–124
    honeymoon period 113
    lack of 'common goal' 124–128

Galilee 51
Ganot, Elazer 91
Gaza-Jericho Agreement *see* Cairo Agreement
Gaza Strip 1, 53, 61, 83
    Israel occupied 67
    occupation 10
Geneva Initiative 153, 155
Gilen, Signe 143
Givat Haviva 141
global capitalism 52
Golan Heights
    Israel occupied 67
Gordon, Neve 150
Gramsci, Antonio 46, 49, 59, 136–137, 159, 180
Gramscian analysis 136, 137, 176
Great Return March, Gaza 24
Green Line 89
Gulf War 13
Gush Emunim (Block of Faith) 73
Gvul, Yesh 86, 87

Haddad, Toufic 60
Haddadin, Yolla 40, 42, 45, 46, 134, 138
Haifa 114
Halper, Jeff 23, 137, 161
Hammami, Rema 93
Hammami, Said 74, 76
Hanieh, Adam 46, 58
Hanssen-Bauer, Jon 8, 32, 40, 106, 124
Haram Al-Sharif 187 n.2
Hassassian, Manuel 84
Hebron Protocol 1, 98
hegemony 49
Helsinki conference 107
Hever, Shir 58
Hilal, Jamil 58
honeymoon period 113
humanitarian law 169

Hussaini, Faisal 80, 88, 90, 92
Hussein, Saddam 91

Idle No More 168, 169
inequality, conceptualization or theorization of 19
institutional reform 59
inter-group contact 38
internalization 49
International Court of Justice (ICJ) 158
international governance 52
International Socialist convention 81
international solidarity 169
interpretative deficiencies 53
Intifadas 9, 10, 11, 23, 28, 36, 51, 58, 78, 84
Iraq–Iran war 78
'Iron Fist' policy 77
Israel
    activists 13
    colonialism 58
    cultural boycott of 3
    ethnic foundations 51
    invasion of Lebanon in 1982 12, 79
    Jerusalem, closed 13
Israeli and Palestinian Planning Groups 33
Israeli Committee Against Demolishing Houses (ICADH) 23, 137, 163
Israeli Communist Party 71
Israeli Council for Israel–Palestine Peace (ICIPP) 74
Israeli crime in 1948 132
Israeli Economic Co-operation Foundation 105
Israeli NGOs 105
Israeli–Palestinian conflict 146 *see also* Palestinian-Israeli conflict
    settler colonial paradigm 167
Israeli–Palestinian cooperation, formalization of 63
Israeli–Palestinian Peace Committee (IPPC) 144
Israeli–Palestinian Peace Project 90
Israeli Planning Group 103
Israeli settlements 2, 12, 16
Israel/Palestine Center for Research and Information (IPCRI) 6, 90, 137
Israel/Palestinian conflict 141

Jabri, V. 136
Jenin 1
Jericho 161
Jerusalem 8, 57, 68, 71, 114
　closed 13
Jerusalem Centre for Women 133
Jerusalem Media & Communications Center (JMCC) 20, 22, 145, 187 n.10
Jerusalem synagogue 144
Jewish democracy 72
Jewish Voice for Peace (JVP) 166
Jobs and Growth Act 168
'Joint Call for Peace' 153
Jones, James M. 37
Jordanian option 68

Kaminer, Reuven 73
Kassis, Nabil 154
Katz, Sheila 7
Kelman, Herbert 75
Kerry, John 16, 132
Khalidi, Raja 68
Khalif, Karim 76
Khatib, Ghassan 86

Larsen, Terje Rod 188 n.6
Levy, Gideon 150
Li, T. M. 59
liberal modernity 52
liberal peacebuilding project 56
liberation 45
　of historical Palestine 73
Lieberman, Avigdor 161
Lonning, Dag 38, 125
Lughod, Abu 84

Machiavellian rationalizations 54
Machsom Watch 163
Madrid Conference 87
Mahshi, Khalil 77
Malki, Ra'id 142
Maoz, Ifat 105
Ma'oz, Moshe 98
market economic actions 59
Masalha, Nur 51
Masri, Hikmat 70
Matzpen 71
Mazen, Abu 143
Melitz 112–113, 114

Memmi, Albert 45, 54, 170
Memmi's depiction 177
Miller, Norma 36
Misk, Adel 165
Mitigation Program Fact Sheet 196 n.17
mobilization 93
Morgensen, Scott Lauria 52
Moroccan Quarter *(Mughrabi)* 68
Morris, Kim T. 37
Mu'allem, Naseef 40
Muslih, Muhammad 85

Nablus 2
Nakba 47, 64, 67, 73, 136, 163, 169
Naser-Najjab, Nadia 137
Nashashibi, Rana 87
Nasir, Hanna 144
Nasrallah, Elias 27, 184
Nathan, Abie 80
Nationality Law 168
Nazzal, Nafez 76
Negev 51
neocolonialism 58
neoliberalism 23
neo-liberal peacebuilding 46–47
neo-liberal projects 168
neo-liberal state-building project 42, 47, 148, 159
Netanyahu, Benjamin 137, 171
non-partisan Jewish education agency 112
non-pecuniary incentives 113
non-violence 85
normalising occupation 48
Norwegian Ministry of Foreign Affairs 32
Nusseibeh, Sari 80, 90

occupation, normalizing 62–63
Occupied Palestinian Territories (OPT) 16, 45, 67, 69, 80, 112
　de-development 71
　humiliating policies 83
　political, economic and security situation 99
October/Yom Kippur War 73
Ofer, Adi 88
One Democratic State Campaign (ODSC) 24
'one-size-fits-all' approaches 99
one-state solution 24, 52

Ophir, A. 150
Orientalism 15
Orient House 127
Orwellian peace 24–29
Oslo Accords 174, 182
Oslo Agreement (1993) 1, 9, 13, 20, 22, 23, 36, 57, 95, 167
    Article XXXI of 101
Oslo II Agreement (1995) 1, 31, 33, 36, 97, 188 n.1
Oslo negotiations 97
Oslo peace process 166
Oslo process 2, 26
Oslo years 67, 97–99, 123
    context of implementation 99–103
    Israeli and Palestinian NGOs 103–108
Oz ve Shalom 73

Palestine
    activists 13
    colonization 11, 51
    counterterrorism 56
    economic development 46
    pre-Oslo period 11–12
    resistance to normalization 25
    right to self-determination 73
Palestine Liberation Organization (PLO) 57, 68, 69
    1974 declaration 73
Palestinian and Israeli NGOs 105, 131
Palestinian Authority (PA) 47, 55–56, 181
    international funding, dependency on 56
Palestinian Central Bureau of Statistics (PCBS) 188 n.12
Palestinian Centre for Peace and Democracy 40
Palestinian Centre for Peace (PCP) 103, 126
Palestinian civil society 93
    during pre-Oslo period 85
    professionalization 11
Palestinian Communist movement 71
Palestinian development 83
Palestinian–Israeli conflict 5, 7, 15, 29, 45, 47, 53, 62, 85, 95, 131, 138
    contact experiences 36
    exigencies of 185
    resolution frameworks 16, 31
Palestinian–Israeli cooperation 11, 39
Palestinian–Israeli cooperative projects 166
Palestinian–Israeli joint projects 161
Palestinian–Israeli peace negotiations 16, 18, 73, 175
Palestinian–Israeli relations 45, 73
Palestinian–Israeli Solidarity initiatives 123
Palestinian Ministry of Education 40
Palestinian National Council 78
Palestinian national movement 93
Palestinian national rights 150
Palestinian negotiator 97
Palestinian NGO Network (PNGO) 143, 156
Palestinian Peace Coalition 154
Palestinian Peace Information Centre (PPIC) 112, 141
Palestinian political parties 84
Palestinian rejectionism 70
Palestinian Right of Return 24
Palestinians in Israel
    compartmentalization 64
Palestinian state-building 56
Palestinian suicide bombs 149
Palestinian Working Women's Society 128
Pappé, Ilan 9, 22, 50, 55, 78–79, 128, 137
Parents' Circle: The Families Forum 164–165
Parliamentary Association for Euro-Arab Co-operation in Britain 76
partition of Palestine, 1948 167
Partnership for Peace Program (2002) 140
PASSIA 101
peacebuilding 49, 64
Peace Coalition 155
Peace Education Department 142
peace negotiations 1
Peace Now 92, 101
peace process 63, 175
    limitation 55
Peace Research Institute in the Middle East (PRIME) 194 n.26
peace/state-building 57
people-to-people diplomacy programme (P2PP) 3, 7, 8, 18–29, 83, 99–100
    Al-Aqsa Intifada, during and after 147–172
    Annex XI of Oslo II 33
    assessments 129, 131–146
    attributes of 32–35

contact in contemporary context 160–167
donor evaluation of 142–145
European Commission on 32
hegemony and consent 136–141
intentions 32–33
internationalization 175
Israeli and Palestinian NGOs 34
limits of cooperation 149–156
narrative and historical context 132–136
neutrality 15
Palestinian and Israeli participants 128
Palestinian non-violent resistance and the 'war of position' 156–160
peacebuilding framework 55
in practice 40–43
resisting colonialism 167–171
social psychology theories 35–40
sponsors and participants 35–36
Perlman, Lee 20, 115, 118, 119, 121, 125
permit system 13
Pettigrew, T. F. 139, 146
Piterberg, G. 51
political expediency 6
Popular Cultural Centre 128
Popular Front for the Liberation of Palestine (PFLP) 77, 84
post-Oslo contact 19
post-Oslo donor 60
post-Oslo joint projects 26
P2PP *see* people-to-people diplomacy programme (P2PP)
pre-Oslo period
Palestinian civil society 85
Preston, James D. 147
professionalization 94, 104
professionalization of Palestinian civil society 93
Protocol Concerning Israeli-Palestinian Cooperation Programme 33
Pundak, Ron 154

Qasis, Nabil 77
Quray, Ahmad 97
Qurei, Ahmad 22

Rabadi, Issa 6
Rabbis for Human Rights 163
Rabbo, Abed 153
Rabin, Yitzhak 13, 18, 67

Rachid, Mohamed 134
racial prejudice 147
racism 92
Ramallah 2, 20, 21
Rantisi, Samir 154
Raz, Avi 70
Reagan Plan, 1982 77
realism 84
recategorization 38
Reconciliation Funds Program 141
refugees 17, 22, 23, 24, 39
Revisionist Zionist 68
Richmond, Oliver 46, 57, 98, 131
Right of Return 123
Right of Return of Palestinian refugees 156, 157
Road Map 141
Roadmap for Peace (2002) 3, 195 n.15
Robinson, Jerry W. 147
Rouhana, Nadim N. 103
Roy, Sara 57, 61, 158
Rundak, Ron 144
Ryan, Joan 142

Sadat, Anwar 69, 74, 174
Said, Edward 15, 25, 85, 182
Saif, Samir 107, 121, 151
Salamanca, Omar Jabary 169
Sarid, Yossi 91
Sartawi, Issam 75, 76, 81
Savir, Uri 57, 97, 100
Scud missiles 91
self-categorization theory 38
self-government initiatives 54
separation wall 18, 100, 102, 147, 150, 157
settler colonialism 7, 15, 17, 22, 28, 44, 45, 47–55, 50, 52, 63, 64
settler colonial theory 51
Shahin, Muhammad 120
Shalom, David Ish 90
Shalom, Gush 74
Shamir, Yitzhak 90
Sharon, Ariel 90
Sharon, Roling 137
Shehadeh, Raja 46
Shikaki, Khalil 1
Shweiki, O. 47
Simpson, Leanne 51

Sinai Peninsula
   Israel occupied 67
social categorization theory 38, 104
social identity theory (SIT) 38, 146
social psychology 35
specific interpretative deficiency 53
Standing Cooperation Committee (SCC) 33
state-building project 180
Svirsky, Gila 163
systematic disregards 53

Taiaiake, Alfred 65
Tajfel, H. 38
Tamari, Salim 27, 155
target groups 93
Tartir, Alaa 46
teacher training 115
Tel Aviv 21, 114, 141
Trew, Karen 37, 39
Trouillot, Michel-Rolph 170
Tulkarm 2
Turner, J. C. 38, 46, 47, 57
two-state solution 17–18, 22, 45, 52, 173

UN General Assembly Resolution
   18 88
   181 90
   194(III) 134
Unified National Leadership of the Uprising (UNLU) 84, 85
Union of Palestinian Women's Committees 161
UN 'peace plan' 24

UNSC Resolutions 242 and 338 68, 90, 123
USAID 15

Veerman, Philip 108, 113
Veracini, Lorenzo 45, 53, 61

Warschawski, Michel 71, 89
Waziyatawin 170, 171
Welfare Association Consortium 107
West Bank 53
   Israel occupied 67
   occupation 10
West Bank settlers 101
Wolfe, Patrick 50
Women in Black (WIB) 89
Women's Intellectual Forum 155
Women's Organization for Women Political Prisoners (WOFWPP) 89
women's organizations 133
Women Wage Peace 161
Workshop on the Israeli-Palestinian Civil Society Co-operative Activities 126
Wretched of the Earth, The 53
Wye River Memorandum 31, 98

Yesh Guvl 12
Yiftachel, Oren 51

Zaida, Sufian Abu 126
Zayyad, Ziad Abu 72
Zhiza, Salah 90
Zionism 10, 17, 45, 50, 77–79, 133, 171
Zochrot 163, 187 n.5
Zucker, Dedi 88, 92

www.ingramcontent.com/pod-product-compliance
Lightning Source LLC
Chambersburg PA
CBHW052035300426
44117CB00012B/1829